MONEY, METHOD, AND THE MARKET PROCESS

The Liberty Fund Library of the Works of Ludwig von Mises

EDITED BY BETTINA BIEN GREAVES

The Anti-capitalistic Mentality
Bureaucracy
Economic Freedom and Interventionism: An Anthology
    of Articles and Essays
Economic Policy: Thoughts for Today and Tomorrow
Epistemological Problems of Economics
Human Action: A Treatise on Economics
Interventionism: An Economic Analysis
Liberalism: The Classical Tradition
Money, Method, and the Market Process: Essays by Ludwig von Mises
Nation, State, and Economy: Contributions to the Politics
    and History of Our Time
Notes and Recollections: With The Historical Setting of the
    Austrian School of Economics
Omnipotent Government: The Rise of the Total State and Total War
On the Manipulation of Money and Credit: Three Treatises on
    Trade-Cycle Theory
Planning for Freedom: Let the Market System Work;
    A Collection of Essays and Addresses
Socialism: An Economic and Sociological Analysis
Theory and History: An Interpretation of Social and
    Economic Evolution
The Theory of Money and Credit
The Ultimate Foundation of Economic Science: An Essay
    on Method

EDITED BY RICHARD M. EBELING

Selected Writings of Ludwig von Mises

Volume 1: Monetary and Economic Policy Problems Before,
    During, and After the Great War
Volume 2: Between the Two World Wars: Monetary Disorder,
    Interventionism, Socialism, and the Great Depression
Volume 3: The Political Economy of International Reform
    and Reconstruction

LUDWIG VON MISES

Money, Method, and the Market Process

Essays by Ludwig von Mises

❧ LUDWIG VON MISES

Selected by Margit von Mises

Edited and with an Introduction by Richard M. Ebeling

LIBERTY FUND   *Indianapolis*

This book is published by Liberty Fund, Inc., a foundation established
to encourage study of the ideal of a society of free and responsible individuals.

𒂼𒄀

The cuneiform inscription that serves as our logo and as the design motif for
our endpapers is the earliest-known written appearance of the word "freedom"
(*amagi*), or "liberty." It is taken from a clay document written about 2300 B.C.
in the Sumerian city-state of Lagash.

Reprinted from the English-language edition of *Money, Method, and the
Market Process: Essays by Ludwig von Mises*, edited by Richard M. Ebeling.
Copyright © 1990, Kluwer Academic Publishers, being a part of Springer
Science + Business Media. This reprint has been authorized by Springer
Science + Business Media for publication in the USA only.

Front cover photograph of Ludwig von Mises used by permission
of the Ludwig von Mises Institute, Auburn, Alabama.

Frontispiece courtesy of Bettina Bien Greaves.

16   17   18   19   20   C   5   4   3   2   1
16   17   18   19   20   P   5   4   3   2   1

Library of Congress Cataloging-in-Publication Data
Von Mises, Ludwig, 1881–1973, author.
  [Essays. Selections]
  Money, method, and the market process : essays / by Ludwig von Mises ; selected
by Margit von Mises ; edited and with an introduction by Richard M. Ebeling.
    pages   cm. — (The Liberty Fund library of the works of Ludwig von Mises)
  Reprint, originally published in 1990.
  Includes bibliographical references and index.
  ISBN 978-0-86597-891-1 (hardcover : alk. paper) — ISBN 978-0-86597-892-8 (pbk.:
alk. paper)
    1. Money.   2. Capitalism.   3. Socialism.   4. Commerce.   5. Comparative
economics.   I. Von Mises, Margit, compiler.   II. Ebeling, Richard M., editor.
III. Title.
  HG221.V63 2016
  330.15'7—dc23   2015026574

Liberty Fund, Inc.
8335 Allison Pointe Trail, Suite 300
Indianapolis, Indiana 46250-1684

CONTENTS

Method

Money

Trade

Comparative Economic Systems

Ideas

FOREWORD

When my husband died in 1973 I had to go through his papers. Some of them were still in manuscript form and had never before been published. I selected several of these, plus a number of other articles that had appeared in periodicals but were no longer in print. This book is the result.

At my request Richard Ebeling wrote an introduction, which he has done in great detail. The depth of Ebeling's understanding of my husband's work is certainly apparent in his writing.

I am pleased to have the Ludwig von Mises Institute present this volume to the public.

Margit von Mises
New York City
September 1989

INTRODUCTION

I

In the 1920s and the 1930s, Ludwig von Mises was recognized as one of the leading economic theorists on the European Continent.[1] F. A. Hayek has said that Mises's critique of the possibilities for economic calculation under socialism had "the most profound impression on my generation. . . . To none of us . . . who read [his] book [*Socialism*] when it appeared was the world ever the same again."[2] Lord Lionel Robbins, in introducing the Austrian School literature on money and the trade cycle to English-speaking readers in 1931, emphasized the "marvelous renaissance" the "School of Vienna" had experienced "under the leadership of . . . Professor Mises."[3] In his comprehensive study *German Monetary Theory*, Howard Ellis insisted that Mises's *Theory of Money and Credit* was "one of the most substantial treatises upon monetary theory in the German literature" and that his personal role in bringing an end to the Austrian hyper-inflation of the early 1920s made "Mises a significant figure."[4] Fritz Machlup pointed out that in

1 Ludwig von Mises was born in Lemberg, Austria-Hungary, on September 29, 1881. After studying with Böhm-Bawerk, he received his doctorate from the University of Vienna in 1906. He taught at the University of Vienna (1913–1938), was Economic Advisor to the Austrian Chamber of Commerce (1909–1934), and served as Director of the League of Nations' Austrian Reparations Commission (1918–1920). In 1927, he founded the Austrian Institute for Trade Cycle Research. Professor Mises also taught at the Graduate Institute for International Studies in Geneva (1934–1940) and at New York University (1945–1969). Professor Mises died on October 10, 1973, at the age of 92.

2 F. A. Hayek, "Tribute to Ludwig von Mises," app. 2, in Margit von Mises, *My Years with Ludwig von Mises* (New Rochelle, N.Y.: Arlington House, 1976), p. 189.

3 Lionel Robbins, foreword to F. A. Hayek, *Prices and Production* (New York: Macmillan, 1932), p. ix.

4 Howard Ellis, *German Monetary Theory, 1905–1933* (Cambridge, Mass.: Harvard University Press, 1934), p. 77.

the early 1920s "Ludwig v. Mises was the first, so far as I know, to point to the phenomenon of the consumption of capital" due to the distortion of capital accounts caused by inflation and the fiscal policies of the Austrian State.[5] And in a study of the evolution of the theory of cost in economics, James M. Buchanan has emphasized that "Ludwig von Mises was one of the chief sources for the subjectivist economics" expounded in the 1930s at the London School of Economics and developed further, more recently, by the latest generation of the Austrian School.[6]

Yet, for most of the post-war period, Mises's writings have been in a general eclipse among economists, even though he continued to lecture widely, published over a half-dozen books during this time, and taught on a regular basis at New York University until his retirement in 1969 at the age of 89. The cause of this peculiar circumstance arose from his position vis-à-vis Keynesian economics. The almost monolithic hold Keynesianism had over economists following 1945 resulted in any individual who challenged either the theoretical edifice or policy proposals of the then "New Economics" experiencing almost certain intellectual death. Yet, this is exactly what Ludwig von Mises did in questioning and unflinchingly criticizing the entire body of Keynesian doctrine. The result was his near total ostracism from the economics profession.

During the 1970s, the intellectual terrain began to shift. In the wake of the dismal failure of Keynesian policy prescriptions, doubts began to be generated about the fundamentals of the Keynesian system. A great amount of scholarly self-criticism emerged as myriad exegetical readings were made in an attempt to divine what Keynes "really meant." The various investigations led to the conclusion that Keynes really meant almost anything, depending upon which of his volumes was read and which passages in any particular book were given emphasis.

The decline of Keynesianism has brought about a new spirit of open, intellectual competition among economists the likes of which has not been seen since the early 1930s. And occupying a prominent place in this competition have been the ideas of Ludwig von Mises and the Austrian School of Economics, of which he was an illustrious member.

5 Fritz Machlup, "The Consumption of Capital in Austria," *Review of Economic Statistics* 17 (January 15, 1935): 13.
6 James M. Buchanan, *Cost and Choice: An Inquiry in Economic Theory* (Chicago: Markham Publishing, 1969), p. 34.

II

The 1871 publication of Carl Menger's *Grundsätze der Volkswirtschafts-lehre*[7] marks the beginning of the Austrian School. Carl Menger is usually classified along with William Stanley Jevons and Léon Walras as one of the co-founders of the "Marginalist Economics" which replaced the Classical School and its labor theory of value. In his landmark volume, however, Menger produced a pioneering contribution to economic theory which distinguishes him uniquely from Jevons and Walras.

All three men had grasped the essential role of marginal utility: value was a matter of relative comparison between alternatives, and each alternative's significance was evaluated by the decision maker at the margin, i.e., the importance of the next unit of a good or service that could be obtained or would have to be given up in an act of choice.

For both Jevons and Walras, however, the value of the marginal utility concept was its power in demonstrating the *conditions for equilibrium* in a *given* exchange environment. For Menger, on the other hand, equilibrium was purely a useful limiting case that portrayed the circumstances under which no further motivations for exchange among traders would exist; the importance of marginal utility, in the Mengerian scheme, was precisely its value in enabling an analysis of the *exchange process* itself, regardless of the concrete manifestation of any eventual equilibrium outcome.[8]

An investigation of exchange sequences and processes in *disequilibrium* circumstances necessarily raised questions concerning the knowledge possessed by the respective market participants, the role of time as it related to adjustment periods and production periods relative to change, and the formation of expectations and foresight as potential traders attempted to anticipate future conditions as a guide for their own actions.

The economic analysis derived from Jevons and Walras took on a fundamentally static quality, being basically an attempt to stipulate the

7 Carl Menger, *Principles of Economics* [1871] (New York: New York University Press, [1950] 1981).
8 William Jaffe, "Menger, Jevons and Walras De-Homogenized," *Economic Inquiry* 14, no. 4 (December 1976): 511–24; and Erich Streissler, "To What Extent Was the Austrian School Marginalist?" in *The Marginalist Revolution in Economics*, R. D. Collision Black, A. W. Coats, and Craufurd D. W. Goodwin, eds. (Durham, N.C.: Duke University Press, 1973), pp. 160–75.

prerequisites for an equilibrium state. The "Austrian" approach derived from Menger had, in comparison, essential dynamic qualities that set it apart from other schools of thought over the years.[9]

The foundations laid by Menger in 1871 were developed further in the last two decades of the nineteenth century and in the first decade of the twentieth century. The two most notable contributors to this endeavor and, in fact, the ones who gave the Austrian School its world-wide recognition, were Eugen von Böhm-Bawerk and Friedrich von Wieser. Böhm-Bawerk extended Menger's analysis to questions concerning the theory of capital and the origin and formation of interest.[10] Wieser, appreciating Menger's insight that marginal utility and valuation are subjective estimates by the individual decision maker, demonstrated that cost was a subjective phenomenon as well, nothing more than the next best alternative or opportunity set aside or forgone when a choice and an exchange are made.[11]

III

Ludwig von Mises's contributions to the Austrian School spanned six decades and touched upon almost every aspect of economic science. The most controversial of Mises's writings have undoubtedly been those devoted to questions of methodology. Yet, at the same time, they are probably the most important of all his works. Indeed, what Mises attempted was the laying of a philosophical foundation for the entire edifice of economic science as it had developed from Adam Smith's first analysis of the spontaneous market order to Carl Menger's restatement of the principles of that spontaneous order on the basis of a conscious use of methodological individualism.[12]

9 Ludwig M. Lachmann, "The Significance of the Austrian School of Economics in the History of Ideas," in *Capital, Expectations, and the Market Process* (Kansas City, Kans.: Sheed Andrews and McMeel, 1977), pp. 45–64. On the evolution of the early Austrian School, see Ludwig von Mises, *The Historical Setting of the Austrian School* (New Rochelle, N.Y.: Arlington House, 1969); also Richard M. Ebeling, "Austrian Economics—An Annotated Bibliography," pt. 1, "The Austrian Economists," *Humane Studies Review* 2, no. 1 (1983).

10 Eugen von Böhm-Bawerk, *Capital and Interest*, 3 vols. (South Holland, Ill.: Libertarian Press, 1959).

11 Friedrich von Wieser, *Natural Value* [1889] (New York: Augustus M. Kelley, [1893] 1971); and Wieser, *Social Economics* [1914] (New York: Augustus M. Kelley, [1927] 1967).

12 Carl Menger, *Problems of Economics and Sociology* [1883] (Urbana, Ill.: University of Illinois Press, 1963). Ludwig von Mises, *Notes and Recollections* (South Holland, Ill.: Libertarian Press, 1978), pp. 122–23; these autobiographical "notes and recollections" were written by Mises in 1940,

Mises's writings on methodology covered practically his entire career. His early statements on the subject were collected in 1933 under the title *Epistemological Problems of Economics*.[13] They were refined and integrated into a general economic treatise, *Nationalökonomie* (1940)[14] and in its English-language counterpart, *Human Action* (1949),[15] and restated in *Theory and History* (1957)[16] and in *The Ultimate Foundation of Economic Science* (1962).[17]

The unique factor that separates the natural sciences from the social sciences, Mises argued, is the purposefulness or intentionality of all human endeavors. Man *above all else* is the being who acts, who inquisitively looks out upon the world, is conscious of opportunities to improve his lot, and proceeds to apply means to achieve ends when circumstances are perceived by the actor as offering the possibility for success.

Purposefulness, perception of circumstances, alertness to opportunities, Mises emphasized, are all attributes assignable only to individuals; and their concrete content are functions of the particular perspectives, circumstances, and interpretations of the respective actors themselves. Social science, therefore, is grounded at its start in methodological individualism and methodological subjectivism. The *alpha* and *omega* of social phenomena is the subjective world of acting man. The laws of nature and the physical environment may be the limits within which human endeavors are possible of accomplishment, but it is the human actor's *perception* of the possible and the attainable that will be the divining rod for action initiated.

We also see in this Misesian schema all the dynamic elements that dominated Menger's *Grundsätze*: imperfect knowledge, time and change, expectations and foresight. Each of these has implied residence

---

shortly after his arrival in the United States from Nazi-occupied Europe; see also, Margit von Mises, *My Years with Ludwig von Mises*, 2nd enl. ed. (Cedar Falls, Iowa: Center for Futures Education, 1984).

13 Ludwig von Mises, *Epistemological Problems of Economics* [1933] (New York: New York University Press, [1960] 1981).

14 Ludwig von Mises, *Nationalökonomie: Theorie des Handelns und Wirtschaftens* [1940] (Munich: Philosophia Verlag, 1980).

15 Ludwig von Mises, *Human Action: A Treatise on Economics*, 3rd rev. ed. [1949] (Chicago: Henry Regnery, 1966).

16 Ludwig von Mises, *Theory and History: An Interpretation of Social and Economic Evolution* [1957] (Auburn, Ala.: The Ludwig von Mises Institute, 1985).

17 Ludwig von Mises, *The Ultimate Foundation of Economic Science: An Essay on Method* (Kansas City, Kans.: Sheed Andrews and McMeel, [1962] 1976).

in the concept of purposeful action, for action—conscious behavior directed toward selected goals—has logical meaningfulness only where choice is seen as possible. And choice, as selection among alternative opportunities, has reality only where certain knowledge of the future is lacking. In turn, time and change, as Mises was wont to emphasize, are inseparable from action, for the very thought of action implies a *becoming* and a *became.*

A methodological subjectivist approach to analyzing the relationship of time to action, or the meaning of "ends possible" and "means available," or costs (as forgone opportunities) and benefits (as prospective gain in psychic improvement) resulted in Mises's rejection of what he saw as Positivist imperialism, i.e., the imposition of the methods considered appropriate in the natural sciences into the social sciences. Application of the Positivist rules of "objective science" would require the abandonment of that aspect that comprises the unique element in human events: appreciation of human action as having subjective meaning from the actor's point of view. The movement of physical objects between individuals only took on the quality of an "exchange," Mises argued, to the extent that that was the meaning the actors respectively assigned to their own action and to that of the other.

Yet, for Mises, this rejection of measurement and quantification as the standards for social science did not at the same time mean a collapse into Historicism, i.e., the argument that there are neither laws nor permanent regularities in the social world. The laws of social phenomena, Mises said, are ultimately derivatives from the *logic of action* which, itself, is one and the same with the logic of thought and reason. The processes of the market that tend to make market prices equal to market costs, for supply to tend toward an equilibrium with demand, are all reducible to the logic guiding the actions of the respective individuals subsumed under the terms "suppliers" and "demanders," i.e., that the value of any particular means should not exceed the value of any particular end they serve.

This accounts, also, for what has usually been perceived as Mises's peculiar insistence that economic theory is both a priori and empirically truthful. It is a priori, for Mises, because the logic of action and its requisite categories of means and ends, costs and benefits, etc., must conceptually precede in thought the selection of any concrete end and the application of any concrete means and, therefore, the designating of something as one or the other. And it is empirically truthful because the logic of human thought precludes the conceiving of any conscious human action not operating within these categories; hence, it empirically reflects the essential qualities of all conscious human conduct.

While the categories of action can serve as the filing system enabling the social scientist and the economist to both order and give intelligible interpretation to the complexity of the social world, the categories remain purely generic in nature; i.e., they do not provide any information about the specific ends and means selected by individuals or the concrete outcomes that may arise from a series of actions. Thus, the "elasticities" of demand and supply and the particular "speeds of adjustment" in prices, output, and expectations will depend upon the historical circumstances. This is lucidly explained by Mises in "The Treatment of 'Irrationality' in the Social Sciences," one of the essays in this volume:

> We have plenty of figures available concerning the German inflation of the years, 1914–1923. Economic theory provides us with all the knowledge needed for a perfect grasp of the causes of price changes. But this knowledge does not give us quantitative definiteness. Economics is . . . qualitative and not quantitative. . . . There are in the sphere of human action no constant relations between magnitudes. . . . The rise of German prices in the years of the First World War was not only due to the increase of the quantity of bank notes. Other changes contributed, too. The supply of commodities went down because many millions of workers were in the army and no longer worked in the plants, because government control of business reduced productivity, because the blockade prevented imports from abroad, and because workers suffered from malnutrition. It is impossible to establish by methods other than *Verstehen* [interpretive "understanding"] how each of these factors—and of some other relevant factors—contributed to the rise of prices. . . . The *Verstehen* is in the realm of history the substitute, as it were, for quantitative analysis and measurement, which are unfeasible with regard to human actions outside the field of technology. (pp. 28–29)

Similarly, economic forecasting, as Mises pointed out, is fundamentally an attempt to act as a "historian of the future."[18] It is an attempt to project oneself into the future and anticipate how market actors over a future period will classify various entities as either means or ends; what expectations they will form about the most advantageous courses of ac-

---

18 Mises, *Theory and History*, p. 320; also, Richard M. Ebeling, "Expectations and Expectations Formation in Mises's Theory of the Market Process," *Market Process* (Spring 1988).

tion to undertake; and to then analyze both the intended and the likely unintended consequences of a multitude of individual plans as they meet and mesh in the social arena over that future period of time.[19]

Mises's contributions to economic science have all been attempts, to one degree or another, to apply this methodology to particular problems. As F. A. Hayek has perceptively pointed out, ". . . most peculiarities of [Mises's] views which at first strike many readers as strange and unacceptable trace to the fact that in the consistent development of the subjectivist approach he has for a long time moved ahead of his contemporaries."[20]

In monetary theory, for instance, Mises made one of the first successful applications of marginal utility analysis to explain the value of money by emphasizing the role of uncertainty and expectations in the actions of market participants. His classic work, *The Theory of Money and Credit* (1912; 1924; 1935),[21] and his monograph *Monetary Stabilization and Cyclical Policy* (1928),[22] as well as portions of *Human Action*,[23] however, contain much more than this. In the parlance of contemporary economics, Mises tried to develop a microeconomic foundation for macroeconomics. Utilizing Böhm-Bawerk's capital theory and Knut Wicksell's distinction between the money and "natural" rates of interest, he devised a dynamic process analysis showing how changes in the money supply could generate shifts in income distribution, cause resource misallocations via relative price distortions, and induce trade cycle fluctuations.

What distinguished Mises's approach, for example, from Irving

19 For an analysis of the relationship between Mises's view of economic science and alternative perspectives in the history of economic thought, see Israel M. Kirzner, *The Economic Point of View* (Kansas City, Kans.: Sheed Andrews and McMeel, [1960] 1976); and for Mises's relationship to other members of the Austrian School, see Lawrence H. White, *The Methodology of the Austrian School Economists* (Auburn, Ala.: The Ludwig von Mises Institute, 1984); and Richard M. Ebeling, "Austrian Economics—An Annotated Bibliography," pt. 2, "Methodology of the Austrian School," *Humane Studies Review* 3, no. 2 (Fall 1985); see also Murray N. Rothbard, "Praxeology as the Method of the Social Sciences," in *Individualism and the Philosophy of the Social Sciences* (San Francisco: Cato Institute, 1979).

20 F. A. Hayek, *The Counter-Revolution of Science* (Indianapolis, Ind.: Liberty Fund, [1952] 1979), p. 52, n. 7.

21 Ludwig von Mises, *The Theory of Money and Credit* [1912; 2nd rev. ed., 1924] (Indianapolis, Ind.: Liberty Fund, [1953] 1981).

22 Ludwig von Mises, "Monetary Stabilization and Cyclical Policy" [1928], in *On the Manipulation of Money and Credit* (Dobbs Ferry, N.Y.: Free Market Books, 1978), pp. 57–171.

23 Mises, *Human Action*, pp. 398–478 and 538–86.

Fisher's quantity theory of money was precisely his refusal to make the analytical jump (made by Fisher and others) from changes in the aggregate money stock to changes in the general "price level." Mises insisted upon a strict adherence to methodological individualism. Any explanation of statistically calculated changes in total employment and output or in the "price level" needed to be dissected into the "step-by-step" sequential process of individual market actions, reactions, and plan adjustments and readjustments following an increase (or decrease) in the money supply. Thus, the macroeconomic aggregates were to be decomposed into their microeconomic components by rigorously analyzing the "transmission mechanism" of a monetary injection.[24]

The same methodological considerations permeate Mises's famous writings on comparative economic systems. Already in the 1880s and 1890s, Wieser and, in particular, Böhm-Bawerk had critically evaluated the Marxian labor theory of value and discovered fundamental defects in both the assumptions and the logic.[25] However, almost no thought had been given by either socialist or non-socialist economists to the efficacy of state economic planning as an alternative to a market economy. In a series of three books, *Socialism* (1922),[26] *Liberalism* (1927),[27] and *A Critique of Interventionism* (1929),[28] Mises took up this very question.

Mises saw the issue as concerning questions of knowledge, change, and adjustment—the Mengerian themes, once again. In the Walrasian world of general equilibrium, on the other hand, where it is assumed that the relevant supply and demand conditions are known and all markets are cleared at equilibrium prices, it superficially appears as if a "market" outcome and a "planned" outcome are interchangeable with

24 Richard M. Ebeling, ed., *The Austrian Theory of the Trade Cycle and Other Essays*, by Ludwig von Mises, Gottfried Haberler, Murray N. Rothbard, and Friedrich A. Hayek (New York: Center for Libertarian Studies, 1978; reprinted by the Ludwig von Mises Institute, 1983).

25 Böhm-Bawerk, "Unresolved Contradiction in the Marxian Economic System" [1976], in *Shorter Classics of Böhm-Bawerk*, vol. 1 (South Holland, Ill.: Libertarian Press, 1962), pp. 201–301; or Böhm-Bawerk, *Karl Marx and the Close of His System* (Clifton, N.J.: Augustus M. Kelley, [1949] 1975), an alternative translation.

26 Ludwig von Mises, *Socialism: An Economic and Sociological Analysis* [1922; rev. ed., 1932] (Indianapolis, Ind.: Liberty Fund, [1951] 1981).

27 Ludwig von Mises, *Liberalism: A Socio-Economic Exposition* [1927] (Kansas City, Kans.: Sheed Andrews and McMeel, [1962] 1978); the original translation was published under the title *The Free and Prosperous Commonwealth*.

28 Ludwig von Mises, *A Critique of Interventionism* [1929] (New Rochelle, N.Y.: Arlington House, 1977).

each other.[29] But what are the implications if, instead, it is assumed that an economy *is not* in equilibrium and that constant changes on both the demand and supply sides are an integral part of the system? In other words, what are the implications in the *real world?* How is the coordination of a multitude of individual human plans and activities to be brought about so as to assure a tendency toward an efficient allocation of scarce consumer goods and means of production?

As Mises explained, in a market economy this is accomplished via the price mechanism: rivalrous entrepreneurs bid for the use or purchase of scarce factors of production based upon their respective anticipations of the relative consumer demands for either existing or new products. Prices for these factors of production are formed out of the interaction of, on the one hand, entrepreneurs who have expectations about the prices consumers would be willing to pay for the final output the productive factors could assist in producing and, on the other hand, owners of the productive factors who form expectations about alternative employment opportunities. In turn, the ongoing process of profit and loss assures that economic control of those scarce factors of production always tends to be in the hands of those entrepreneurs who demonstrate a greater capacity for forming a more nearly correct foresight about changes in underlying market conditions.[30]

Socialism, Mises argued, negated the entire market process. Without private ownership of the means of production, no markets would exist upon which prices for scarce resources could be generated. And without real market-created prices, reflecting ever-changing supply and demand conditions, no rational technique would exist for carrying out the economic calculations required for the estimation of various least-cost methods of production. Hence, concluded Mises, the establishment of universal socialism would necessitate the demise of all rational economic planning.[31]

---

29 This is not to suggest that Walras believed that a "planned" solution was interchangeable with a "market" solution. Indeed, he emphasized that the problem was too complex for any solution other than that provided by the competitive market; see Léon Walras, *Elements of Pure Economics* (New York: Augustus M. Kelley, [1954] 1969), p. 106.

30 Mises, *Human Action*, pp. 257–397; and Ludwig von Mises, "Profit and Loss," in *Planning for Freedom*, enl. ed. (South Holland, Ind.: Libertarian Press, 1980), pp. 108–50.

31 Mises, *Human Action*, pp. 689–715; also, Ludwig von Mises, "Economic Calculation in the Socialist Commonwealth" [1920], in *Collectivist Economic Planning*, F. A. Hayek, ed. (London: Routledge and Sons, 1935), pp. 87–130. For an extended summary of Mises's contribution to the socialist calculation debate, see Murray N. Rothbard, "Ludwig von Mises and Economic

Government intervention within a market order, Mises reasoned, ultimately created the same problems as did socialism, only in a more moderate form. To the extent that the interventions infringed upon the free-market formation of prices and direction of production, to that extent, market forces—i.e., entrepreneurial attempts to competitively satisfy consumer demands in the most efficient manner—were thwarted. Furthermore, as each government intervention would distort and disrupt the competitive market price structure, the government would continually face the problem of either extending its controls and regulations in an attempt to compensate for the imbalances its previous interventions had caused or repealing the existing interventions and allowing a return to a competitive market arrangement. Thus, Mises insisted, an interventionist "mixed-economy" was inherently unstable; logically it required either an extension of the interventions until all-round planning was established via a continuing piecemeal process or else the interventionist state would have to contract until a free-market order once again predominated.[32]

Mises's conclusion that a market economy was the only reasonable solution to the problem of economic order was not meant by him to be taken as a personal value judgment on his part. Quite to the contrary, he saw it as a purely scientific conclusion to a scientific problem. Once a society is beyond a primitive economic state, or more exactly, if it is to get beyond such a state, there must exist a certain set of institutional structures that enable advantageous utilization of extensive division of labor. The growing complexity and dispersion of knowledge that emerges with the division of labor precludes any successful coordination via some central directing authority. Some mechanism must assist in this endeavor, and the price mechanism, argued Mises, was

Calculation Under Socialism," in *The Economics of Ludwig von Mises: Toward a Critical Reappraisal*, Lawrence S. Moss, ed. (Kansas City, Kans.: Sheed Andrews and McMeel, 1976), pp. 67–77; Karen I. Vaughn, "Economic Calculation under Socialism: The Austrian Contribution," *Economic Inquiry* 18 (October 1980): 535–54; Don Lavoie, *Rivalry and Central Planning: The Socialist Calculation Debate Reconsidered* (New York: Cambridge University Press, 1985); and Richard M. Ebeling, "Economic Calculation under Socialism: Ludwig von Mises and His Predecessors," in *The Meaning of Ludwig von Mises* (Auburn, Ala.: The Ludwig von Mises Institute, forthcoming).

32 Ludwig von Mises, "Middle-of-the-Road Policy Leads to Socialism," in *Planning for Freedom*, pp. 18–35. For an elaboration of Mises's critique of intervention linked to his criticism of economic calculation under socialism, see Israel M. Kirzner, "The Perils of Regulation: A Market-Process Approach," *Discovery and the Capitalist Process* (Chicago: University of Chicago Press, 1985), pp. 119–49.

just such an apparatus. Information about a multitude of consumer preferences and entrepreneurial expectations could be successfully transmitted across a nation, across a continent, and, indeed, across the world through changes in market prices for both finished goods and the factors of production.

Real market prices—reflecting *real* preferences, *real* expectations, *real* information about scarcity conditions—were impossible if private ownership of the factors of production was outlawed, for without ownership there could be no trades, without the ability to trade there could be no bids and offers, and without bids and offers there were no *real* prices. Interventions in a market economy, on the other hand, did not abrogate prices, but they could distort and disrupt the informational flow, thus seriously diminishing the efficiency of the society's extended use of the division of labor. Thus, as a scientist, Mises felt confident in saying that ultimately there was no alternative to a thoroughgoing market order.

We also see in Mises's critique of interventionism the same microeconomic process analysis that is visible in his monetary studies. An intervention impinges upon the economic system at some point. The relative price and production relations of the market are disturbed, resulting in modifications in the actions of various market participants that distort the market order. These modified actions, in turn, influence the behavior and response of still others, resulting in even further imbalances and distortions between various supplies and demands. The implication that Mises drew was that the longer-term, complex ramifications from any specific intervention can, therefore, tend to have the consequence of making worse any initial market condition that the intervention was meant to remedy. Thus, with the tools of modern economic theory, Mises was able to construct a sophisticated sequence analysis that reinforced the older arguments of the Classical Economists concerning the importance of understanding both what is seen (the initial, short-run effect of an intervention) and what is unseen (the longer-run consequences) in the implementation of economic policy.

IV

In the post-war years, the methodological thrust implicit in Mises's writings was inevitably bound to conflict with the Keynesian spirit of the times. For a wide range of theoretical and policy issues, microeconomics was declared a defective analytical device. A "subjectivist" microeconomic approach such as Mises's was certain to be rejected. Instead, for special "macro"-economic problems, different tools, it was said, needed to be forged. The search was made to discover quantitative "functional" relationships that were postulated to exist between certain economic aggregates, e.g., total investment and total employment, and total income and total consumption. The search has ended in dismal failure; it was bound to fail.

From the beginning its failure was preordained because Keynesianism was shot through and through with the fallacy of "conceptual realism," i.e., the imputing to statistically derived magnitudes, attributes, and qualities independent of and separate from their component parts. As Mises's fellow Austrian economist F. A. Hayek has pointed out, the application of such a macroeconomic approach has, in fact, been "a positive hindrance to further progress" in monetary and business-cycle theory. Indeed, economic theory, itself, is abrogated by attempts

> to establish direct causal connections between the *total* quantity of money, the *general* level of prices and . . . also the *total* amount of production. For none of these magnitudes as such ever exerts an influence on the decisions of individuals; yet, it is on the assumption of a knowledge of the decisions of individuals that the main propositions of . . . economic theory are based. It is to this "individualistic" method that we owe whatever understanding of economic phenomena we possess. . . . If, therefore, monetary theory still attempts to establish causal relations between aggregates and general averages, this means that monetary theory lags behind the development of economics in general. In fact, neither aggregates nor averages do act upon one another, and it will never be possible to establish necessary connections of cause and effect between them as we can between individual phenomena, individual prices, etc.[33]

The crucial point against this still-prevailing macroeconomic approach is that the aggregate components entering into the analysis are all elements having no existence of their own outside the economist's own calculations of the chosen magnitudes. The "price level," for example, is a statistical averaging at a point in time of a group of selected and weighted prices. But the individuals in the marketplace are never confronted by such a statistical "price level." What they *do*

---

33 Friedrich A. Hayek, *Prices and Production* [1935] (New York: Augustus M. Kelley, 1967), pp. 4–5.

face is an array of particular prices representing the exchange ratios between money and every good or service against which the medium of exchange is traded. Any calculated change in the "price level" can only be an *ex post* statistical averaging of a series of individual price changes. The causal links generating changes in market decisions will have been the alterations in the specific, individual exchange ratios between money and various goods, not a statistical "price level" created by the economic analyst *after* all the individual price changes have already worked, or are still in the process of working, their effects upon the economy.

The same reasoning applies to any measured changes in total output and total employment. Such statistical calculations are, again, purely the *ex post* summations and averaging of an array of changes in particular and individual outputs and specific and individual employment opportunities. One cannot, in any meaningful sense, separate the "total" changes from the particular circumstances in each sector of the economy that has contributed to the measured "total" outcome. Any attempt to do so must necessarily eliminate practically all possibility of analyzing the conditions that have generated these changes as well as the forces that would have to come into operation to either maintain or change further the output and employment "levels" already attained.[34]

The inevitable conclusion that the bulk of macroeconomics must be seen as having shunted economic theory on to a wrong track has been too much for some economists to take. In a methodological discussion that included a critical evaluation of Mises and the Austrian School, Professor Mark Blaug perceived "what methodological individualism strictly interpreted . . . would imply for economics. In effect, it would rule out all macroeconomic propositions that cannot be reduced to microeconomic ones, and since few have yet been so reduced, this amounts in turn to saying goodbye to almost the whole of received macroeconomics." In exasperation, Blaug declares, "[t]here must be something wrong with a methodological principle that has such devastating implications."[35]

In reply to Blaug, I can do no better than to quote another economist, Arthur W. Marget, who, like Mises, was washed away in the tidal

34 See Roger W. Garrison, "Intertemporal Coordination and the Invisible Hand: An Austrian Perspective on the Keynesian Vision," *History of Political Economy* 17, no. 2 (Summer 1985): 309–21.
35 Mark Blaug, *The Methodology of Economics, or How Economists Explain* (Cambridge: Cambridge University Press, 1980), pp. 51 and 91–93.

wave of Keynesian euphoria because he, too, questioned the very foundation of Keynes's system:

> It is a fundamental methodological proposition of "modern" versions of the *"general" Theory of Value* that all categories with respect to "supply" and "demand" must be unequivocally related to categories which present themselves to the minds of those "economizing" *individuals* (or individual business *firms*) whose calculations make the "supplies" and "demands" realized in the market what they are. . . . [T]he type of problem raised by the necessity for establishing a relation between these "microeconomic" decisions and these "macroeconomic" processes is not solved by the arbitrary introduction of an "aggregate supply function" and an "aggregate demand function" for industry *as a whole*, in defiance of the fact that neither of these "functions" deals with elements which enter directly into the calculations of the individual entrepreneurs whose "microeconomic" decisions and actions make "macroeconomic" processes what they are. On the contrary, it must be said, of such an attempt at "solution," that it misconceives entirely the true nature of the relation between microeconomic analysis and macroeconomic analysis.[36]

Up until recently, a good many macro-theorists abdicated any responsibility for even trying to establish microeconomic linkages. While the last few years have seen the development of a new literature with this goal as its motivating force, it has developed along mostly "static" lines, i.e., an analysis of the choice theoretics that serve as the logic guiding the market participants in selecting particular pricing, output, and employment options, with the microeconomic quantities then being summed into macroeconomic totals.

The Austrians, following the directions suggested by Mises, have attempted a much more dynamic analysis. The heart of Mises's "step-by-step" procedure is to show how *changes* in the various microeconomic elements set in motion *sequential effects through time* that generate modifications in individual actions, which, in turn, result in changes not only in the "aggregate" quantities but in the *relative price and production structures*, as well.[37]

---

36 Arthur W. Marget, *The Theory of Prices*, vol. 2 [1942] (New York: Augustus M. Kelley, 1966), pp. 541 and 544.

37 Cf. Richard M. Ebeling, "Ludwig von Mises and the Gold Standard," in *The Gold Standard: An Austrian Perspective*, by Llewellyn H. Rockwell, Jr., ed. (Lexington, Mass.: Lexington Books, 1985), pp. 35–59; also Richard M. Ebeling, "Ludwig von Mises and Some Contemporary Economic Themes," in *Homage to Mises: The First Hundred Years*, by John K. Andrews, ed. (Hillsdale, Mich.: Hillsdale College Press, 1981), pp. 38–44.

This has been clearly explained by another Austrian, Oskar Morgenstern. Using an inflationary process as an example, Morgenstern argued that if,

> no account is given *where* this additional money originates from, *where* it is injected, with *what* different magnitudes and *how* it penetrates (through *which* paths and channels and with *what* speed), into the body economic, very little information is given. The same total addition will have different consequences if it is injected via consumer's loans, or producer's borrowings, via the Defense Department, or via unemployment subsidies, etc. Depending on the existing conditions of the economy, each point of injection will produce different consequences for the same aggregate amount of money, so that the monetary analysis will have to be combined with an equally detailed analysis of changing flows of commodities and services.[38]

The emphasis placed by Mises and the Austrians on analyzing macroeconomic phenomena in terms of microeconomic processes led Joseph Schumpeter to conclude that "the Austrian way of emphasizing the behavior or decisions of individuals and of defining exchange value of money with respect to individual commodities rather than with respect to a price level of one kind or another has its merits, particularly in the analysis of an inflationary process; it tends to replace a simple but inadequate picture by one which is less clear-cut but more realistic and richer in results."[39]

Such an approach, it is important to bring out, has significance for more than "pure theory" alone. The continuing crisis in macroeconomic theory reflects the consequences of ignoring these very aspects of microeconomic dynamics. Directing all their attention to policy effects on "total" demand, "aggregate" employment, and the general "price-level," the Praetorian Guard of the aging "New Economics" still remains blind to the warping effect their policies have had on the entire structure of the economy. Perpetual monetary injections by the central bank (the Federal Reserve System) have disrupted the market price structure, creating artificial employment opportunities and, thus,

38 Oskar Morgenstern, "Thirteen Critical Points in Contemporary Economic Theory: An Interpretation," *Journal of Economic Literature* 10, no. 4 (December 1972): 1184; reprinted in *Selected Economic Writings by Oskar Morgenstern*, Andrew Schotter, ed. (New York: New York University Press, 1976), p. 288.
39 Joseph A. Schumpeter, *History of Economic Analysis* (New York: Oxford University Press, 1954), p. 1090.

inducing massive misdirections of labor and capital. Fiscal policies have so distorted incentive structures that savings in the United States is among the lowest in the Western World. And layers of interventions and regulatory acts have severely curtailed effective utilization of existing productive capacity as well as narrowing the range of opportunities open to new entrepreneurial discovery and innovation.

The present times, however, seem to offer a chance for a change. With orthodox Keynesianism in disrepute, with a new and growing awareness and sympathy for the free market among economists, and with increasing concern among the general public over the degree of government intervention in social and economic affairs, a reversal might just be possible.

V

The present volume, by one of the leading figures of twentieth-century economic thought, and touching on almost every major issue of the day, could serve as an important handbook in bringing about such a reversal in both theory and policy.

The essays contained in this collection, many previously unpublished, offer a convenient composite of "Misesian economics." They include discussions of almost every aspect of economic and social theory that Mises considered of paramount importance. Furthermore, in many instances they offer applications of Mises's schema that are not to be found in his other writings.

The first three essays, on method, carefully delineate the differences between the social and natural sciences, discuss the importance of value-freedom in social analysis, and explain the distinction that Mises saw between his science of human action—*praxeology*—and the methods of the German Historical School.

The next five essays, on money, discuss the unique position of money in economic exchange, the distortive effects of monetary expansion on market activity, and the devastating consequences of ever-worsening inflation. Of particular interest is an analysis by Mises of the limits of any attempt to stabilize economic activity via stabilization of the price level.

The following four essays, on trade, focus on the economic distortions and inefficiencies arising in a world of economic nationalism. Though mostly written in the 1940s and early 1950s, these essays are more relevant than ever. With third-world countries aggressively pursuing policies of economic self-sufficiency and with a rising tide of protectionism in the industrialized western nations, Mises's warnings of the danger of international conflict and war in a world without free trade will be found particularly cogent.

The seven essays on comparative economic systems analyze the political-economic clash between the free-market order and collectivist economic planning. Included are detailed studies of socialism, the cooperatives movement, and the economic basis for group conflicts.

The final two essays, on ideas, emphasize that the ultimate contest in politics and economics is not between nations and armies, but between the ideas that rule the actions of men.

The noted German economist Wilhelm Röpke once recounted how the reading of Mises's post–World War I book *Nation, State, and Economy* (1919) had been "in many ways the redeeming answer to the questions tormenting a young man who had just come back from the trenches.[40] With the collapse of Keynesian supremacy and the initiation of a new battle of ideas among economists and policy-makers, the writings of Ludwig von Mises might once again be of assistance to the new generation of combatants who will be manning the intellectual trenches. It is with this idea in mind that this volume of essays, *Money, Method, and the Market Process*, is offered to the public.

Richard M. Ebeling
Ludwig von Mises Assistant Professor of Economics
Hillsdale College
Hillsdale, Michigan
September 1989

---

40 Wilhelm Röpke, "Homage to a Master and a Friend," *The Mont Pelerin Quarterly* (October 1961): 6.

❧ Method

CHAPTER 1

Social Science and Natural Science

I

The foundations of the modern social sciences were laid in the eighteenth century. Up to this time we find history only. Of course, the writings of the historians are full of implications which purport to be valid for all human action irrespective of time and milieu, and even when they do not explicitly set forth such theses, they necessarily base their grasp of the facts and their interpretation on assumptions of this type. But no attempt was made to clarify these tacit suppositions by special analysis.

On the other hand the belief prevailed that in the field of human action no other criterion could be used than that of good and bad. If a policy did not attain its end, its failure was ascribed to the moral insufficiency of man or to the weakness of the government. With good men and strong governments everything was considered feasible.

Then in the eighteenth century came a radical change. The founders of Political Economy discovered regularity in the operation of the market. They discovered that to every state of the market a certain state of prices corresponded and that a tendency to restore this state made itself manifest whenever anything tried to alter it. This insight opened a new chapter in science. People came to realize with astonishment that human actions were open to investigation from other points of view than that of moral judgment. They were compelled to recognize a regularity which they compared to that with which they were already familiar in the field of the natural sciences.

Since the days of Cantillon, Hume, the Physiocrats, and Adam Smith, economic theory has made continuous—although not steady—

[Reprinted from *Journal of Social Philosophy and Jurisprudence* 7, no. 3 (April 1942).—Ed.]

progress. In the course of this development it has become much more than a theory of market operations within the frame of a society based on private ownership of the means of production. It has for some time been a general theory of human action, of human choice and preference.

II

The elements of social cognition are abstract and not reducible to any concrete images that might be apprehended by the senses. To make them easier to visualize, one likes to have recourse to metaphorical language. For some time the biological metaphors were very popular. There were writers who overworked this metaphor to ridiculous extremes. It will suffice to cite the name of Lilienfeld.[1]

Today the mechanistic metaphor is much more in use. The theoretical basis for its application is to be found in the positivist view of social science. Positivism blithely waved aside everything which history and economics taught. History, in its eyes, is simply not science; economics, a special kind of metaphysics. In place of both, positivism postulates a social science which has to be built up by the experimental method as ideally applied in Newtonian physics. Economics has to be experimental, mathematical and quantitative. Its task is to measure, because science is measurement. Every statement must be open to verification by facts.

Every proposition of this positivist epistemology is wrong.

The social sciences in general and economics in particular cannot be based on experience in the sense in which this term is used by the natural sciences. Social experience is historical experience. Of course every experience is the experience of something passed. But what distinguishes social experience from that which forms the basis of the natural sciences is that it is always the experience of a complexity of phenomena. The experience to which the natural sciences owe all

---

1 Cf., for instance, Paul von Lilienfeld, *La Pathologie Sociale* [Social Pathology] (Paris, 1896). ["When a government takes a loan from the House of Rothschild organic sociology conceives the process as follows: . . . 'The House of Rothschild's operation, on such an occasion, is precisely similar to the action of a group of body cells which cooperate in the production of the blood necessary for nourishing the brain, in hope of being compensated by a reaction of the gray matter cells which they need to reactivate and to accumulate new energies,' Ibid., p. 104," in Ludwig von Mises, *Socialism*, J. Kahane, trans. (Indianapolis, Ind.: Liberty Fund, 1981), p. 257 n. — Ed.]

their success is the experience of the experiment. In the experiments the different elements of change are observed in isolation. The control of the conditions of change provides the experimenter with the means of assigning to each effect its sufficient cause. Without regard to the philosophical problem involved he proceeds to amass "facts." These facts are the bricks which the scientist uses in constructing his theories. They constitute the only material at his disposal. His theory must not be in contradiction with these facts. They are the ultimate things.

The social sciences cannot make use of experiments. The experience with which they have to deal is the experience of complex phenomena. They are in the same position as acoustics would be if the only material of the scientist were the hearing of a concerto or the noise of a waterfall. It is nowadays fashionable to style the statistical bureaus laboratories. This is misleading. The material which statistics provides is historical; that means the outcome of a complexity of forces. The social sciences never enjoy the advantage of observing the consequences of a change in one element only, other conditions being equal.

It follows that the social sciences can never use experience to verify their statements. Every fact and every experience with which they have to deal is open to various interpretations. Of course, the experience of a complexity of phenomena can never prove or disprove a statement in the way in which an experiment proves or disproves. We do not have any historical experience whose import is judged identically by all people. There is no doubt that up to now in history, only nations which have based their social order on private ownership of the means of production have reached a somewhat high stage of welfare and civilization. Nevertheless, nobody would consider this as an incontestable refutation of socialist theories. In the field of the natural sciences there are also differences of opinion concerning the interpretation of complex facts. But here freedom of explanation is limited by the necessity of not contradicting statements satisfactorily verified by experiments. In the interpretation of social facts no such limits exist. Everything could be asserted about them provided that we are not confined within the bounds of principles of whose logical nature we intend to speak later. Here however we already have to mention that every discussion concerning the meaning of historical experience imperceptibly passes over into a discussion of these principles without any further reference to experience. People may begin by discussing the lesson to be learnt from an import duty or from the Russian Soviet system; they will very quickly be discussing the general theory of interregional trade or the no less pure theory of socialism and capitalism.

The impossibility of experimenting means concomitantly the impossibility of measurement. The physicist has to deal with magnitudes and numerical relations, because he has the right to assume that certain invariable relations between physical properties subsist. The experiment provides him with the numerical value to be assigned to them. In human behavior there are no such constant relations, there is no standard which could be used as a measure, and there are no experiments which could establish uniformities of this type.

What the statistician establishes in studying the relations between prices and supply or between supply and demand is of historical importance only. If he determines that a rise of 10 percent in the supply of potatoes in Atlantis in the years between 1920 and 1930 was followed by a fall in the price of potatoes by 8 percent, he does not say anything about what happened or may happen with a change in the supply of potatoes in another country or at another time. Such measurements as that of elasticity of demand cannot be compared with the physicist's measurement, e.g., specific density or weight of atoms. Of course everybody realizes that the behavior of men concerning potatoes and every other commodity is variable. Different individuals value the same things in different ways, and the valuation changes even with the same individual with changing conditions. We cannot categorize individuals in classes which react in the same way, and we cannot determine the conditions which evoke the same reaction. Under these circumstances we have to realize that the statistical economist is a historian and not an experimenter. For the social sciences, statistics constitutes a method of historical research.

In every science the considerations which result in the formulation of an equation are of a non-mathematical character. The formulation of the equation has a practical importance, because the constant relations which it includes are experimentally established and because it is possible to introduce specific known values in the function to determine those unknown. These equations thus lie at the basis of technological designing; they are not only the consummation of the theoretical analysis but also the starting point of practical work. But in economics, where there are no constant relations between magnitudes, the equations are void of practical application. Even if we could dispose of all qualms concerning their formulation we would still have to realize that they are without any practical use.

But the chief objection which must be raised to the mathematical treatment of economic problems comes from another ground: it really does not deal with the actual operations of human actions but with a fictitious concept that the economist builds up for instrumental purposes. This is the concept of static equilibrium.

For the sake of grasping the consequences of change and the nature of profit in a market economy, the economist constructs a fictitious system in which there is no change. Today is like yesterday and tomorrow will be like today. There is no uncertainty about the future, and activity therefore does not involve risk. But for the allowance to be made of interest, the sum of the prices of the complementary factors of production exactly equals the price of the product, which means there is no room left for profit. But this fictitious concept is not only unrealizable in actual life; it cannot even be consistently carried to its ultimate conclusions. The individuals in this fictitious world would not act; they would not have to make choices; they would just vegetate. It is true that economics, exactly because it cannot make experiments, is bound to apply this and other fictitious concepts of a similar type. But its use should be restricted to the purposes which it is designed to serve. The purpose of the concept of static equilibrium is the study of the nature of the relations between costs and prices and thereby of profits. Outside of this it is inapplicable, and occupation with it vain.

Now all that mathematics can do in the field of economic studies is to describe static equilibrium. The equations and the indifference curves deal with a fictitious state of things, which never exists anywhere. What they afford is a mathematical expression of the definition of static equilibrium. Because mathematical economists start from the prejudice that economics has to be treated in mathematical terms, they consider the study of static equilibrium as the whole of economics. The purely instrumental character of this concept has been overshadowed by this preoccupation.

Of course, mathematics cannot tell us anything about the way by which this static equilibrium could be reached. The mathematical determination of the difference between any actual state and the equilibrium state is not a substitute for the method by which the logical or non-mathematical economists let us conceive the nature of those human actions which necessarily would bring about equilibrium provided that no further change occurs in the data.

Occupation with static equilibrium is a misguided evasion of the study of the main economic problems. The pragmatic value of this equilibrium concept should not be underrated, but it is an instrument for the solution of one problem only. In any case the mathematical elaboration of static equilibrium is mere by-play in economics.

The case is similar with the use of curves. We may represent the price of a commodity as the point of intersection of two curves, the curve of demand and the curve of supply. But we have to realize that we do not know anything about the shape of these curves. We know *a posteriori* the prices, which we assume to be the points of intersection, but we do not know the form of the curve either in advance or for the past. The representation of the curves is therefore nothing more than a didactic means of rendering the theory graphic and hence more easily comprehensible.

The mathematical economist is prone to consider the price either as a measurement of value or as equivalent to the commodity. To this we have to say that prices are not measured in money but that they are the amount of money exchanged for a commodity. The price is not equivalent to the commodity. A purchase takes place only when the buyer values the commodity higher than the price, and the seller values it lower than the price. Nobody has the right to abstract from this fact and to assume an equivalence where there is a difference in valuation. When either one of the parties considers the price as the equivalent of the commodity no transaction takes place. In this sense we may say every transaction is for both parties a "bargain."

III

Physicists consider the objects of their study from without. They have no knowledge of what is going on in the interior, in the "soul," of a falling stone. But they have the opportunity to observe the falling of the stone in experiments and thereby to discover what they call the laws of falling. From the results of such experimental knowledge, they build up their theories proceeding from the special to the more general, from the concrete to the more abstract.

Economics deals with human actions not, as it is sometimes said, with commodities, economic quantities, or prices. We do not have the power to experiment with human actions. But we have, being human ourselves, a knowledge of what goes on within acting men. We know something about the meaning which acting men attach to their actions. We know why men wish to change the conditions of their lives. We know something about that uneasiness which is the ultimate incentive of the changes which they bring about. A perfectly satisfied man or a man who although unsatisfied did not see any means of improvement would not act at all.

Thus the economist is, as Cairnes says, at the outset of his research already in possession of the ultimate principles governing the phenomena which form the subject of his study; whereas mankind has no direct knowledge of ultimate physical principles.[2] Herein lies the radical difference between the social sciences (moral sciences, *Geisteswissenschaften*) and the natural sciences. What makes natural science possible is the power to experiment; what makes social science possible is the power to grasp or to comprehend the meaning of human action.

We have to distinguish two quite different kinds of this comprehension of the meaning of action: we conceive and we understand.

We conceive the meaning of an action; that is to say, we take an action to be such. We see in the action the endeavor to reach a goal by the use of means. In conceiving the meaning of an action, we consider it as a purposeful endeavor to reach some goal, but we do not regard the quality of the ends proposed and of the means applied. We conceive activity as such, its logical (praxeological) qualities and categories. All that we do in this conceiving is by deductive analysis to bring to light everything which is contained in the first principle of action and to apply it to different kinds of thinkable conditions. This study is the object of the theoretical science of human action (praxeology) and in particular of its hitherto most developed branch, economics (economic theory).

Economics therefore is not based on or derived (abstracted) from experience. It is a deductive system, starting from the insight into the principles of human reason and conduct. As a matter of fact all our experience in the field of human action is based on and conditioned by the circumstance that we have this insight in our mind. Without this a priori knowledge and the theorems derived from it we could not

2 [John E. Cairnes, *The Character and Logical Method of Political Economics* [1875] (New York: Augustus M. Kelley, 1965), pp. 89–97.—Ed.]

at all realize what is going on in human activity. Our experience of human action and social life is predicated on praxeological and economic theory.

It is important to be aware of the fact that this procedure and method are not peculiar only to scientific investigation but are the mode of ordinary daily apprehension of social facts. These aprioristic principles and the deductions from them are applied not only by the professional economist but by everybody who deals with economic facts or problems. The layman does not proceed in a way significantly different from that of the scientist; only he sometimes is less critical, less scrupulous in examining every step in the chain of his deductions, and therefore sometimes more subject to error. One need only observe any discussion on current economic problems to realize that its course turns very soon toward a consideration of abstract principles without any reference to experience. You cannot, for instance, discuss the Soviet system without falling back on the general principles of both capitalism and socialism. You cannot discuss a wage and hours bill without falling back on the theory of wages, profits, interests, and prices; that means the general theory of a market society. The "pure fact"—let us set aside the epistemological question whether there is such a thing—is open to different interpretations. These interpretations require elucidation by theoretical insight.

Economics is not only not derived from experience; it is even impossible to verify its theorems by appeal to experience. Every experience of a complex phenomenon, we must repeat, can be and is explained in different ways. The same facts, the same statistical figures, are claimed as confirmations of contradictory theories.

It is instructive to compare the technique of dealing with experience in the social sciences with that in the natural sciences. We have many books on economics which, after having developed a theory, annex chapters in which an attempt is made to verify the theory developed by an appeal to the facts. This is not the way which the natural scientist takes. He starts from facts experimentally established and builds up his theory in using them. If his theory allows a deduction that predicts a state of affairs not yet discovered in experiments, he describes what kind of experiment would be crucial for his theory; the theory seems to be verified if the result conforms to the prediction. This is something radically and significantly different from the approach taken by the social sciences.

To confront economic theory with reality, we do not have to try to explain in a superficial way facts interpreted differently by other people so that they seem to verify our theory. This dubious procedure is not the way in which reasonable discussion can take place. What we have to do is this: we have to inquire whether the special conditions of action which we have implied in our reasoning correspond to those we find in the segment of reality under consideration. A theory of money (or rather of indirect exchange) is correct or not without reference to the question of whether the actual economic system under examination employs indirect exchange or only barter.

The method applied in these theoretical aprioristic considerations is the method of speculative constructions. The economist—and likewise the layman in his economic reasoning—builds up an image of a non-existent state of things. The material for this construction is drawn from an insight into the conditions of human action. Whether the state of affairs which these speculative constructions depict corresponds or could correspond to reality is irrelevant for their instrumental efficiency. Even unrealizable constructions can render valuable service in giving us the opportunity to conceive what makes them unrealizable and in what respect they differ from reality. The speculative construction of a socialist community is indispensable for economic reasoning notwithstanding the question of whether such a society could or could not be realized.

One of the best-known and most frequently applied speculative constructions is that of a state of static equilibrium mentioned above. We are fully aware that this state can never be realized. But we cannot study the implications of changes without considering a changeless world. No modern economist will deny that the application of this speculative concept has rendered invaluable service in elucidating the character of entrepreneur's profits and losses and the relation between costs and prices.

All our economic reasoning operates with these speculative concepts. It is true that the method has its dangers; it easily lends itself to errors. But we have to use it because it is the only method available. Of course, we have to be very careful in using it.

To the obvious question of how a purely logical deduction from aprioristic principles can tell us anything about reality, we have to reply that both human thought and human action stem from the same root in that they are both products of the human mind. Correct results from our aprioristic reasoning are therefore not only logically irrefutable, but are at the same time applicable with all their apodictic certainty to reality provided that the assumptions involved are given in reality. The only way to refute a conclusion of economics is to demonstrate that it contains a logical fallacy. It is another question whether the results obtained apply to reality. This again can be decided only by the demonstration that the assumptions involved have or do not have any counterpart in the reality which we wish to explain.

The relation between historical experience—for every economic experience is historical in the sense that it is the experience of something past—and economic theory is therefore different from that generally assumed. Economic theory is not derived from experience. It is on the contrary the indispensable tool for the grasp of economic history. Economic history can neither prove nor disprove the teachings of economic theory. It is on the contrary economic theory which makes it possible for us to conceive the economic facts of the past.

IV

But to orient ourselves in the world of human actions we need to do more than merely conceive the meaning of human action. Both the acting man and the purely observing historian have not only to conceive the categories of action as economic theory does; they have besides to understand (verstehen) the meaning of human choice.

This understanding of the meaning of action is the specific method of historical research. The historian has to establish the facts as far as possible by the use of all the means provided both by the theoretical sciences of human action—praxeology and its hitherto most developed part, economics—and by the natural sciences. But then he has to go farther. He has to study the individual and unique conditions of the case in question. Individuum est ineffabile. Individuality is given to the historian; it is exactly that which cannot be exhaustively explained or traced back to other entities. In this sense individuality is irrational. The purpose of specific understanding as applied by the historical disciplines is to grasp the meaning of individuality by a psychological process. It establishes the fact that we face something individual. It fixes the valuations, the aims, the theories, the beliefs, and the errors, in a word, the total philosophy of the acting individuals and the way in which they envisaged the conditions under which they had to act. It puts us into the milieu of the action. Of course this specific understanding cannot be separated from the philosophy of the interpreter. That degree of scientific objectivity which can be reached in the natural sciences and in the aprioristic sciences of logic and praxeology can never be attained by the moral or historical sciences (*Geisteswissenschaften*) in the field of the specific understanding. You can understand in different ways. History can be written from different points of view. The historians may agree in everything that can be established in a rational way and nevertheless widely disagree in their interpretations. History therefore has always to be rewritten. New philosophies demand a new representation of the past.

The specific understanding of the historical sciences is not an act of pure rationality. It is the recognition that reason has exhausted all its resources and that we can do nothing more than to try as well as we may to give an explanation of something irrational which is resistant to exhaustive and unique description. These are the tasks which the understanding has to fulfill. It is, notwithstanding, a logical tool and should be used as such. It should never be abused for the purpose of smuggling into the historical work obscuranticism, mysticism, and similar elements. It is not a free charter for nonsense.

It is necessary to emphasize this point because it sometimes happens that the abuses of a certain type of historicism are justified by an appeal to a wrongly interpreted "understanding." The reasoning of logic, of praxeology, and of the natural sciences can under no circumstances be invalidated by the understanding. However strong the evidence supplied by the historical sources may be, and however understandable a fact may be from the point of view of theories contemporaneous with it, if it does not fit into our rationale, we cannot accept it. The existence of witches and the practice of witchcraft are abundantly attested to by legal proceedings; yet we will not accept it. Judgments of many tribunals are on record asserting that people have depreciated a country's currency by upsetting the balance of payments; yet we will not believe that such actions have such effects.

It is not the task of history to reproduce the past. An attempt to do so would be vain and would require a duplication not humanly possible. History is a representation of the past in terms of concepts. The specific concepts of historical research are type concepts. These types of the historical method can be built up only by the use of the specific understanding, and they are meaningful only in the frame of the understanding to which they owe their existence. Therefore not every type-concept which is logically valid can be considered as useful for the purpose of understanding. A classification is valid in a logical sense if all the elements united in one class are characterized by a common feature. Classes do not exist in actuality; they are always a product of the mind which in observing things discovers likenesses and differences. It is another question whether a classification which is logically valid and based on sound considerations can be used for the explanation of given data. There is for instance no doubt that a type or class "Fascism" which includes not only Italian Fascism but also German Nazism, the Spanish system of General Franco, the Hungarian system of Admiral Horthy, and some other systems can be constructed in a logically valid way and that it can be contrasted to a type called "Bolshevism," which includes the Russian Bolshevism and the system of Bela Kun in Hungary and of the short Soviet episode of Munich. But whether this classification and the inference from it which sees the world of the last twenty years divided into the two parties, Fascists and Bolsheviks, is the right way to understand present-day political conditions is open to question. You can understand this period of history in a quite different way by using other types. You may distinguish Democracy and Totalitarianism, and then let the type Democracy include the Western Capitalist system and the type Totalitarianism include both Bolshevism and what the other classification terms Fascism. Whether you apply the first or the second typification depends on the whole mode in which you see things. The understanding depends upon the classification to be used, and not the classification upon the understanding.

The type-concepts of the historical or moral sciences (*Geisteswissenschaften*) are not statistical averages. Most of the features used for classification are not subject to numerical determination, and this alone renders it impossible to construct them as statistical averages. These type-concepts (in German one uses the term *Ideal-Typus* in order to distinguish them from the type-concepts of other sciences, especially of the biological ones) ought not to be confused with the praxeological concepts used for the conceiving of the categories of human action. For instance: the concept "entrepreneur" is used in economic theory to signify a specific function, that is, the provision for an uncertain future. In this respect everybody has to some extent to be considered as an entrepreneur. Of course, it is not the task of this classification in economic theory to distinguish men, but to distinguish functions and to explain sources of profit or loss. Entrepreneur in this sense is the personification of the function which results in profit or loss. In economic history and in dealing with current economic problems, the term "entrepreneur" signifies a class of men who are engaged in business but who may in many other respects differ so much that the general term entrepreneur seems to be meaningless and is used only with a special qualification, for instance big (medium-sized, small) business, "Wall Street," armaments business, German business, etc. The type entrepreneur as used in history and politics can never have the conceptual exactitude which the praxeological concept entrepreneur has. You never meet in life men who are nothing else than the personification of one function only.[3]

V

The preceding remarks justify the conclusion that there is a radical difference between the methods of the social sciences and those of the natural sciences. The social sciences owe their progress to the use of their particular methods and have to go further along the lines which the special character of their object requires. They do not have to adopt the methods of the natural sciences.

It is a fallacy to recommend to the social sciences the use of mathematics and to believe that they could in this way be made more "exact." The application of mathematics does not render physics more exact or more certain. Let us quote Einstein's remark: "As far as mathematical propositions refer to reality they are not certain and as far as they are certain they do not refer to reality." It is different with praxeological propositions. These refer with all their exactitude and certainty to the reality of human action. The explanation of this phenomenon lies in the fact that both—the science of human action and human action itself—have a common root, i.e., human reason. It would be a mistake to assume that the quantitative approach could render them more exact. Every numerical expression is inexact because of the inherent limitations of human powers of measurement. For the rest we have to refer to what has been said above on the purely historical character of quantitative expressions in the field of the social sciences.

---

3 For the sake of completeness we have to remark that there is a third use of the term entrepreneur in law which has to be carefully distinguished from the two mentioned above.

The reformers who wish to improve the social sciences by adopting the methods of the natural sciences sometimes try to justify their efforts by pointing to the backward state of the former. Nobody will deny that the social sciences and especially economics are far from being perfect. Every economist knows how much remains to be done. But two considerations must be kept in mind. First, the present unsatisfactory state of social and economic conditions has nothing to do with an alleged inadequacy in economic theory. If people do not use the teachings of economics as a guide for their policies, they cannot blame the discipline for their own failure. Second, if it may someday be necessary to reform economic theory radically, this change will not take its direction along the lines suggested by the present critics. The objections of these are thoroughly refuted forever.

CHAPTER 2

The Treatment of "Irrationality" in the Social Sciences

I

One of the manifestations of the present-day "revolt against reason" is the tendency to find fault with the social sciences for being purely rational. Life and reality, say the critics, are irrational; it is quite wrong to deal with them as if they were rational and open to interpretation by reasoning. Rationalism fixes its eyes upon accessory matters only; its cognition is shallow and lacks profundity; it does not penetrate to the essence of things. It is an absurdity to press into dry rational schemes and into bloodless abstractions the finite variety of life's phenomena. What is needed is a science of irrationality and an irrational science.

The main target of these attacks is the theoretical science of human action, praxeology, and especially its hitherto best-developed part, economics or catallactics. But their scope includes the historical discipline too.

It should be realized that political motives have prompted this storm. Political parties and pressure groups whose programs cannot stand criticism based on dispassionate reasoning grasp at the straw of such an evasion. But science does not have the right to dispose of any objection merely on account of the motives which instigated it; it is not entitled to assume beforehand that a disapprobation must needs be unfounded because some of its supporters are imbued by party bias. It is bound to reply to every censure without any regard to its underlying motives and its background.

The challenge to reason and rationality did not rise in Germany. Like all other social doctrines and philosophies, it had its origin in Western Europe. But it has prospered better on German soil than any-

[Reprinted from *Philosophy and Phenomenological Research* 4, no. 4 (June 1944).—Ed.]

where else. It has for a long time been the official doctrine of the Prussian universities. It has fashioned present-day German mentality, and the Nazi philosophers proudly style it "German social philosophy." German *Staatswissenschaften* have refuted economics wholesale as a spurious product of the British and the Austrian minds, and German historians have disparaged the achievements of Western historiography. However, we should not forget that a long line of German philosophers and historians have brilliantly succeeded in the elucidation of the epistemological problems of history.[1] Of course, to the men to whom we are indebted for these contributions no place is assigned in present-day Germany's Hall of Fame.

It would be logical to provide at the outset of a study devoted to the problems of "rationality" and "irrationality" a precise definition of the two terms. But it is impossible to conform to this legitimate requirement. It is precisely the characteristic feature of the objections with which we have to deal that they apply terms in a vague and ambiguous manner. They defy definiteness and logical strictness as inappropriate means for grasping of life and reality and cling to obscurity on purpose. They do not aim at clarity, but at depth *(Tiefe)*. They are proud of being inexact and of talking in metaphors.

The problem which we have to investigate is this. Is it true or not that the social sciences lost the right way because they apply discursive reasoning? Do we have to look for other avenues of approach than those provided by ratiocination and historical experience?

II

The scope of the social sciences is human action. History deals with past events, representing them from the viewpoint of various aspects. It embraces history proper, philology, ethnology; anthropology is a branch of history as far as it is not a part of biology, and psychology as far as it is neither physiology nor epistemology or philosophy. Economic history, descriptive economics, and economic statistics are, of course, history. The term sociology is used in two different meanings. Descriptive sociology deals with those historical phenomena of human action which

1 For a critical presentation of these theories, cf. Talcott Parsons, *The Structure of Social Action* (New York: Macmillan, 1937); Raymond Aron, *German Sociology* [1938] (Westport, Conn.: Greenwood Press, 1954).

are not viewed in descriptive economics; it overlaps to some extent the field claimed by ethnology and anthropology. General sociology, on the other hand, approaches historical experience from a more nearly universal viewpoint than that of the other historical branches. History proper, for instance, deals with an individual town or with towns in a definite period or with an individual people or with a certain geographical area. Max Weber, in his main treatise, deals with the town in general, i.e., with the whole historical experience concerning towns without any limitation to historical periods, geographical areas, or individual peoples, nations, races, and civilizations.[2] The subject matter of all historical sciences is the past; they cannot teach us anything which would be valid for all human actions, that means for the future too.

The natural sciences, too, deal with past events. Of course, every experience is an experience of something passed away; there is no experience of future happenings. But the experience to which the natural sciences owe all their success is the experience of the experiment in which the various elements of change can be observed in isolation. The facts amassed in this way can be used for induction, a peculiar procedure of inference which has given evidence of its expediency, although its epistemological and logical qualification is still an unsolved problem.

The experience with which the social sciences have to deal is always the experience of complex phenomena. They are open to various interpretations. They do not provide us with facts which could be used in the manner in which the natural sciences use the results of their experiments for the forecast of future events. They cannot be used as building materials for the construction of theories.

Praxeology is a theoretical and systematic, not historical, science. Its scope is human action as such, irrespective of all environmental and incidental circumstances of the concrete acts. It aims at knowledge valid for all instances in which the conditions exactly correspond to those implied by its assumptions and inferences. Whether people exchange commodities and services directly by barter or indirectly by using a medium of exchange is a question of the particular institutional setting which can be answered by history only. But whenever

2 [Max Weber, *The City*, Don Martindale and Gertrud Neuwirth, trans. and eds. (New York: The Free Press, 1958).—Ed.]

and wherever a medium of exchange is in use, all the laws of monetary theory are valid with regard to the exchanges thus transacted.[3]

It is not the task of this article to enquire what makes such a science of praxeology possible, what its logical and epistemological character is, and what methods it applies. The study of the epistemological problems of the social sciences has been neglected for a long time. Even those authors who like David Hume, Archbishop Whately, John Stuart Mill, and William Stanley Jevons were themselves eminent economists, dealt in their logical and epistemological writings only with the natural sciences, and did not bother about the peculiar character of the sciences of human action. The epistemology of the social sciences is the youngest branch of knowledge. Moreover, most of its work refers only to history; the existence of a theoretical science was long entirely ignored. The pioneer work of Senior and of Cairnes has only lately borne fruit.[4] The economists mostly lack philosophical training, and the philosophers are not familiar with economics. The importance of phenomenology for the solution of the epistemological problems of praxeology has not been noticed at all.[5]

But this article is not concerned with these tasks. We have to deal with those critics who blame the economists and the historians for having neglected the fact of "irrationality."

Action means conscious behavior or purposive activity. It differs as such from the biological, physiological, and instinctive processes going on within human beings. It is behavior open to the regulation and direction by volition and mind. Its field coincides with the sphere within which man is free to influence the course of events. As far as man has

---

3 The term "praxeology" was first used by Espinas in an essay published in the *Revue Philosophique*, vol. 30, pp. 114ff., and in his book *Les Origines de la Technologie* (Paris: F. Alcon, 1897), pp. 7ff. It was later applied by Slutsky in his essay "Ein Beitrag zur formal-praxeologischen Grundlegung der Ökonomik," Academie Oukräienne des Sciences, *Annales de la Classe des Sciences Sociales-Economiques* 4 (1926).

4 Cf. Nassau W. Senior, *Political Economy*, 6th ed. (London: J. J. Griffen, 1872); John E. Cairnes, *The Character and Logical Method of Political Economy*, 2nd ed. (London: Macmillan, 1875); Lionel Robbins, *An Essay on the Nature and Significance of Economic Science*, 2nd ed. (London: Macmillan, 1935); Mises, *Epistemological Problems of Economics* [1933] (New York, 1981); *Human Action*, 3rd ed. (Chicago: Henry Regnery, 1966); Alfred Schutz, *The Phenomenology of the Social World* [1932] (Evanston, Ill.: Northwestern University Press, 1967); F. A. Hayek, *The Counter-Revolution of Science* ([1952]; Indianapolis, Ind.: Liberty Fund, 1979).

5 The book of Josef Back, *Die Entwicklung der reinen Ökonomie zur nationalökonomischen Wesenswissenschaft* (Jena: Gustav Fischer, 1929), is unsatisfactory because of the author's poor knowledge of economics. All the same, this book would deserve a better appreciation than it received.

power to bring about an effect or a change, he necessarily acts, whether he does something or refrains from doing anything. Inactivity and passivity, letting things alone, are the outcome of a choice, are therefore action whenever a different form of behavior would be possible. He who endures what he could change acts no less than he who interferes in order to attain another result. A man who abstains from influencing the operation of physiological and instinctive factors which he could influence also acts. Action is not only doing but no less omitting to do what possibly could be done.

Most of a man's daily behavior is simple routine. He performs certain acts without paying special attention to them. He does many things because he was trained in his childhood to do them, because other people behave in the same way, and because it is customary in his environment. He acquires habits, he develops automatic reactions. But he indulges in these habits only because he welcomes their outcome. As soon as he discovers that the pursuit of the habitual way may hinder the attainment of ends considered as more desirable, he changes his attitude. A man brought up in an area in which the water is clean acquires the habit of heedlessly drinking, washing, and bathing. When he moves to a place in which the water is polluted by morbific germs, he will devote the most careful attention to procedures about which he never bothered before. He will watch himself permanently in order not to hurt himself by indulging unthinkingly in his automatic reactions and in his traditional routine. The abandonment of a settled practice into which a man has fallen is not an easy task. It is the main lesson to be learned by all those who aspire to achievements above the level of the masses. (To break off the consumption of habit-creating drugs often requires the employment of therapeutical procedures.) The fact that an act is in the regular course of affairs performed spontaneously, as it were, does not mean that it is not due to conscious volition. Indulgence in a routine which possibly could be changed is action.

Action is the mind's response to stimuli, i.e., to the conditions in which nature and other people's actions place a man. It differs as such from the functional reaction of the bodily organs. It is the outcome of a man's will. Of course, we do not know what will is. We simply call *will* man's faculty to choose between different states of affairs, to prefer one and to set aside the other, and we call action, behavior aiming at one state and forsaking another. Action is the attitude of a human being aiming at some ends.

Praxeology is not concerned with the metaphysical problem of free will as opposed to determinism. Its fundamental insight is the incontestable fact that man is in a position to choose among different states of affairs with regard to which he is not neutral and which are incompatible with each other, i.e., which he can not enjoy together. It does not assert that a man's choice is independent of antecedent conditions, physiological and psychological. It does not enter into a discussion of the motives determining the choice. It does not ask why a customer prefers one pattern of a necktie to another or a motor-car to a horse and buggy. It deals with the choosing as such, with the categorical elements of choice and action.

Neither does praxeology concern itself about the ultimate goals of human activity. We will have to deal with this problem too. For the moment we have only to emphasize that praxeology does not have to question ultimate ends, but only to study the means applied for the attainment of any ends. It is a science of means, not of ends.

The investigation of the fitness of concrete means to attain, by complying with the laws of nature, definite ends in the field of the practical arts is the task of the various branches of technology. Praxeology does not deal with technological problems, but with the categorical essence of choice and action as such, with the pure elements of setting aims and applying means.

Praxeology is not based on psychology and is not a part of psychology. It was a bad mistake to call the modern theory of value a psychological theory, and it was a confusion to link it up with the Weber-Fechner Law of Psychophysics.[6]

Praxeology deals with choice and action and with their outcome. Psychology deals with the internal processes determining the various choices in their concreteness. It may be left undecided whether psychology can succeed in explaining why a man in a concrete case preferred red to blue or bread to lyrics. At any rate such an explanation

---

6 Cf. Max Weber, "Marginal Utility Theory and the So-Called Fundamental Law of Psychophysics" [1905], *Social Science Quarterly* (1975): 21–36; and Mises, *Human Action*, 3rd ed. (Chicago: Henry Regnery, 1966), pp. 125–27. ["Ernst H. Weber (1795–1878) proclaimed in his law of psychophysics that the least noticeable increase in the intensity of a human sensation is always brought about by a constant proportional increase in the previous stimulus. Gustav T. Fechner (1801–1887) developed this into the Weber-Fechner Law that said to increase the intensity of a sensation in arithmetical progression, it is necessary to increase the intensity of the stimulus in geometric progression," *Mises Made Easier: A Glossary for Ludwig von Mises' Human Action*, Percy L. Greaves, Jr., comp. (Dobbs Ferry, N.Y.: Free Market Books, 1974), p. 147.—Ed.]

has nothing to do with a branch of knowledge for which the concrete choices are data not needing further explanation or analysis. Not what a man chooses, but that he chooses counts for praxeology.

The motives and springs of action are without concern for the praxeological investigation. It is immaterial for the formation of the price of silk whether people ask for silk because they want to be protected against cold weather or because they find it beautiful or because they want to get more sexual attractiveness. What matters is that there is a demand of a given intensity for silk.

Yet, modern psychology has brought about some results which may arouse the interest of praxeology. It was once usual to consider the behavior of lunatics and neurotics as quite nonsensical and "irrational." It is the great merit of Breuer and Freud that they have disproved this opinion. Neurotics and lunatics differ from those whom we call sane and normal with regard to the means which they choose for the attainment of satisfaction and with regard to the means which they apply for the attainment of these means. Their "technology" is different from that of sane people, but they do not act in a categorically different way.[7] They aim at ends and they apply means in order to attain their ends. A mentally troubled person with whom there is still left a trace of reason and who has not been literally reduced to the mental level of an animal is still an acting being. Whoever has the remnants of a human mind cannot escape the necessity of acting.

III

Every human action aims at the substitution of more satisfactory conditions for less satisfactory. Man acts because he feels uneasy and believes that he has the power to relieve to some extent his uneasiness by influencing the course of events. A man perfectly content with the state of his affairs would not have any incentive to change things; he would have neither wishes nor desires, he would not act, because he would be perfectly happy. Neither would a man act who, although not content with his condition, does not see any possibility of improving it.

Strictly speaking, only the increase of satisfaction (decrease of un-

---

7 It may be of some interest for the history of ideas that young Sigmund Freud collaborated as a translator in the German edition of John Stuart Mill's collected works edited by Theodor Gomperz, the Austrian historian of ancient Greek philosophy. Joseph Breuer too was, as the present writer can attest, well familiar with the standard works of utilitarian philosophy.

easiness) should be called *end*, and accordingly all states which bring about such an increase *means*. In daily speech people use a loose terminology. They call ends things which should be rather called means. They say: This man knows only one end, namely, to accumulate more wealth, instead of saying: He considers the accumulation of more wealth as the only means to get more satisfaction. If they were to apply this more adequate mode of expression, they would avoid some current mistakes. They would realize that nobody else than the individual himself can decide what satisfies *him* better and what less. They would conceive that judgments of value are purely subjective and that there is no such thing as an absolute state of satisfaction or happiness irrespective of the desires of the individual concerned. In fact, he who passes a judgment of an alleged end reduces it from the rank of an end to that of a means. He values it from the viewpoint of a (higher) end and asks whether it is a suitable means to attain this (higher) end. But the highest end, the ultimate goal of human action, is always satisfaction of an individual's desire. There is no other standard of greater or lesser satisfaction than the individual judgments of value, different with various people and with the same people at various times. What makes a man feel uneasy or less uneasy is established by every individual from the standard of his own will and judgment, from his personal valuation. Nobody is in a position to decree what could make a fellow man happier. The innate spirit of intolerance and the neurotic "dictatorship complex" instigate people to dispose blithely of other people's will and aspirations. Yet, a man who passes a judgment on another man's aims and volitions does not declare what would make this other man happier or less discontented; he only asserts what condition of this other man would better suit himself, the censor.

From this point of view we have to appreciate the statements of eudaemonism, hedonism, and utilitarianism. All the objections raised against these schools are invalid if one attaches to the terms happiness, pain, pleasure, and utility formal meaning. Happiness and pleasure are what people consider as such; useful are things which people consider as appropriate means for the attainment of aims sought. The concept of utility as developed by modern economics means suitability to render some services which are deemed as useful from any point of view. This is the meaning of the axiological subjectivism [subjectivism in value theory] of modern economics. It is at the same time the test of its impartiality and scientific objectivity. It does not deal with the *ought*, but with the *is*. Its subject matter is, e.g., the explanation of the formation of prices as they really are, not as they should be or would be if men were to act in a way different from what they really do.

IV

Praxeology does not employ the term *rational*. It deals with purposive behavior, i.e., human action. The opposite of action is not *irrational behavior*, but a reactive response to stimuli on the part of the bodily organs and of the instincts, which cannot be controlled by volition. If we were to assign a definite meaning to the term *rationality* as applied to behavior, we could not find a meaning other than: the attitude of men intent on bringing about some effects.

The terms *irrational* and *irrationality* are mostly used for censuring concrete modes of action. An action is called irrational either because the censor disapproves of the end (i.e., of the way in which the acting individual wants to attain satisfaction) or because the censor believes that the means employed were not fit to produce the immediate effect aimed at. But often the qualification of an action as irrational involves praise; actions aiming at altruistic ends, inspired by noble motives, and executed to the detriment of the acting man's material well-being are considered as irrational.

We do not have to dwell upon the contradictions and logical inconsistencies involved in this use of words. The qualification of ends is without significance for praxeology, the science of means, not ends. That mortal men are not infallible and that they sometimes choose means which cannot bring about the ends sought is obvious.

It is the task of technology and of therapeutics to find the right means for the attainment of definite ends in the field of the practical arts. It is the task of applied economics to discover the appropriate methods for the attainment of definite ends in the realm of social cooperation. But if the scientists fail in these endeavors or if the acting men do not correctly apply the means recommended, the outcome falls short of the expectations of the acting individuals. Yet, an action unsuited to the end sought is still an action. If we call such an unsuitable and inexpedient action *irrational*, we do not deprive it of its qualification as purposive activity, and we do not at all invalidate the assertion that the only way to conceive it essentially and categorically is provided by praxeology.

Economics does not deal with an imaginary *homo oeconomicus* as ineradicable fables reproach it with doing, but with *homo agens* as he really is, often weak, stupid, inconsiderate, and badly instructed. It does not matter whether his motives and emotions are to be qualified as noble or as mean. It does not contend that man strives only after more material wealth for himself and for his kin. Its theorems are neutral with regard to ultimate judgments of value and are valid for all actions irrespective of their expediency.

It is the scope of history and not of praxeology to investigate what ends people aim at and what means they apply for the realization of their plans.

V

It is a frequent mistake to assume that the desire to procure the base necessities of life and health is more rational than the striving after other amenities. It is true that the appetite for food and warmth is common to men and other mammals and that as a rule a man who lacks food and shelter concentrates his efforts upon the satisfaction of these urgent needs and does not care for other things. The impulse to live, to preserve one's own life, and to take advantage of every opportunity of strengthening one's vital force is a primal feature of life, present in every living being. However, to yield to this impulse is not—for man—an inextricable necessity.

All other animals are unconditionally driven by the impulse to preserve their own life and by the impulse of proliferation. They are, without a will of their own, bound to obey the impetus which at the instant prevails. It is different with man. Man has the faculty of mastering his instincts. He can rein both his sexual appetites and his will to live. He can give up his life when the conditions under which alone he could preserve it seem intolerable. Man is capable of dying for a cause or of committing suicide. To live is for man the outcome of a choice, of a judgment of value.

It is the same with the desire to live in affluence. The very fact of asceticism evidences that the striving after more amenities is not inextricable but rather the result of a choice. Of course, the immense majority prefer life to death and wealth to poverty.

On the other hand, it is arbitrary to consider only the satisfaction of the body's physiological needs as "natural" and therefore as "rational" and everything else as "artificial" and therefore as "irrational." It is the characteristic feature of human nature that man seeks not only food and shelter like all other animals, but aims also at other kinds of satisfaction, that he has specifically human needs too. It was the fundamental error of the iron law of wages that it ignored this fact.

VI

The concrete judgments of value are not open to further analysis. We may assume that they are absolutely dependent upon and conditioned by their causes. But as long as we do not know how external (physical and physiological) facts produce in a human "soul" definite thoughts and volitions resulting in concrete acts, we have to face an insurmountable dualism. In the present state of our knowledge, the fundamental statements of positivism and monism are mere metaphysical postulates devoid of any scientific foundation. Reason and experience show us two separate realms: the external world of physical and physiological events and the internal world of thought, feeling, and purposeful action. No bridge connects—as far as we can see today—these two spheres. Identical external events result sometimes in different human responses, and different external events produce sometimes the same human response. We do not know why.

We have not yet discovered other methods for dealing with human action than those provided by praxeology and by history. The suggestion of pan-physicalism that the methods of physics be applied to human actions is futile. The sterility of the pan-physicalist recipe is beyond doubt. In spite of the fanatical propaganda of its advocates, nobody has ever made use of it. It is simply inapplicable. Positivism is the most conspicuous failure in the history of metaphysics.

The concrete judgments of value and the resulting acts are for history ultimate data. History tries to collect all relevant facts, and it has, in this attempt, to make use of all knowledge provided by logic, mathematics, the natural sciences, and especially by praxeology. But it can never succeed in reducing all historical facts to external events open to an interpretation by physics and physiology. It must always reach a point beyond which all further analysis fails. Then it cannot establish anything else than that it is faced with an individual or unique case.

The mental act for dealing with such historical facts is, in the philosophy of Bergson, "une intuition," namely, "la sympathie par laquelle on se transporte a l'intérieur d'un objet pour coincider avec ce qu'il a d'unique, et par conséquent d'inexprimable."[8] German epistemology calls the act *das spezifische Verstehen der Geisteswissenschaften*, or simply *Verstehen*. I suggest it be translated into English as "specific understanding" or simply as "understanding." The *Verstehen* is not a method or a mental process which the historians should apply or which epistemology advises them to apply. It is the method which all historians and all other people always apply in commenting upon social events of the past and in forecasting future events. The discovery and the delimitation of the *Verstehen* was one of the most important contributions of epistemology. It is not a blueprint for a science which does not yet exist and is to be founded.

The uniqueness and individuality which remains at the bottom of every historical fact when all the means for its interpretation provided by logic, praxeology, and the natural sciences have been exhausted is an ultimate datum. But, whereas the natural sciences cannot say anything else about their ultimate data than that they are such, history can try to make its data intelligible. Although it is impossible to reduce them to their causes—they would not be ultimate data, if such a reduction were possible—the observer can understand them because he is himself a human being. We may call this faculty to understand, congeniality and sympathetic intelligence. But we have to guard against the error to confuse the understanding with approval, be it only conditional and circumstantial. The historian, the anthropologist, and the psychologist sometimes register actions which are for their feelings simply repulsive and disgusting; they understand them only as actions, i.e., in establishing the underlying aims and the technological and praxeological methods applied. To understand an individual case does not mean to explain it, still less to excuse it.

Neither must understanding be confused with the act of aesthetic empathy by virtue of which an individual aims at an aesthetic enjoyment of a phenomenon. *Einfühlung* [empathy] and *Verstehen* are two radically different attitudes. It is a different thing, on the one hand, to understand historically a work of art, to determine its place, its mean-

---

8 Cf. Henri Bergson, *La Pensée et le mouvant*, 4th ed. (Paris: F. Alcan, 1934), p. 205. [Passage translated as "The sympathy with which one enters inside an object in order to identify thereby what it has that is unique and therefore inexpressible," *Mises Made Easier: A Glossary for Ludwig von Mises' Human Action*, Percy L. Greaves, Jr., comp. (Dobbs Ferry, N.Y.: Free Market Books, 1974), p. 76.—Ed.]

ing, and its importance in the chain of events and, on the other hand, to appreciate it emotionally as a work of art. One can look at a cathedral with the eyes of a historian. But one can look at the same cathedral either as an enthusiastic admirer or as an unaffected and indifferent tourist. One can look at a mountain range with the eyes of a naturalist—a geologist, a geographer, or a zoologist—or with the eye of a beauty-seeker—with disgust as the ancients used to do, or with the modern enthusiasm for the picturesque. The same individuals are capable of different modes of reaction, of the aesthetic appreciation and of the scientific grasp either of the *Verstehen* or of the natural sciences.

The understanding establishes the fact that an individual or a group of individuals have engaged in a definite action emanating from definite judgments of value and choices and aiming at definite ends. It further tries to appreciate the effects and the intensity of the effects brought about by an action. It tries to assign to every action its relevance, i.e., its bearing upon the course of events.

The historian gives us an account of all facts and events concerning the battle of Waterloo as complete and exact as the material available allows. As far as he deals with the forces engaged and with their equipment, with the tactical operations, with the figures of soldiers killed, wounded, and made prisoners, with the temporal sequence of the various happenings, with the plans of the commanders and with their execution, he is grounded on historical experience. What he asserts is either correct or contrary to fact, is either proved or disproved by the documents available or vague, because the sources do not provide us with sufficient information. Other experts will either agree with him or will disagree, but they will agree or disagree on the ground of a reasonable interpretation of the evidence available. So far the whole discussion must be conducted with reasonable affirmations and negations. But that is not the total work to be achieved by the historian.

The battle resulted in a crushing defeat of the French army. There are many facts, indubitably established on the basis of documentary evidence, which could be taken to account for this outcome. Napoleon suffered from illness, he was nervous, he lacked self-confidence. His judgment and his comprehension of the situation were no longer what they used to be. His plans and orders were in many respects inappropriate. The French army was hastily organized, numerically too weak, and its soldiers were partly veterans tired from the endless wars, partly inexperienced recruits. Its generals were not equal to their task;

there was especially Grouchy's serious blunder.[9] On the other hand, the British and the Prussians fought under the imminent leadership of Wellington and of Gneisenau; their morale was excellent; they were well organized, richly equipped, and strong in number. To what extent did these various circumstances and many others contribute to the outcome? This question cannot be answered from the information derived from the data of the case; it is open to various interpretations. The historian's opinions concerning them can be neither confirmed nor refuted in the same way in which we can confirm or refute his statement that the vanguard or Blücher's[10] army arrived at a certain hour on the battlefield.

Let us take another example. We have plenty of figures available concerning the German inflation of the years 1914–1923. Economic theory provides us with all the knowledge needed for a perfect grasp of the causes of price changes. But this knowledge does not give us quantitative definiteness. Economics is, as people say, qualitative and not quantitative. This is not due to an alleged backwardness of economics. There are in the sphere of human action no constant relations between magnitudes. For a long time many economists believed that there exists one relation of this character. The thorough demolition of this unfounded assumption was one of the most important achievements of modern economic research. Monetary theory has proved in an irrefutable way that the rise of prices caused by an increase of the quantity of money can never be proportional to this increase. Thus it destroyed by its process analysis the only stronghold of an inveterate error. There cannot be any such thing as measurement in the field of economics. All statistical figures available have importance only for economic history; they are data of history like the figures concerning the battle of Waterloo; they tell us what happened in a unique and non-repeatable historical case. The only way to utilize them is to interpret them by *Verstehen*.

The rise of German prices in the years of the First World War was not only due to the increase of the quantity of bank notes. Other changes contributed too. The supply of commodities went down because many millions of workers were in the army and no longer worked in the

9 [Emmanuel Grouchy, one of Napoleon's generals, through an error of judgment delayed notifying Napoleon of movements of the British forces in what would become the French army's last attempt to stave off the defeat at Waterloo.—Ed.]

10 [Gebhard von Blücher was commander of the Prussian forces that aided the German, British, and Dutch armies to defeat Napoleon at Waterloo in 1815.—Ed.]

plants, because government control of business reduced productivity, because the blockade prevented imports from abroad, and because the workers suffered from malnutrition. It is impossible to establish by methods other than by *Verstehen* how much each of these factors— and of some other relevant factors—contributed to the rise of prices. Quantitative problems are in the sphere of human action not open to another solution. The historian can enumerate all the factors which cooperated in bringing about a certain effect and all the factors which worked against them and may have resulted in delaying and mitigating the final outcome. But he can never coordinate the various causes in a quantitative way to the effects produced. The *Verstehen* is in the realm of history the substitute, as it were, for quantitative analysis and measurement which are unfeasible with regard to human actions outside the field of technology.

Technology can tell us how thick a steel plate must be in order not to be pierced by a bullet fired at a distance of 300 yards from a Mauser rifle. It thus can answer the question why a man who took shelter behind a steel plate of a known thickness was hurt or not hurt by a shot fired. History is at a loss to explain with the same assurance why Louis Philippe lost his crown in 1848 or why the Reformation succeeded better in the Scandinavian countries than in France. Such problems do not allow any other treatment than that of the specific understanding.

The understanding is not a method which could be used as a substitute for the aprioristic reasoning of logic, mathematics, and praxeology or the experimental methods of the natural sciences. Its field lies where these other methods fail: in the description of a unique and individual case not open to further analysis—its qualitative service—and in the appraisal of the intensity, importance, and strength of the various factors which jointly produced an effect—its service as a substitute for the unfeasible quantitative analysis.

The subject of the historical understanding is the mental grasp of phenomena which cannot be totally elucidated by logic, mathematics, praxeology, and the natural sciences and as far as they cannot be elucidated by science and reason. It establishes the fact that scientific enquiry has reached a point beyond which it cannot go further and tries to fill the gap by *Verstehen*.[11] One may, if one likes, qualify the *Ver-*

---

11 The important problem of various conflicting modes of *Verstehen* (for instance: the Catholic and the Protestant interpretation of the Reformation, or the various interpretations of the rise of German Nazism) must be treated in a special essay.

stehen as irrational, because it involves individual judgments not amenable to criticism by purely rational methods. However, the method of understanding is not a free charter to deviate from the certified results obtained from the documentary evidence and from its interpretation through the teachings of the natural sciences and of praxeology. The *Verstehen* oversteps its due limits if it ventures to contradict physics, physiology, logic, mathematics, or economics. The abuses which many German scholars made of the *geisteswissenschaftliche Methode* and the spurious attempts of the German Historical School to substitute an imaginary *verstehende Nationalökonomie* for praxeological economics cannot be charged to the method itself.

German *Geisteswissenschaften* have preached the gospel of what should be an irrational science. They have substituted arbitrary judgments for reason and experience. They derive from intuition knowledge about historical events which the documents available do not provide or which are contrary to the facts as established by careful examination of the documents available. They do not refrain from drawing conclusions contradicting the statements of economic theory which they cannot refute on logical grounds. They are not afraid to produce absurdities. Their only justification is the reference to the irrationality of life.

Let us take an example from a serious and scholarly book available in English translation. Mr. Ernst Kantorowicz, a historian of the esoteric circle of the poet and visionary Stephen George, in his biography of the German emperor Frederick II, gives a correct account of the constitutional changes which took place in the reign of this Hohenstaufen monarch. Frederick's position in Germany was extremely precarious because his hereditary Norman kingdom of Sicily drew him into conflicts with the Pope and the Italian republican cities. He lacked the strength to preserve his royal authority in Germany and was forced to abandon most of the crown's rights and to grant ample privileges to the princes. What followed, says Kantorowicz quite correctly, "was the almost sovereign independence of each individual prince in his territory," which "definitely hindered the amalgamation of the German people into one *German State*."[12] So far, Kantorowicz is still on the basis of sound *Verstehen* and in perfect agreement will all other serious

---

12 Cf. E. Kantorowicz, *Frederick the Second*, 1194–1250, E. O. Lorimer, trans. (London: Constable, 1931), pp. 381–82.

historians. But then comes the amazing interpretation of the visionary and mystic; he adds: "Yet in a higher sense Frederick II perfected and completed the unified German Empire. He strengthened the princes' power . . . with more exalted statesmanship believing that the power and the brilliance of his own imperial sceptre would not pale in giving forth light but would gain radiance and would shine the brighter the more mighty and brilliant and majestic were the princes whom Caesar Imperator beheld *as equals round his judgment seat.* The princes are no longer columns bearing as a burden the weight of the throne. . . . They become piers and pillars expressive of upward-soaring strength, preparing the glorious elevation of *the prince of princes and king of kings* who is borne aloft on the shoulders of his peers, and who in turn exalts both kings and princes."[13] It is true that some phrases used by the princes at the Diet preceding the extortion of the privilege had a similar ring. The princes were polite; they did not want to fill the emperor with too much bitterness and were anxious to gild the pill which they forced him to swallow. When Hitler reduced Czechoslovakia to vassalage status he too sugared the pill by the establishment of the protectorate. Yet, hardly any historian would dare to say that "in a higher sense" Hitler "perfected and completed" the country's independence by granting it the protection of the mighty Reich. Frederick II disintegrated the Holy Empire by the privileges granted to the princes. It is absurd to assert that "in a higher sense" he perfected and completed it. No metaphorical speech and no appeal to the irrational can render such a dictum any more tenable.

Understanding entitles the historian to determine the role played by the two privileges in question in the evolution of the Empire's political structure, to determine, as it were, the quantity of their effect. He might, for instance, express the opinion that the role usually attributed to them has been exaggerated and that other events were more destructive than these privileges, and he could try to prove his thesis, his mode of understanding. But it is inadmissible to say: yes, this happened, such were its consequences; yet "in a higher sense" it was just the contrary.

Human knowledge can never transcend the cognition conveyed by reason and experience. If there is any "higher sense" in the course of events, it is inaccessible to the human mind.

13 Cf. ibid., pp. 386–87.

VII

A school of thought teaches that there is an eternal, irreconcilable antagonism between the interests of the individual and those of the collectivity. If the individual selfishly seeks after his own happiness, society comes to grief. Social cooperation and civilization are only possible at the cost of the individual's well-being. The existence of society and its flowering require permanent sacrifices on the part of its members. Therefore, it is unthinkable to imagine a human and purely rational origin of moral law and social cooperation. Some supernatural being has blessed mankind with the revelation of the moral code and has entrusted great leaders with the mission of enforcing this law. History is not the interplay of natural factors and purposive human activity which, within certain limits, are open to an elucidation by reason, but the result of the interference of transcendental factors, repeated again and again. History is destiny, and reason can never fathom its depths.

The conflict between the good and the evil, between collectivism and individualism, is therefore eternal and insoluble. What separates social and moral philosophies and political parties is a divergence of world views, a disparity of ultimate judgments of value. This discord is rooted in the deepest recesses of a man's soul and innate character; no ratiocination or discursive reasoning can brush it away or reconcile its contrasts. Some men are born with the divine call to leadership, others with the endowment to espouse spontaneously the cause of the great whole and to subordinate themselves of their own accord to the rule of its champions; but the many are incapable of finding the right way; they aim at the happiness of their own wretched selves and have to be tamed and subjugated by the conquering dictators. Social philosophy can consist in nothing else than in the cognition of the eternal truth of collectivism and in the unmasking of the spurious fallacies and pretensions of individualism. It is not the result of a rational process, but rather an illumination with which intuition blesses the elect. It is vain to strive after genuine social and moral truth by the application of the rational methods of logic. To the chosen, God, or *Weltgeist*, gives the right intuition; the rest of mankind has simply to forsake thinking and to obey blindly the God-given authority. True wisdom and the counterfeit doctrines of rationalistic economics and rationalistic history can never agree in the appreciation of historical and social facts, of political measures, and of an individual's actions. Human reason is not an appropriate tool to acquire true knowledge of the social totality; rationalism and its derivatives, economics and critical history, are fundamentally erroneous.[14]

The fundamental assumption of this doctrine, namely, that social cooperation is contrary to the interests of the individuals and can be achieved only at the expense of the individual's welfare, has long since been exploded. It was one of the great achievements of British social philosophy and classical economics that they developed a theory of social evolution which does not need to refer to the miraculous appearance of leaders endowed with superhuman wisdom and powers. Social cooperation and its corollary, division of labor, serve better the selfish interests of all individuals concerned than isolation and conflict. Every step toward peaceful cooperation brings all concerned an immediate and discernible advantage. Men cooperate and are eager to intensify cooperation exactly because they are anxious to pursue their selfish interests. The sacrifices which the individual makes for the maintenance of social cooperation are only temporary; if he abstains from antisocial actions which could give him small immediate gains, he profits much more by the advantages which he derives from the higher productivity of work performed in the peaceful cooperation of the division of labor. Thus, the principle of association elucidates the forces which integrated the primitive hordes and tribes and step by step widened out the social units until finally the oecumenical Great Society came into being. There is in the long run no irreconcilable conflict between the rightly understood selfish interests of the individuals and those of society. Society is not a Moloch to whom man has to sacrifice his own personality. It is, on the contrary, for every individual the foremost tool for the attainment of well-being and happiness. It is man's most appropriate weapon in his struggle for survival and improvement. It is not an end, but a means, the most eminent means for the attainment of all human desires.

We do not have to enter into a detailed critique of the statements

---

14 Such are the teachings of the German Historical School of the Social Sciences, whose latest exponents are Werner Sombart and Othmar Spann. It may be worthwhile to note that Catholic philosophy does not endorse the collectivist doctrine. According to the teachings of the Roman Church, natural law is nothing but the dictates of reason properly exercised, and man is capable of acquiring its full knowledge even if unaided by supernatural revelation. "God so created man as to bestow on him endowments amply sufficient for him to attain his last end. Over and above this He decreed to make the attainment of beatitude yet easier for man by placing within his reach a far simpler and far more certain way of knowing the law on the observance of which his fate depended." Cf. G. H. Joyce, "Revelation," in *The Catholic Encyclopedia*, vol. 13 (New York: Encyclopedia Press, 1913), pp. 1–5.

of the collectivist doctrine. We have only to establish the fact that the acts of the allegedly collectivist parties do not comply with the tenets of this philosophy. The political representatives of these parties occasionally in their speeches referred to collectivist slogans and connived at the propagation of party songs of the same tenor. But they do not ask their followers to sacrifice their own happiness and well-being at the altar of the collectivity. They are anxious to demonstrate by ratiocination that the methods which they recommend will in the long run serve best the selfish interests of their followers. They do not ask any other sacrifices than temporary ones which, as they promise, will at a later time be rewarded by hundredfold booty. The Nazi professors and the Nazi rhymesters say: "Efface yourself for Germany's splendor, give your wretched lives in order to make the German Nation live forever in glory and grandeur." But the Nazi politicians use a different argument: "Fight for your own preservation and for your future well-being. The enemies are firmly resolved to exterminate the noble race of Aryan heroes. If you do not resist, you all are lost. But if you take up the challenge courageously, you have a chance of defeating the onslaught. Many will be killed in action, but they would not have survived if the devilish plans of our foes were not to meet any resistance. Much more will be saved if we fight. We have the choice between two alternatives only: certain extermination of us all, if the enemies conquer, on the one hand, and the survival of the great majority in case of our victory on the other hand."

There is no appeal to the "irrational" in this purely rational—although not reasonable—reasoning. But even if the collectivist doctrine were correct, and people, in forsaking other advantages, aimed at the flowering of the collective only under the persuasion or compulsion exercised on the part of the superhuman leaders, all the statements of praxeology would remain unshaken and history would not have any reason to change its methods of approach.

VIII

The real reason for the popular disparagement of the social sciences is reluctance to accept the restrictions imposed by nature on human endeavors. This reluctance is potentially present in everybody and is overwhelming with the neurotic. Men feel unhappy because they cannot have two incompatible things together, because they have to pay a price for everything and can never attain full satisfaction. They blame the social sciences for demonstrating the scarcity of the factors which preserve and strengthen the vital forces and remove uneasiness. They disparage them for describing the world as it really is and not as they would like to have it, i.e., as a cosmos of unlimited opportunities. They are not judicious enough to comprehend that life is exactly an active resistance against adverse conditions and manifests itself only in this struggle, and that the notion of a life free from any limitations and restrictions is even inconceivable for a human mind. Reason is man's foremost equipment in the biological struggle for the preservation and expansion of his existence and survival. It would not have any function and would not have developed at all in a fool's paradise.[15]

It is not the fault of the social sciences that they are not in a position to transform society into a utopia. Economics is not a "dismal science," because it starts from the acknowledgment of the fact that the means for the attainment of ends are scarce. (With regard to human concerns which can be fully satisfied because they do not depend on scarce factors, man does not act, and praxeology, the science of human action, does not have to deal with them.) As far as there is scarcity of means, man behaves rationally, i.e., he acts. So far there is no room left for "irrationality."

That man has to pay a price for the maintenance of social institutions enabling him to attain ends which he deems as more valuable than this price made, than these sacrifices brought for them, is obvious. It is futile to disguise the impotent dissatisfaction with this state of affairs as a revolt against an alleged dogmatic orthodoxy of the social sciences.

If the "rational" methods of economic theory demonstrate that an a results in a p, no appeal to irrationality can make a result in a q. If the theory was wrong, only a correct theory can refute it and substitute a correct solution for an incorrect one.

IX

The social sciences have not neglected to give full consideration to all those phenomena which people may have in mind in alluding to irrationality. History has developed a special method for dealing with

15 Cf. Benedetto Croce, *History as the Story of Liberty*, S. Sprigge, trans. (New York: W. W. Norton, 1941), p. 33.

them: understanding. Praxeology has built up its system in such a way that its theorems are valid for all human action without any regard to whether the ends aimed at are qualified, from whatever point of view, as rational or irrational. It is simply not true that the social sciences are guilty of having left untouched a part of the field which they have to elucidate. The suggestions for the construction of a new science whose subject matter has to be the irrational phenomena are of no account. There is no untilled soil left for such a new science.

The social sciences are, of course, rational. All sciences are. Science is the application of reason for a systematic description and interpretation of phenomena. There is no such thing as a science not based on reason. The longing for an irrational science is self-contradictory.

History will one day have to understand historically the "revolt against reason" as one of the factors of the history of the last generations. Some very remarkable contributions to this problem have already been published.

Economic theory is not perfect. No human work is built for eternity. New theorems may supplement or supplant the old ones. But what may be defective with present-day economics is certainly not that it failed to grasp the weight and significance of factors popularly qualified as irrational.

CHAPTER 3

Epistemological Relativism in the Sciences of Human Action

I

Up to the eighteenth century, historians paid little or no attention to the epistemological problems of their craft. In dealing with the subject of their studies, they again and again referred to some regularities that—as they themselves and their public assumed—are valid for any kind of human action irrespective of the time and the geographical scene of the action as well as of the actors' personal qualities and ideas. But they did not raise the question whether these regularities were of an extraneous character or inherent in the very nature of human action. They knew very well that man is not able to attain all that he wants to attain. But they did not ask whether the limits of a man's power are completely described by reference to the laws of nature and to the Deity's miraculous interference with them, on the one hand, and to the superior power of more puissant men, on the other hand.

Like all other people, the historians too distinguished between behavior complying with the moral law and behavior violating it. But, like all other people, they were fully aware of the fact that nonobservance of the laws of ethics did not necessarily—in this life—result in failure to attain the ends sought. Whatever may happen to the sinner in the life hereafter and on the day of the Last Judgment, the historian could not help realizing that on earth he could sometimes fare very well, much better than many pious fellow men.

Entirely new perspectives were opened when the economists discovered that there prevails a regularity in the sequence and interdependence of market phenomena. It was the first step to a general theory of

[Reprinted from *Relativism and the Study of Man*, Helmut Schoeck and James W. Wiggins, eds. (Princeton, N.J.: D. Van Nostrand, 1962).—Ed.]

human action, praxeology. For the first time people became aware of the fact that in order to succeed, human action must comply not only with what are called the laws of nature, but also with specific laws of human action. There are things that even the most efficient constabulary of a formidable government cannot bring about, although they may not appear impossible from the point of view of the natural sciences.

It was obvious that the claims of this new science could not fail to give offense from three points of view. There were first of all the governments. Despots as well as democratic majorities are not pleased to learn that their might is not absolute. Again and again they embark upon policies that are doomed to failure and fail because they disregard the laws of economics. But they do not learn the lesson. Instead they employ hosts of pseudo-economists to discredit the "abstract," i.e., in their terminology, vain teachings of sound economics.

Then there are ethical doctrines that charge economics with ethical materialism. As they see it, economics teaches that man ought to aim exclusively or first of all at satisfying the appetites of the senses. They stubbornly refuse to learn that economics is neutral with regard to the choice of ultimate ends, as it deals only with the methods for the attainment of ends chosen, whatever these ends may be.

There are, finally, authors who reject economics on account of its alleged "unhistorical approach." The economists claim absolute validity for what they call the laws of economics; they assert that in the course of human affairs something is at work that remains unchanged in the flux of historical events. In the opinion of many authors this is an unwarranted thesis, the acceptance of which must hopelessly muddle the work of historians.

In dealing with this brand of relativism, we must take into account that its popularity was due not to epistemological, but to practical considerations. Economics pointed out that many cherished policies cannot result in the effects aimed at by the governments that resorted to them, but bring about other effects—from the point of view of those who advocated and applied those policies—that were even more unsatisfactory than the conditions that they were designed to alter. No other conclusion could be inferred from these teachings than that these measures were contrary to purpose and that their repeal would benefit the rightly understood or long-run interests of all the people. This explains why all those whose short-run interests were favored by these measures bitterly criticized the "dismal science." The epistemological qualms of some philosophers and historians met with an enthusiastic response on the part of aristocrats and landowners who wanted to preserve their old privileges and on the part of small business and employees who were intent upon acquiring new privileges. The European "historical schools" and American Institutionalism won political and popular support, which is, in general, denied to theoretical doctrines.

However, the establishment of this fact must not induce us to belittle the seriousness and importance of the problems involved. Epistemological relativism as expressed in the writings of some of the historicists, e.g., Karl Knies and Max Weber, was not motivated by political zeal. These two outstanding representatives of historicism were, as far as this was humanly possible in the milieu of the German universities of their age, free from an emotional predilection in favor of interventionist policies and from chauvinistic prejudice against the foreign, i.e., British, French, and Austrian science of economics. Besides, Knies[1] wrote a remarkable book on money and credit, and Weber[2] gave the deathblow to the methods applied by the schools of Schmoller and Brentano[3] by demonstrating the unscientific character of judgments of value. There were certainly in the argumentation of the champions of historical relativism points that call for an elucidation.

II

Before entering into an analysis of the objections raised against the "absolutism" of economics, it is necessary to point out that the rejection of economics by epistemological relativism has nothing to do with the positivist rejection of the methods actually used by historians.

In the opinion of positivism, the work of the historians is mere gossip or, at best, the accumulation of a vast amount of material that they do not know how to use. What is needed is a science of the laws that determine what happens in history. Such a science has to be developed

---

1 [Karl Knies, *Geld und Kredit*, 3 vols. (Berlin: Weidmann, 1873–79). — Ed.]

2 [Max Weber, *Wirtschaft und Gesellschaft*, vol. 1 of *Grundriss der Sozialökonomik* (Tübingen, 1922). English-language edition, *The Theory of Social and Economic Organization*, A. M. Henderson and Talcott Parsons, trans. (Glencoe, Ill.: Free Press, 1947). — Ed.]

3 [Gustav Schmoller was the founder of the "Younger" German Historical, or "Historicoethical," School. Its program combined a historical approach to economic phenomena with the pursuit of economic and social politics grounded in "moral principles." Lujo Brentano was a prominent proponent and follower of Schmoller but disagreed on matters of methodology. — Ed.]

by the same methods of research that made it possible to develop out of experience the science of physics.

The refutation of the positivistic doctrine concerning history is an achievement of several German philosophers, first of all of Wilhelm Windelband and of Heinrich Rickert. They pointed out in what the fundamental difference between history, the record of human action, and the natural sciences consists. Human action is purposive, it aims at the attainment of definite ends chosen, it cannot be treated without reference to these ends, and history is in this sense—we must emphasize, *only* in this sense—finalistic. But to the natural sciences the concept of ends and final causes is foreign.

Then there is a second fundamental difference. In the natural sciences, man is able to observe in the laboratory experiment the effects brought about by a change in one factor only, all other factors the alteration of which could possibly produce effects remaining unchanged. This makes it possible to find what the natural sciences call experimentally established facts of experience. No such technique of research is available in the field of human action. Every experience concerning human action is historical, i.e., an experience of complex phenomena, of changes produced by the joint operation of a multitude of factors. Such an experience cannot produce "facts" in the sense in which this term is employed in the natural sciences. It can neither verify nor falsify any theorem. It would remain an inexplicable puzzle if it could not be interpreted by dint of a theory that had been derived from other sources than historical experience.

Now, of course, neither Rickert and the other authors of the group to which he belonged, the "Southwestern German philosophers," nor the historians who shared their conception went as far as this last conclusion. To them, professors of German universities at the end of the nineteenth and the beginning of the twentieth century, the very idea that there could be any science claiming for its theses universal validity for all human action irrespective of time, geography, and the racial and national characteristics of people remained unknown. For men living in the spiritual climate of the second German Reich, it was an understood thing that the pretensions of "abstract" economic theory were vain and that German *wirtschaftliche Staatswissenschaften* (the economic aspects of political science), an entirely historical discipline, had replaced the inane generalization of the school of Hume, Adam Smith, and Ricardo. As they saw it, human action—apart from theology, ethics, and jurisprudence—could be dealt with scientifically only by history. Their radical empiricism prevented them from paying any attention to the possibility of an a priori science of human action.

The positivist dogma that Dilthey, Windelband, Rickert, and their followers demolished was not relativistic. It postulated a science—sociology—that would derive from the treatment of the empirical data provided by history a body of knowledge that would render to the mind the same services with regard to human action that physics renders with regard to events in the sphere of nature. These German philosophers demonstrated that such a general science of action could not be elaborated by a posteriori reasoning. The idea that it could be the product of a priori reasoning did not occur to them.

III

The deficiency of the work of the classical economists consisted in their attempt to draw a sharp line of demarcation between "purely economic activities" and all other human concerns and actions. Their great feat was the discovery that there prevails in the concatenation and sequence of market phenomena a regularity that can be compared to the regularity in the concatenation and sequence of natural events. Yet, in dealing with the market and its exchange ratios, they were baffled by their failure to solve the problem of valuation. In interpersonal exchange transactions, objects are not valued according to their utility, they thought, because otherwise "iron" would be valued more highly than "gold." They did not see that the apparent paradox was due only to the vicious way they formulated the question. Value judgments of acting men do not refer to "iron" or to "gold" as such, but always to definite quantities of each of these metals between which the actor is forced to choose because he cannot have both of them. The classical economists failed to find the law of marginal utility. This shortcoming prevented them from tracing market phenomena back to the decisions of the consumers. They could deal only with the actions of the businessmen, for whom the valuations of the consumers are merely data. The famous formula "to buy on the cheapest and to sell on the dearest market" makes sense only for the businessman. It is meaningless for the consumer.

Thus forced to restrict their analysis to business activities, the classical economists constructed the concept of a science of wealth or the production and distribution of wealth. Wealth, according to this definition, meant all that could be bought or sold. The endeavors to get wealth were seen as a separate sphere of activities. All other human concerns appeared from the vantage point of this science merely as disturbing elements.

Actually, few classical economists were content with this circumscription of the scope of economics. But their search for a more satisfactory concept could not succeed before the marginalists substituted the theory of subjective value from the various abortive attempts of the classical economists and their epigones. As long as the study of the production and distribution of wealth was considered as the subject matter of economic analysis, one had to distinguish between the economic and the noneconomic actions of men. Then economics appeared as a branch of knowledge that dealt with only one segment of human action. There were, outside of this field, actions about which the economists had nothing to say. It was precisely the fact that the adepts of the new science did not deal with all those concerns of man which in their eyes were qualified as extraeconomic that appeared to many outsiders as a depreciation of these matters dictated by an insolent materialistic bias.

Things are different for modern economics, with its doctrine of the subjective interpretation of valuation. In its context the distinction between economics and allegedly noneconomic ends becomes meaningless. The value judgments of the ultimate consumers express not only the striving after more tangible material goods, but no less the striving after all other human concerns. The narrow viewpoint of a science of—material—wealth is surpassed. Out of the discipline of wealth evolves a general theory of all choices made by acting men, a general theory of every kind of human action, praxeology. In their behavior on the market, people evidence not only their wishes to acquire more material goods, but no less all their other preferences. Market prices reflect not only the "materialistic side" of man, but his philosophical, ethical, and religious ideas as well. The observance of religious commandments—to build and maintain houses of worship, to cease working on holidays, to avoid certain foods either always or on specific days and weeks, to abstain from intoxicating beverages and tobacco, to assist those in need, and many others—is one of the factors that determine the supply of and the demand for consumers' goods and thereby the conduct of business. Praxeology is neutral with regard to the ultimate ends that the individuals want to attain. It does not deal with ultimate ends, but with the means chosen for their attainment. It is merely interested in the question whether or not the means resorted to are fitted to attain the ends sought.

The enormous quantity of anti-economic literature published in the last hundred and fifty years turns around one argument only. Its authors repeat again and again that man as he really is and acts strives not only after more material amenities, but also after some other—higher or loftier or ideal—aims. From this point of view the self-styled Historical School attacked what they called the absolutism of the economic doctrine and advocated a relativistic approach. It is not the theme of this paper to investigate whether the economists of the classical school and their epigones were really guilty of having neglected to pay due attention to the nonmaterialistic concerns of man. But it is to be emphasized that all the objections raised by the Historical School, e.g., by Knies in his famous book,[4] are futile and invalid with regard to the teachings of modern economics.

It is customary in German political literature to distinguish between an older and a later Historical School.[5] As the champions of the older school, Roscher, Bruno Hildebrand, and Knies are named. The younger school consists of the followers of Schmoller, who after the establishment of the Reich in 1870 held the chairs of economics at the German universities. This way of subdividing into periods the history of ideas is an outcome of the parochialism that induced German authors to slight all that was accomplished abroad. They failed to realize that the "historical" opposition against what was called the absolutism of economics was inaugurated outside of Germany. Its outstanding representative was Sismondi[6] rather than Roscher and Hildebrand. But it is much more important to realize the fact that all those who in Germany as well as in other countries after the publication of the books of Jevons,

4 The first edition was published in 1853 under the title *Die politische Ökonomie vom Standpunkte der geschichtlichen Methode*. The second edition was published in 1883 under the title *Die politische Ökonomie vom geschichtlichen Standpunkte*. It is by and large a reprint of the earlier edition enlarged by many additions.

5 [The "older" Historical School proponents did not advocate politics as a means of intervention, nor a basis for economic reasoning as did the "younger" Historical School advocates.—Ed.]

6 [Jean Charles Leonard Sismondi was a Swiss economist and historian. He thought that the focus of economics should be man and social reform not wealth and laissez faire. Sismondi was the first to practice modern period analysis in 1819.—Ed.]

Menger, and Walras criticized economic doctrine on account of its alleged materialism were fighting against windmills.

IV

Max Weber's concept of a general science of human action—to which he applied the name sociology—no longer refers to the distinction between economic action and other activities. But Weber virtually endorsed the objections raised by historicism against economics by distinguishing between genuinely rational action, on the one hand, and other kinds of action. His doctrine is so closely connected with some untranslatable peculiarities of the German language that it is rather difficult to expound it in English.

The distinction that Weber makes between "social action" and other action is, from the point of view of our problem, of little importance. The main thing is that Weber quite correctly distinguishes between *sinnhaftes Handeln* and the merely physiologically determined reactions of the human body. *Sinnhaftes Handeln* is directed by the *Sinn* the acting individual attaches to it; we would have to translate: by the meaning the actor attaches to it and by the end he wants to attain by it. This definition would appear as a clear distinction between human action, the striving after a definite end, on the one hand, and the physiological—quasi-automatic—reactions of the nerves and cells of the human body, on the other hand. But then Weber goes on to distinguish within the class of *sinnhaftes Handeln* four different subclasses. The first of these subclasses is called *zweckrationales Handeln* and is defined as action aiming at a definite end. The second subclass is called *wertrationales Handeln* and is defined as action determined by the belief in the unconditional intrinsic value *(unbedingter Eigenwert)* of a certain way of conduct as such, without regard to its success, from the point of view of ethics, aesthetics, religion, or other principles. What Weber failed to see is the fact that also the striving after compliance with definite ethical, aesthetical, and religious ideas is no less an end than any other end that men may try to attain. A Catholic who crosses himself, a Jew who abstains from food and drink on the Day of Atonement, a lover of music who forgoes dinner in order to listen to a Beethoven symphony, all aim at ends that from their point of view are more desirable than what they have to renounce in order to get what they want. Only a personal judgment of value can deny to their actions the qualification *zweckrational*, i.e., aiming at a definite end. And what in Weber's definition do the words "without regard to its success" mean? The Catholic crosses himself because he considers such behavior as one link in a chain of conduct that will lead him to what for him is the most important success of man's earthly pilgrimage. It is tragic that Max Weber, the eminent historian of religion, the man who tried to free German sociological thought from its naive commitment to judgments of value, failed to see the contradictions of his doctrine.[7]

Other attempts to distinguish between rational action and nonrational or irrational action were likewise based on crass misconstructions and failed. Most of them called "irrational," conduct directed by mistaken ideas and expectations concerning the effects of definite methods of procedure. Thus, magic practices are today styled as irrational. They were certainly not fitted to attain the ends sought. However, the people who resorted to them believed that they were the right technique in the same way in which physicians up to the middle of the past century believed that bleeding is a method of preventing and curing various diseases. In speaking of human action, we have in mind conduct that, in the opinion of the actor, is best fitted to attain an end he wants to attain, whether or not this opinion is also held by a better-informed spectator or historian. The way in which contemporary physicians deal with cancer is not irrational, although we hope that one day more efficacious therapeutic and prophylactic methods will be discovered. A report concerning other people's actions is confusing if it applies the term irrational to the activities of people whose knowledge was less perfect than that of the reporter. As no reporter can claim for himself omniscience, he would at least have to add to his qualification of an action as irrational the proviso "from my personal point of view."

Another way in which the epithet "irrational" is often employed refers, not to the means but to the ends of definite modes of conduct. Thus, some authors call, either approvingly or disapprovingly, "irrational" the behavior of people who prefer religious concerns, national independence, or other goals commonly called noneconomic to a more

---

7 There is no need to enter into an analysis of the two other subclasses enumerated by Weber. For a detailed critique of Weber's doctrine, see my essay "Sociologie und Geschichte," in *Archiv für Sozialwissenschaft*, vol. 61 [1929], reprinted in my book *Grundprobleme der Nationalökonomie* (Jena: Gustav Fischer, 1933), pp. 64–121. In the English-language translation of this book, *Epistemological Problems of Economics*, George Reisman, trans., and Arthur Goddard, ed. (Princeton, N.J.: D. Van Nostrand, 1960), this essay appears on pp. 68–129.

abundant supply of material satisfactions. Against this highly inexpedient and confusing terminology there is need to emphasize again and again the fact that no man is called to sit in judgment on other people's judgments of value concerning ultimate ends. When the Huguenots preferred the loss of all their earthly possessions, the most cruel punishments, and exile to the adoption of a creed that in their opinion was idolatrous, their behavior was not "irrational." Neither was Louis XIV "irrational" when he deprived his realm of many of its most worthy citizens in order to comply with the precepts of his conscience. The historian may disagree with the ultimate ends that the persecutors and their victims were aiming at. But this does not entitle him to call the means to which they resorted in order to attain their ends irrational. The terms "rational" and "irrational" are just as much out of place when applied to ends as when applied to means. With regard to ultimate ends, all that a mortal man can assert is approval or disapproval from the point of view of his own judgments of value. With regard to means, there is only one question, viz., whether or not they are fitted to attain the ends sought.

Most of our contemporaries are guided by the idea that it is the worst of all crimes to force a man, by recourse to violence, to behave according to the commandments of a religious or political doctrine that he despises. But the historian has to record the fact that there were ages in which only a minority shared this conviction, and unspeakable horrors were committed by fanatical princes and majorities. He is right in pointing out that Louis XIV, in outlawing Protestantism, inflicted irreparable evils on the French nation. But he must not forget to add that the king was not aware of these consequences of his policy and that, even if he had anticipated them, he would perhaps nonetheless have considered the attainment of religious uniformity as a good for which the price paid was not too high.

The surgeons who accompanied the armies of ages past did their best to save the lives of the wounded warriors. But their therapeutic knowledge was pitifully inadequate. They bled the injured man whom only a transfusion of blood could have saved and thus virtually killed him. Because of their ignorance, their treatment was contrary to purpose. It would be misleading and inexpedient to call it irrational. Present-day doctors are not irrational, although probably better-informed physicians of the future will qualify some of their therapeutic techniques as detrimental and contrary to purpose.

V

Whenever the distinction between rational and irrational is applied to ultimate ends, the meaning is that the judgments of value underlying the choice of the end in question meet with approval or disapproval on the part of the speaker or writer. Now the promulgation of judgments of value is not the business of a man in his capacity as a praxeologist, economist, or historian. It is rather the task of religion, metaphysics, or ethics. History of religion is not theology, and theology is not history of religion.

When the distinction between rational and irrational is applied to means, the meaning is that the speaker or writer asserts that the means in question are not serving their purpose, i.e., that they are not fit to attain the ends sought by the people who resort to such means. It is certainly one of the main tasks of history to deal with the serviceableness of the means people employed in their endeavors to attain the ends sought. It is also certain that the main practical goal of praxeology and its hitherto best developed part, economics, is to distinguish between means that are fit to attain the ends sought and those that are not. But it is, as has been pointed out, not expedient and rather confusing to use for this distinction the terms "rational" and "irrational." It is more appropriate to speak of means answering the intended purpose and those not answering it.

This holds true also with regard to the way in which the terms "rational" and "irrational" are employed by psychoanalysts. They "call behavior irrational that is predominately emotional or instinctual," and furthermore, "all unconscious functions," and in this sense distinguish between "irrational (instinctual or emotional) action as opposed to rational action, and irrational as opposed to rational thinking."[8] Whether this terminology is expedient for the treatment of the therapeutic problems of psychoanalysis may be left to the psychoanalysts. From the praxeological point of view, the spontaneous reactions of the human body's organs and the activity of instinctual drives are not action. On the other hand, it is manifestly the outcome of a personal judgment of value to call emotional actions—e.g., the action with which a man may react to the awareness of his fellow men's distress—irrational. It is

8 H. Hartmann, "On Rational and Irrational Action," in *Psychoanalysis and the Social Sciences,* vol. 1 (1947), p. 371.

further obvious that no other meaning can be ascribed to the term "irrational thinking" than that it is logically invalid thinking and leads to erroneous conclusions.

VI

The philosophy of historical relativism—historicism—fails to see the fact that there is something unchanging that, on the one hand, constitutes the sphere of history or historical events as distinct from the spheres of other events and, on the other hand, enables man to deal with these events, i.e., to record their succession and to try to find out their concatenation, in other words, to understand them. This unchanging phenomenon is the fact that man is not indifferent to the state of his environment (including the conditions of his own body) and that he tries, as far as it is possible for him to do so, to substitute by purposive action a state that he likes better for a state he likes less. In a word: man acts. This alone distinguishes human history from the history of changes going on outside the field of human action, from the study of "natural history" and its various subdivisions as, e.g., geology or the evolution of various species of living beings. In human history we are dealing with the ends aimed at by the actors, that is, with final causes.[9] In natural history, as in the other branches of the natural sciences, we do not know anything about final causes.

All human wisdom, science, and knowledge deal only with the segment of the universe that can be perceived and studied by the human mind. In speaking of human action as something unchanging, we refer to the conditions of this segment only. There are authors who assume that the state of the universe—the cosmos—could change in a way about which we simply do not know anything and that all that our natural sciences say about the behavior of sodium and levers, for example, may be invalid under this new state. In this sense they deny "any kind of universality to chemical and mechanical statements" and suggest that they be treated "as historical ones."[10] With this brand of

9 When the sciences of human action refer to ends, they always mean the ends that acting men are aiming at. This distinguishes these sciences from the metaphysical doctrines known under the name of "philosophy of history" that pretend to know the ends toward which a superhuman entity—for instance, in the context of Marxism, the "material productive forces"—directs the course of affairs independent of the ends the acting men want to attain.

10 Otto Neurath, "Foundations of the Social Sciences," *International Encyclopedia of Unified Science*, vol. 2, no. 1 (Chicago: University of Chicago Press, 1956), p. 9.

agnostic hyperhistoricism that deals in its statements with visionary conditions about which—as they freely admit—we do not know and cannot know anything, reason and science have no quarrel.

Thinking man does not look upon the world with a mind that is, as it were, a Lockian paper upon which reality writes its own story. The paper of his mind is of a special quality that enables man to transform the raw material of sensation into perception and the perceptual data into an image of reality. It is precisely this specific quality or power of his intellect—the logical structure of his mind—that provides man with the faculty of seeing more in the world than nonhuman beings see. This power is instrumental in the development of the natural sciences. But it alone would not enable man to discover in the behavior of his fellow men more than he can see in the behavior of stars or of stones, in that of amoebae or in that of elephants.

In dealing with his fellow men, the individual resorts not only to the a priori of logic, but besides to the praxeological a priori. Himself an acting being, he knows what it means to strive after ends chosen. He sees more in the agitation and the stir of his fellow men than in the changes occurring in his nonhuman environment. He can search for the ends their conduct is aiming at. There is something that distinguishes in his eyes the movements of germs in a liquid as observed in the microscope from the movements of the individuals in the crowd he may observe in the rush hour at New York's Grand Central Terminal. He knows that there is some "sense" in a man's running around or sitting still. He looks upon his human environment with mental equipment that is not required or, to say it more precisely, is downright obstructive in endeavors to explore the state of his nonhuman environment. This specific mental equipment is the praxeological a priori.

The radical empiricism of the historicists went astray in ignoring this fact. No report about any man's conduct can do without reference to the praxeological a priori. There is something that is absolutely valid for all human action irrespective of time, geography, and the racial, national, and cultural characteristics of the actors. There is no human action that can be dealt with without reference to the categorical concepts of ends and means, of success and failure, of costs, of profit or loss. What the Ricardian law of association, better known as the law of comparative cost, describes is absolutely valid for any kind of voluntary human cooperation under the division of labor. What the much derided economic laws describe is precisely what must always and everywhere happen provided the special conditions presupposed by them are present.

Willy-nilly, people realize that there are things they cannot achieve because they are contrary to the laws of nature. But they are loath to admit that there are things that even the most powerful government cannot achieve because they are contrary to praxeological law.

VII

Different from the case of the historians who are loath to take cognizance of the praxeological a priori is the case of the authors who belong to the various historical, "realistic," and institutional schools of economics. If these scholars were consistent, they would limit their studies to what is called economic history; they would deal exclusively with the past and would carefully abstain from asserting anything about the future. Prediction about events to come can be made only on the ground of knowledge of a regularity in the succession of events that is valid for every action irrespective of the time and the geographical and cultural conditions of its occurrence. Whatever economists committed to historicism or institutionalism do, whether they advise their own governments or those backward foreign countries, is self-contradictory. If there is no universal law that describes the necessary effects of definite ways of acting, nothing can be predicted, and no measure to bring about any definite results can be recommended or rejected.

It is the same with those authors who, while rejecting the idea that there are economic laws valid for all times, everywhere, and for all people, assume that every period of history has its own economic laws that have to be found a posteriori by studying the history of the period concerned. These authors may tell us that they have succeeded in discovering the laws governing events up to yesterday. But—from the point of view of their own epistemological doctrine—they are not free to assume that the same laws will also determine what will happen tomorrow. All that they are entitled to affirm is: experience of the past shows that A brought about B; but we do not know whether tomorrow A will not bring about some other effects than B.

Another variety of the denial of economics is the trend doctrine. Its supporters blithely assume that trends of evolution as manifested in the past will go on. However, they cannot deny that in the past, trends did change and that there is no reason whatever to assume that present trends will not one day change too. Thus, this becomes especially manifest when businessmen, concerned about the continuation of prevailing trends, consult economists and statisticians. The answer they get is invariably this: statistics show us that the trend you are interested in was still continuing on the day to which our most recent statistical data refer; if no disturbing factors turn up, there is no reason why the trend should change; however, we do not know anything about the question whether or not such new factors will present themselves.

VIII

Epistemological relativism, the essential doctrine of historicism, must be clearly distinguished from the ethical relativism of other schools of thought. There are authors who combine praxeological relativism with ethical relativism. But there are also authors who display ethical absolutism while rejecting the concept of universally valid praxeological laws. Thus, many adepts of the Historical School of economics and of institutionalism judge the historical past from the point of view of what they consider as indisputable, never-changing moral precepts, e.g., equality of wealth and incomes. In the eyes of some of them private property is as such morally objectionable. They blame the economists for an alleged praise of material wealth and disparagement of more noble concerns. They condemn the system of private enterprise as immoral and advocate socialism on account of its presumed higher moral worth. As they see it, Soviet Russia complies better with the immutable principles of ethics than do the nations of the West committed to the cult of Mammon.

As against all this emotional talk there is need to point out again: praxeology and economics, its up to now best-developed branch, are neutral with regard to any moral precepts. They deal with the striving after ends chosen by acting men without any regard whether these ends are approved or disapproved from any point of view. The fact that the immense majority of men prefer a richer supply of material goods to a less ample supply is a datum of history; it does not have any place in economic theory. Economics neither advocates capitalism nor rejects socialism. It merely tries to show what the necessary effects of each of these two systems are. He who disagrees with the teachings of economics ought to try to refute them by discursive reasoning, not by abuse, insinuations, and the appeal to arbitrary, allegedly ethical standards.

❧ Money

CHAPTER 4

The Position of Money among Economic Goods

Karl Knies has recommended replacing the traditional division of economic goods into consumer goods and producer goods with a threefold classification: producer goods, consumer goods, and means of exchange.[1] Terminological questions of this kind, however, should be decided solely on the basis of their usefulness for furthering scientific work; definitions, concepts, and the taxonomy of phenomena have to prove their usefulness in the results of the research which makes use of them. When these criteria are applied to the classification and terminology suggested by Knies, it becomes apparent that they are extremely appropriate. Indeed, there is no theory of catallactics[2] which does not make use of them. The theory of the value of money is always reserved for special treatment and separated for the explanation of the price formation of producer goods as well as consumer goods, although it is obviously part of a uniform theory of value and price. Even if we do not use the Kniesian terminology and classification consciously, in all significant discussions we act as if we had adopted them completely.

But it is also necessary to note that the special role of money among economic goods has, if anything, been over-emphasized. The problems of the determination of the purchasing power of money have mostly been treated as if they had nothing or very little in common with the problems of non-monetary exchange. This led to a special status of monetary theory and has been detrimental to the development

[Originally published in Die Wirtschaftstheorie der Gegenwart, vol. 2, Hans Mayer, Frank A. Fetter, and Richard Reisch, eds. (Vienna: Julius Springer, 1932). Translated for this volume by Albert H. Zlabinger.—Ed.]

1 Karl Knies, Geld und Kredit, 2nd ed. (Berlin: Weidmann, 1885), pp. 20ff.

2 [Catallactics is that part of praxeology that deals specifically with market phenomena. The term was first used by Bishop Richard Whately in his Introductory Lectures in Political Economy (1831).—Ed.]

of economic understanding. Even today, we continually encounter attempts to defend certain unjustified peculiarities of monetary theory.

Roscher's often quoted remark, "[that] the wrong definitions of money can be divided into two main groups: Those which think of it as more and those which think of it as less than the most saleable good,"[3] applies not only to the question of the definition of money. Even a number of those who consider the theory of money a part of catallactics go too far in emphasizing its special position. This branch of our science offers plenty of difficulties, and it is not necessary to construct artificial problems; the existing ones provide enough challenge.

I   Monetary Services and the Value of Money

It is clear that the naive conception of the layman that things have value in themselves, i.e., intrinsic value, necessarily leads to a position which draws the dividing line between money and money substitutes differently from the position according to which the value of a thing is derived from its usefulness. Those who conceive of value as the result of properties inherent in things must necessarily make a distinction between physically valuable money and means of exchange which provide monetary services but are without material value. This approach inescapably leads to a contrasting of normal money with bad and abnormal money, which, in reality, is not money at all.

Today there is no need to deal with this theory. For the modern subjective theory of value, the question has long been decided. No one would still openly defend a concept according to which the whole or a portion of value and price theory was based upon intrinsic exchange value, i.e., independent of the valuations of acting men. Once this is admitted, one has already adopted the fundamental principle of subjective value theory, i.e., the theory of marginal utility.

For prescientific economists—the predecessors of the Physiocrats and the Classical Economists—it was a significant problem to integrate the theory of the value of money with that of the value of other goods. Holding a crudely materialistic bias, they saw the source of value in the "objective" usefulness of goods. From this point of view, it is obvious why bread, which can still hunger, and cloth, which can protect

---

3 Wilhelm Roscher, *Grundlagen der Nationalökonomie*, 25th ed. (Stuttgart and Berlin: J. G. Cotta'sche Buchhandlung Nachtfolger, 1918), p. 340.

from the cold, will have value. But from where does money, which can neither nourish people nor keep them warm, derive its value? Some responded that it arose "from convention," and others maintained that the value of money was "imaginary."

The error in this view was discovered early. John Law had put it most succinctly. If all value is derived from usefulness, then it must be true that the adoption of the precious metals as means of exchange must generate a value for it. If one wishes to call the value of the metal used as money, insofar as it is derived from its monetary services, imaginary, one has to regard all value as imaginary,

> Car aucune chose n'a de valeur que par l'usage auquel on l'applique, et a raison des demandes qu'on en fait, proportionellement a sa quantite.[4]

With these words, Law anticipated the subjective theory of value; he should not be denied the place he deserves in the history of our science. The importance of his accomplishment is not reduced by his inability to develop all the implications from his fundamental idea or that he got lost in the impenetrable thicket of error or, perhaps, even of guilt.

Researchers who came after him were also unable to make full use of the content of the clearly developed fundamental idea advanced by Law. In three respects we still encounter misconceptions.

First, some writers categorically deny that the service provided by money can generate value. Unfortunately, they do not provide a justification why monetary services should be different from the services provided by food and clothing. The difficulty posed by "paper money" is circumvented by viewing "paper money" as a claim on genuine, i.e., "materially" valuable, metallic money. Fluctuations in the rate of exchange of "paper money" are explained by changes in the probability of payment in species. In view of the development of monetary theory during the last decades, I consider it superfluous to challenge this theory. I have attempted an empirical refutation and have not encountered adequate opposition.[5]

In a way, the second error is connected with the first: the denial

---

4 John Law, *Considerations sur le Numeraire et le Commerce* (Paris: Buisson, 1851), pp. 447ff. The passage translates as: The value of a thing is only in the use we make of it and the expectations we put into it, proportional to its quantity.
5 See Mises, *The Theory of Money and Credit*, 2nd ed. (Indianapolis, Ind.: Liberty Fund, 1981), pp. 146–53.

of the possibility of there being a money whose "substance" only produces monetary services and nothing else. It is usually granted that monetary services can generate value, just as every other service, in general. Without reservation, we have to agree with Knies when he argues, "[that] gold and silver would have been as unsuitable for the purpose of performing the functions of money as any other commodity, if they had not previously—before their adoption for monetary services—served as economic goods for the satisfaction of human wants, a 'general' economic need, a need that was widely felt and persistent."[6] But Knies is in error when he continues, "it is not sufficient that this primary use of the precious metals has preceded their use for monetary services; it is necessary that this use continues, lest the pieces of precious metal lose their usefulness as money. . . . If people ceased to use gold and silver to satisfy their desire for jewelry or ornamentation, etc., then the other use of the precious metals, their use as a means of exchange, would be eliminated, also."[7] Knies did not succeed in proving the validity of this assertion. It is by no means evident why an economic good, which performs the services of a commonly used means of exchange, should lose its ability to serve as money simply because its use for other purposes is gradually discontinued.

That the adoption of a good as a medium of exchange requires the good's previous use or consumption for other purposes results from the fact that the specific demand for its services as a means of exchange presupposes an already existing objective exchange value. This objective exchange value, which subsequently will be modified by the demand for the good as a medium of exchange in addition to the demand for it in its "other" use, will be based exclusively upon its "other" use when it begins to be used as a means of exchange. But once an economic good has become money, then the specific demand for money can tie into an already existing exchange relationship between money and goods in the market, even if the demand for the money-good, as motivated by the other use, disappears.

Only very slowly and with difficulty has the human spirit freed itself from the crude materialistic mode of thought that has resulted in a prolonged resistance to the idea that the use of a good as a medium of exchange, like any other possible use for the good, generates a demand that establishes a price and is capable of changing that price. If the

6 Knies, *Geld und Kredit*, p. 322.
7 Ibid., pp. 322ff.

ability of a thing to satisfy a human need, as well as the *recognition* of this ability, is made the prerequisite for establishing the goods-quality of a thing,[8] then one comes close to distinguishing between "real" and "unreal" goods among the objects of economic action. As soon as the economist steps upon this ground, he loses his footing and slides unintentionally out of the domain of scientific objectivity; he enters the realm of ethical valuations, morality, and policy. There, he will compare the "objectively useful" things to those which are merely "thought to be useful." He will examine whether and to what extent the things which are thought to be useful (and therefore are treated accordingly) are indeed so in an "objective" sense. As soon as one has come this far, it is only logical to ask whether the usefulness provided by a good satisfies a genuine need or merely a fictitious one. This way of thinking may subsequently lead to the view that the value of precious metals (which serve "only" the desire for jewelry and do not satisfy a physiological need as, e.g., food and clothing undeniably do from a crude materialistic point of view) is entirely imaginary, a result of inappropriate social institutions and human vanity. On the other hand, the result can be that the value of precious metals is admitted as legitimate, since even the desire for jewelry is "genuine" and "justified." The objective utility of the precious metals is not denied; rather, the general validity of the requirement for the services of money is questioned, since society had once existed without money and, in any case, such a society is imaginable. It is an untenable assumption that the "goods-quality" requires a "natural" utility not limited to the particular requirements of any presupposed social order.

But an even cruder materialism was the view which wanted to deny monetary services their value-creating power because money in its performance of this service did not lose its ability to serve other purposes; in other words, because its "substance" was not used up in its services as money.

All of those who denied the ability of the services of money to determine its exchange value failed to recognize that the only decisive element is demand. The fact that there exists a demand for money—the most marketable (most saleable) good, for which the owners of other goods are prepared to exchange—means that the monetary function is capable of creating value.

---

8 This is even done by Menger; see his *Principles of Economics* [1871] (New York: New York University Press, 1981), pp. 52–53.

II Money Supply and Money Demand: The "Velocity of Circulation" of Money

The most disastrous of the unjustified deviations of monetary theory from the theory of direct exchange was the failure to base the analysis of the fundamental problem of the theory of the value of money on the relation between the stock of money and the demand for it by the individual economic units, or between the demand for money and the supply of money on the market. Rather, the analysis began with the objective usefulness of the monetary unit for the aggregate economy, which was expressed as the velocity of money relative to the money stock and which was then compared to the sum of transactions.

The old tendency, taken over from the Cameralists,[9] to base the analysis of economic problems of the "national economy," on the "totality" and not on the acting human subjects, seems hard to eradicate. In spite of all the warnings of the subjective economists, we continue to observe relapses. It is one of the lesser evils that ethical judgments regarding phenomena are presented under the guise of scientific objectivity. For example, productive activity (i.e., activity carried out in an imagined socialist community led by the critic) is contrasted with profit-seeking activity (i.e., the activity of individuals in a society based on private property in the means of production). The former will be viewed as the "just" and the latter as the "unjust" mode of production. Much more important is the fact that if one thinks in terms of the totality of a society's economy, one can never understand the operation of a society based on private property in the means of production. It is erroneous to maintain that the necessity for the collectivist method can be proved by showing that actions of the individuals can only be understood within the framework of that individual's environment. This is so because economic analysis does not depend on the psychological understanding of the motives of action, but on only an understanding of action itself. It is unimportant for catallactics why bread, clothes, books, cannons, or religious items are desired on the market; it is only important that a certain demand does exist. The mechanism of the

9 [The Cameralist school, in the countries of central Europe during the seventeenth and eighteenth centuries advocated a total paternalistic state. Their program centered on how best to regulate industry, trade, and fiscal matters to fund the growing military and administrative state. The school held the basic tenets of Mercantilism, advocated the dissolution of the guild system, and standardization of laws.—Ed.]

market and, therefore, the laws of the capitalistic economy can only be grasped if one begins with the forces operating on the market. But on the market there are only individuals acting as buyers and sellers, never the "totality." In economic theory, the totality can be taken only in the sense of an economic collective where the means of production are entirely outside the orbit of exchange and, therefore, cannot be sold for money. Here there is neither room for price theory nor a theory of money. But if we wish to grasp the value problems of a collective economy, we can—ironically—only use that method of analysis which has come to be known as the "individualistic method."

The attempts to solve the problem of the value of money with reference to the aggregate economy, rather than through market factors, culminated in a tautological equation without any epistemological value. Only a theory which shows how subjective value judgments of buyers and sellers are influenced by changes in the different elements of the equation of exchange can legitimately be called a theory of the value of money.

Buyers and sellers on the market never concern themselves with the elements in the equation of exchange, of which two—velocity of circulation and the price level—do not even exist before market parties act and the other two—the quantity of money (in the whole economy) and the sum of transactions—could not possibly be known to the parties in the market. Only the importance which the various actors in the market attach, on the one hand, to the maintenance of a cash balance of a certain magnitude and, on the other hand, to the ownership of the various goods in question determines the formation of the exchange relationship between money and goods.

Connected with the concept of the velocity of circulation of money is the mental image that money generates its usefulness only at the instant of transaction, but is "idle" and useless at other times. A distinction between active and idle money is also made when one speaks of money hoarding and proceeds to a comparison between the "hoarded" quantity of money and the quantity of money that would be necessary to perform the monetary services; what distinguishes this from the previous case is the way in which the boundary between active and idle money is drawn. Both distinctions must be rejected.

The service of money is not confined to transactions. It fulfills its task not only at the moment it passes from one hand to the next. It also performs services when it rests in the till, as the most marketable good, in anticipation of its future use in trade as a generally used means of exchange. The demand for money by individuals, as well by as the entire economy, is determined by the desire to maintain a cash balance and not by the aggregate of transactions to be carried out during a certain time period.[10]

It is an arbitrary procedure to divide the money stock into two parts: that which is designated to perform money services proper and that which serves as a money hoard. Of course, no damage will be done if, on the one hand, the demand for money is separated into a demand for hoarding and a demand to perform the monetary service proper. But a formula which portrays and solves only an arbitrarily delineated part of the problem must be rejected if we are able to show another one which will deal with and solve the whole problem in a uniform fashion.

III   Fluctuations in the Value of Money

One of the most peculiar phenomena in the history of monetary theory is the stubborn resistance encountered by the quantity theory. The imperfect formulation given to it by many of its advocates inevitably ran into opposition, with many—as, for example, Benjamin Anderson[11]—ascribing to the concept a meaning quite different from that commonly accepted. As a result, what they call the quantity theory, and oppose as such, is not the theory itself but only a variation of it. This is not particularly astonishing. But what is quite surprising is that an attempt was made and sometimes is still made today to deny that changes in the relation between money supply and money demand will modify the purchasing power of the monetary unit. It is not sufficient to base an explanation on the special interests of inflationists, statists and socialists, of civil servants and politicians who would be harmed by a spreading of knowledge concerning monetary policy. We will never arrive at an answer by following the path of the Historical-Realistic School, which (following the Marxian example) explains all ideas by ideologies. It had never been a problem to explain why a particular ideology is developed and advocated by certain classes who believe they can benefit from it directly (even if this direct advantage is more than outweighed by indirect disadvantages). What has to be explained,

10 Also see Edwin Cannan, *Money*, 4th ed. (Westminister: P. S. King and Son, 1932), pp. 72ff.
11 Benjamin Anderson, *The Value of Money* (New York: Macmillan, 1917).

however, is rather how incorrect theories come about and find followers. How does it come about that many people, without justification, come to assume that a certain policy benefits either the entire society or many groups in that society?

However, the theory of money as such is not interested in these psychological aspects which explain the reasons for the unpopularity of the quantity theory and the tendency to adopt other explanations for the value of money. Rather, it is interested in the question: which elements of the doctrines opposing the quantity theory could be useful? Since it was equally inadmissible to deny the importance of changes in supply for the formation of exchange relations in the area of indirect exchange as it was in the area of direct exchange, one could oppose the quantity theory only by admitting its correctness in principle, but arguing that notwithstanding its general validity another principle would regularly eliminate its effectiveness. This attempt was made by the Banking School with its famous theory of hoarding, and its offshoot, the theory of the automatic adjustment of the circulation of money substitutes to the demand for money in the broader sense. Today, both theories are overthrown.

As is the case with so many theories, the advocates of the quantity theory have harmed it more than its enemies. We have already mentioned the inadequacy of those theories based on the concept of the velocity of circulation of money. It was not any less erroneous to interpret the quantity theory as saying that the changes in the quantity of money resulted in proportional changes in the prices of goods. It was overlooked that every change in the relationship between the supply of money and the demand for money would necessarily bring about .a shift in the distribution of wealth and income and that, therefore, the prices of the different goods and services could not be affected proportionally and simultaneously.

Nowhere has the practice of working with formulas modeled after mechanics, instead of paying attention to the problem of the influence of market factors, taken a greater toll than in this case. Economists wanted to operate with the equation of exchange without noticing that the changes in the volume of money and the demand for money can come about in only one way: at first, the evaluations and with them the actions of only a few economic subjects will be influenced, with the resulting changes in the purchasing power of the monetary unit only spreading through the economy in a step-by-step pattern. In other words, the problem of changes in the value of money has been treated with the method of "statics," although there should never have been any doubt concerning the dynamic character of the problem.

IV   Money Substitutes

The most difficult and most important special problem of monetary theory is that of money substitutes. The fact that money services can also be rendered by secure money claims redeemable on demand, presents considerable difficulties to the monetary theorists' attempt to define the supply of money and the demand for money. This difficulty could not be overcome as long as money substitutes were not clearly defined and separated into money certificates and fiduciary media, in order to treat the granting of credit through the issue of fiduciary media separately from all other types of credit.

Loans which do not involve the issuing of fiduciary media (i.e., bank notes or deposits which are not backed by money) are of no consequence for the volume of money. The demand for money can be influenced by lending as much as by any other institution of the economic order. Without knowledge of the data of the specific case, we cannot say in which direction this influence will operate. The widely held opinion that an expansion of credit will always lead to a reduction in the demand for money is not correct. If many of the loan contracts provide for large repayments on certain days (for example, at the end of the month or quarter), the result will be an increase and not a reduction in the demand for money. The consequences of this increase in the demand for money will be expressed in prices, if it were not for clearing arrangements, on the one hand, and the practice of banks to increase the volume of fiduciary media on critical days, on the other hand.

Everything depends on the clear separation of money from money substitutes and within the category of money substitutes a distinction between money certificates (a money substitute fully backed by money) and the fiduciary medium (the money substitute not backed by money). But this is above all a question of terminological appropriateness. However, this question gains in importance in view of the difficulty and complexity of the problems. It is not—as so often is still maintained—the "granting of credit" but the issuing of fiduciary media which causes those effects on prices, wages, and interest rates, which banking theory has to deal with. It is, therefore, not inappropriate to refer to banking theory as the theory of fiduciary media.

V   Economic Calculation and the Problem of "Value Stability"

The old and widely accepted conception of money as a measure of price and value is out of the question for modern theory. But it was not an entirely harmless oversight of the subjective theory that it has not paid more attention to the importance of money for economic calculation, as well as the problem of economic calculation in general.

Traditionally, theoretical economics separates the theory of unintermediated (direct) exchange from the theory of intermediated (indirect) exchange. This division of catallactics is indispensable, and without it, it would have been impossible to ever produce useful results. But one must always be aware that the assumption that economic goods are exchanged without the intermediation of a generally used means of exchange is realistic only for the cases involving the exchange of consumer goods and those producer goods of the lowest order, i.e., those closest to consumer goods. The direct exchange of consumer goods and closely related producer goods is, of course, possible; it exists today and did so in the past. However, the exchange of goods of a more remote order presupposes the use of money. The concept of the market as the essence of coordination of all elements of demand and supply, upon which modern theory does and must depend, is unthinkable without the use of money. Only with the use of money is it possible to compare the marginal utility of goods in all alternative employments. Only where money exists can we clearly analyze the difference in value between present and future goods. Only within a money economy can this value difference be comprehended in the abstract and separated from changes in the valuation of individual concrete economic goods. In a barter economy, the phenomenon of interest could never be isolated from the evaluation of future price movements of individual goods. To assume the existence of a highly developed market system without the intermediation of a generally accepted means of exchange would be a scientific fiction like Vaihinger's "as if" theory.[12]

We will not deal here with the significance of monetary calculation for rational action and social cooperation; this is not a task for catallactics but one for sociology. The field of monetary theory is large enough

---

12 [Hans Vaihinger (1852–1933) was a German philosopher who maintained that "An idea whose theoretical untruth or incorrectness, and therewith its falsity, is admitted, is not for that reason particularly valueless and useless; for an idea in spite of its theoretical nullity may have great practical importance," *The Philosophy of "As If,"* C. K. Ogden, trans. (New York: Harcourt, Brace, 1935), p. viii.—Ed.]

if it confines itself to an exhaustive treatment of questions of its own immediate concern.

The paramount role of money within the sphere of economic goods was established by the practice of calculating in terms of money, by expressing the price of all other economic goods in terms of the corresponding amount of money, and by basing economic decisions solely on the value of the monetary unit. One result of this practice is the contrast between money and goods as we encounter it in the phrase "the high cost of living" and even more clearly in mercantilist theory. But a more serious consequence of assigning such prominence to money has been the development of the idea of a "stable value" of money, which in spite of its naivete and vagueness has been a permanent influence on monetary policy.

As it came to be recognized that money is not of "stable value," the political postulate arose that money *should* be of stable value or at least be designed in such a way that it would approximate this ideal as closely as possible. The advocates of the gold standard, as well as those of the bimetallic standard, have touted their monetary systems as the best guarantee for the greatest possible stability of the value of money. A number of proposals are based on the idea that the greatest possible constancy of the purchasing power of money is the ultimate and the most important goal of monetary policy. One such proposal foresees the creation of a commodity currency (tabular standard) for long-term contracts to supplement precious metal currency. The proposals by Irving Fisher[13] and John Maynard Keynes[14] go even farther by recommending a "manipulated currency" based on a system of index numbers.

The shortcomings of the "stable value" notion and the contradictions in a monetary policy based upon it do not have to be shown again.[15] In everyday life, the actions of economizing subjects regarding value estimates usually cover only short periods of time, if we ignore for the moment long-term loan contracts with which we will have to deal in more detail later. The economic calculations of the entrepreneur are confined to the months and years ahead. Only conditions in

---

13 Irving Fisher, *Stabilizing the Dollar* (New York: Macmillan, 1925), pp. 79ff.
14 John Maynard Keynes, *A Tract on Monetary Reform* (London: Macmillan, 1923), pp. 177ff.
15 [Ludwig von Mises, *Monetary Stabilization and Cyclical Policy* (1928), in *On the Manipulation of Money and Credit*, Percy L. Greaves, Jr., ed. (Dobbs Ferry, N.Y.: Free Market Books, 1978), pp. 83–103. — Ed.]

the immediate future can be forecasted and considered in economic calculations. Apart from the difficulties which changes in the purchasing power of money present, it would be impossible to forecast the economic situation of a more distant future with any degree of reliability.

The desire for a "stable" store of purchasing power originated with attempts to protect wealth and income from the vicissitudes of the market. The goal was to maintain wealth and income for "eternity." The agrarian mentality thought it had found such a store of wealth in the form of land. Land would always be land, and the fruits of agriculture would always be desirable; thus, it was believed that the ownership of land was a form of wealth which would assure a steady income. It is easy for us today, in an age of capitalistically organized agriculture, to show the error of this view. A self-sufficient farmer working on his own land might be able to insulate himself "forever" from the changes taking place around him. But for a business operating in a society based on an extensive division of labor, the situation is quite different. Capital and labor must only be applied to the best plots of land. To produce on land of lesser quality fails to yield any net returns. Even plots of land can fall drastically in value or lose it altogether when higher quality land becomes available in large amounts.

This type of thinking was soon transferred from land to claims secured by property in land. Later claims against the "State" and other creatures of public law were added to the secured claims. The State was thought to have eternal existence, and its promises to pay were accorded unconditional faith. Consequently, government bonds appeared as a means to remove wealth and income from the uncertainties of life into the sphere of "eternity." We need not waste any more words on the fallacy of this idea. It is sufficient to point out that even States can fall and that States repudiate their debts.

Contrary to prevailing opinion, in the capitalistic social order no wealth exists which automatically produces a return. In order to derive income from property in the means of production, property either has to be employed in a successful venture or has to be loaned to a promising entrepreneur. But for entrepreneurs, success is never "certain." It can happen that a firm will decline and the capital invested vanishes, either partly or entirely. The capitalist who is not an entrepreneur himself, but merely lends to entrepreneurs, is less exposed to the danger of loss than is the entrepreneur; but even he bears the risk that the loss of the entrepreneur becomes so substantial that he is unable to repay the borrowed capital. Ownership of capital is not the source of automatically accruing income but a means whose successful application can produce income. To derive income from property in capital, one has to have the ability to invest it advantageously. He who does not have this ability, cannot count on income from his capital ownership and may lose it entirely.

To reduce these difficulties and uncertainties to the lowest possible level, capitalists acquire land, government obligations, and mortgage bonds. But here the shortcomings of a money lacking "stable value" begin to cause problems. In the case of short-term credit, the effects of changes in the purchasing power of money on the value of the claim will be eliminated or at least reduced by the fact that market interest rates for short-term loans will rise and fall with the fluctuations in the prices of goods. This adjustment is not possible in the case of long-term loans.

The ultimate reason behind the striving for money of a "stable value" is to be found in the desire to create a medium capable of removing the ownership of capital from the domain of the temporal into the domain of the eternal. But the solution to the problem of value stability can only be accomplished if all movement and change is eliminated from the economic system. It is not sufficient to stabilize the exchange relationship between money and an average of commodity prices; one would also have to fix the exchange ratios between all goods.

If monetary policy abstains from everything which could cause violent changes in the exchange relationship between money and other economic goods which originate from the "money side"; if it chooses a commodity currency which is not subject to sudden fluctuations in value stemming either from its own supply or from its demand for industrial and other non-monetary uses; if it exercises restraint in the issue of fiduciary media: then it has done everything that can be done toward a mitigation of the harmful effects that flow from changes in the purchasing power of money. If monetary policy were confined to these tasks, it would contribute more to the elimination of these perceived evils than by conscious efforts to realize an unreachable ideal. No one who understands the meaning and implications of the theoretical concept of a "stationary state" can deny that all attempts to transplant this conceptualization from the world of economic theory into real life must remain unsuccessful.

CHAPTER 5

The Non-Neutrality of Money

The monetary economists of the sixteenth and seventeenth centuries succeeded in dissipating the popular fallacies concerning an alleged stability of money. The old error disappeared, but a new one originated, the illusion of money's neutrality.

Of course, classical economics did its best to dispose of these mistakes. David Hume, the founder of British Political Economy, and John Stuart Mill, the last in the line of classical economists, both dealt with the problem in a masterful way. And then we should not forget Cairnes, who in his essay on the course of depreciation paved the way for a realistic view of the issue involved.[1]

Notwithstanding these first steps toward a more correct grasp, modern economists incorporated the fallacy of money neutrality into their system of thought.

The reasoning of modern marginal utility economics begins from the assumption of a state of pure barter. The mechanism of exchanging commodities and of market transactions is considered on the supposition that direct exchange alone prevails. The economists depict a purely hypothetical entity, a market without indirect exchange, without a medium of exchange, without money. There is no doubt that this method is the only possible one, that the elimination of money is necessary, and that we cannot do without this concept of a market with direct exchange only. But we have to realize that it is a hypothetical concept which has no counterpart in reality. The actual market is necessarily a market of indirect exchange and money transactions.

[This essay was delivered as a lecture to a group in Paris in 1938 and again to the New York City Economics Club in 1945; previously unpublished. — Ed.]
1 [David Hume, "On Money," in *Writings on Economics*, Eugene Rotwein, ed. (University of Wisconsin Press, Madison, 1970), pp. 33–46; John Stuart Mill, *Principles of Political Economy*, Sir William Ashley, ed. (1909), bk. 3, chap. 8; John E. Cairnes, *Essays in Political Economy* (London: MacMillan, 1873), pp. 1–65. — Ed.]

From this assumption of a market without money, the fallacious idea of neutral money is derived. The economists were so fond of the tool which this hypothetical concept provided that they overestimated the extent of its applicability. They began to believe that all problems of catallactics could be analyzed by means of this fictitious concept. In accordance with this view, they considered that the main work of economic analysis was the study of direct exchange. After that all that was left was to introduce the monetary terms into the formulas obtained. But this was, in their eyes, a work of only secondary importance, because, as they were convinced, the introduction of monetary terms did not affect the substantial operation of the mechanism they had described. The functioning of the market mechanism as demonstrated by the concept of pure barter was not affected by monetary factors.

Of course, the economists knew that the exchange ratio between money and commodities was subject to change. But they believed—and this is exactly the essence of the fallacy of money's neutrality—that these changes in purchasing power were brought about simultaneously in the whole market and that they affected all commodities to the same extent. The most striking expression of this point of view is to be found in the current metaphorical use of the term "level" in reference to prices. Changes in the supply or demand of money—other things remaining equal—make all prices and wages simultaneously rise or fall. The purchasing power of the monetary unit changes, but the relations among the prices of individual commodities remain the same.

Of course, economists have developed for more than a hundred years the method of index numbers in order to measure changes in purchasing power in a world where the ratios between the prices of individual commodities are in continuous transition. But in doing so, they did not give up the assumption that the consequences of a change in the supply or demand of money were a proportional and simultaneous modification of prices. The method of index numbers was designed to provide them with a means of distinguishing between the consequences of those changes in prices which take their origins from the side of the demand for or supply of individual commodities and those which start from the side of demand for or supply of money.

The erroneous assumption of money neutrality is at the root of all endeavors to establish the formula of a so-called equation of exchange. In dealing with such an equation the mathematical economist assumes that something—one of the elements of the equation—changes and that corresponding changes in the other values must needs follow. These elements of the equation are not items in the individual's economy, but items of the whole economic system, and consequently the changes occur not with individuals but with the whole economic system, with the *Volkswirtschaft* as a whole. Proceeding thus, the economists apply unawares for the treatment of monetary problems a method radically different from the modern catallactic method. They revert to the old manner of reasoning which doomed to failure the work of older economists. In those early days philosophers dealt in their speculations with universal concepts, such as mankind and other generic notions. They asked: What is the value of gold or of iron, that is: value in general, for all times and for all people, and again gold or iron in general, all the gold or iron available or even not yet mined. They could not succeed in this way; they discovered only alleged antinomies which were insoluble for them.

All the successful achievements of modern economic theory have to be ascribed to the fact that we have learned to proceed in a different way. We realize that individuals acting in the market are never presented with the choice between all the gold existing and all the iron existing. They do not have to decide whether gold or iron is more useful for mankind as a whole, but they have to choose between two limited quantities both of which they cannot have together. They decide which of these two alternatives is more favorable for them under the conditions and at the moment when they make their decision. These acts of choice performed by individuals faced with alternatives are the ultimate causes of the exchange ratios established in the market. We have to direct our attention to these acts of choice and are not at all interested in the metaphysical and purely academic, nay, vain question of which commodity in general appears more useful in the eyes of a superhuman intelligence surveying earthly conditions from a transcendental point of view.

Monetary problems are economic problems and have to be dealt with in the same way as all other economic problems. The monetary economist does not have to deal with universal entities like volume of trade meaning total volume of trade or quantity of money meaning all the money current in the whole economic system. Still less can he make use of the nebulous metaphor "velocity of circulation." He has to realize that the demand for money arises from the preferences of individuals within a market society. Because everybody wishes to have a certain amount of cash, sometimes more, sometimes less, there is a demand for money. Money is never simply in the economic system, in the *Volkswirtschaft*, money is never simply circulating. All the money available is always in the cash holdings of somebody. Every piece of money may one day—sometimes oftener, sometimes more seldom—pass from one man's cash holding to another man's. But at every moment it is owned by somebody and is a part of his cash holdings. The decisions of individuals regarding the magnitude of their cash holdings constitute the ultimate factor in the formation of purchasing power.

Changes in the quantity of money and in the demand for money for cash holding do not occur in the economic system as a whole if they do not occur in the households of individuals. These changes in the households of individuals never occur for all individuals at the same time and to the same degree, and they therefore never affect their judgments of value to the same extent and at the same time. It is exactly the merit of Hume and Mill that they tried to construct a hypothetical case where the changes in the supply of money could affect all individuals in such a way that the prices of all commodities would rise or fall at the same time and in the same proportion. The failure of their attempts provided a negative proof, and modern economics has added to this the positive proof that the prices of different commodities are not influenced at the same time and to the same extent. The oversimple formula both of the old quantity theory and of contemporary mathematical economists according to which prices—that is, all prices—rise or fall in the proportion of the increase or decrease in the quantity of money is disproved.

To simplify and to shorten our analysis let us look at the case of inflation only. The additional quantity of money does not find its way at first into the pockets of all individuals; not every individual of those benefited first gets the same amount and not every individual reacts to the same additional quantity in the same way. Those first benefited—in the case of gold, the owners of the mines, in the case of government paper money, the treasury—now have greater cash holdings, and they are now in a position to offer more money on the market for goods and services they wish to buy. The additional amount of money offered by them on the market makes prices and wages go up. But not all the prices and wages rise, and those which do rise do not rise to the same degree. If the additional money is spent for military purposes, the prices of some commodities only and the wages of only some kinds of labor rise; others remain unchanged or may even temporarily fall. They may fall because there are now on the market some groups of men whose incomes have not risen but who nevertheless are obliged to pay more for some commodities, namely, for those asked by the men first benefited by the inflation. Thus, price changes which are the result of the inflation start with some commodities and services only, and are diffused more or less slowly from one group to the others. It takes time till the additional quantity of money has exhausted all its price-changing possibilities. But even in the end the different commodities are not affected to the same extent. The process of progressive depreciation has changed the income and the wealth of the different social groups. As long as this depreciation is still going on, as long as the additional quantity of money has not yet exhausted all its possibilities of influencing prices, as long as there are still prices left unchanged at all or not yet changed to the extent that they will be, there are in the community some groups favored and some at a disadvantage. Those selling the commodities or services whose prices rise first are in a position to sell at the new higher prices and to buy what they want to buy at the old still-unchanged prices. On the other hand, those who sell commodities or services whose prices remain for some time unchanged are selling at the old prices whereas they already have to buy at the new higher prices. The former are making a specific gain, they are profiteers; the latter are losing, they are the losers, out of whose pockets the extra gains of the profiteers must come. As long as the inflation is in progress, there is a perpetual shift in income and wealth from some social group to other social groups. When all price consequences of the inflation are consummated, a transfer of wealth between social groups has taken place. The result is that there is in the economic system a new dispersion of wealth and income, and in this new social order the wants of individuals are satisfied to different relative degrees than formerly. Prices in this new order cannot simply be a multiple of the previous prices.

The social consequences of a change in the purchasing power of money are twofold: first, as money is the standard of deferred payments, the relations between creditors and debtors is changed. Second, as the changes in purchasing power do not affect all prices and wages at the same moment and to the same extent, there is a shift of wealth and income between different social groups. It was one of the errors of all proposals to stabilize purchasing power that they did not take into account this second consequence. We may say that economic theory in general did not pay enough attention to this matter. As far as it did, it principally considered it only in reference to the reaction of a change in a country's currency on its foreign trade. But this is only a special application of a problem which has a much wider scope.

What is fundamental for economic theory is that there is no constant relation between changes in the quantity of money and in prices. Changes in the supply of money affect individual prices and wages in different ways. The metaphorical use of the term price level is misleading.

The erroneous opinion to the contrary was based on a consideration which may be represented thus: let us think of two absolutely independent systems of static equilibrium A and B. Both are in every respect alike except that to the total quantity of money (M) in A and to every individual cash holding (m) in A, there correspond in B a total quantity of Mn and individual cash holdings mn. On these assumptions of course all the prices and wages in B are n times those in A. But they are exactly thus because these are our hypothetical assumptions. But nobody can devise a way by which the system A can be transformed into the system B. Of course it is impermissible to operate with static equilibrium if we wish to approach a dynamic problem.

Setting aside all qualms about the use of the terms dynamic and static, I wish to say: money is necessarily a dynamic agent, and it was a mistake to deal with monetary problems in a static way.

Of course there is no room left for money in a concept of static equilibrium. In forming the concept of a static society we assume that no changes are taking place. Everything is going on in the same old manner. Today is like yesterday and tomorrow will be like today. But under these conditions nobody needs a cash holding. Cash holding is necessary only when the individual does not know what situation he will have to face in an uncertain future. If everybody knows when and what he will have to buy, he does not need a private cash holding and can entrust all his money to the central bank as time deposits due on the dates and in the amounts necessary for his future payments. As everybody would proceed in the same way, the central bank does not need any reserves to meet its obligations. Of course, the total amount which it has to pay out to the buyers every day exactly balances the amount which it receives as deposits from the sellers. If we assume that in this world of static equilibrium once, before the equilibrium was attained, there was metallic currency only, let us say gold, we have to assume that with the gradual approach toward conditions of equilibrium, the citizens deposited more and more of their gold and that the bank, which had no need for it, sold the gold to jewelers and others for industrial consumption. With the advent of equilibrium there is no more metallic money; there is in fact no more money at all, but an unsubstantial and immaterial clearing system, which cannot be considered as money in the ordinary sense. It is rather an unrealizable and even unthinkable system of accounting, a numeraire as some economists believed ideal money ought to be. This, if it could be called money, would be neutral money. But we should never forget, that the state of equilibrium is purely hypothetical, that this concept is nothing but a tool for our mental work. Not being able to make experiments, the social sciences have to forge such tools. But we must be very careful in their use. We have to be aware that the state of static equilibrium can never be attained in real life. Still more important is the fact that in this hypothetical state the individual does not make choices, does not act, and does not have to decide between incompatible alternatives. Life in this hypothetical state is therefore robbed of its essential element. In constructing this hypothetical state, we want merely to understand the incentives of action, which always implies change, by conceiving conditions in which no action takes place. But a changeless world would be a dead world. We do not just have to deal with death, but with life, action, and change. In a living world there is no room for neutrality of money.

Money, of course, is a dynamic factor and as such cannot be discussed in terms of static equilibrium.

Let me now briefly point out some of the major conclusions derived from an insight into the non-neutrality of money.

First we have to realize that the abandonment of the fallacious concept of neutral money destroys the last stronghold of the advocates of quantitative economics. For a very long time eminent economists have believed that it will be possible one day to replace qualitative economics by quantitative economics. What renders these hopes vain is the fact that in economic quantities we never have any constant ratios among magnitudes. What the economist discovers when he studies relations between demand and prices is not comparable with the work of the natural scientist who determines by experiments in his laboratory constant relations, e.g., the specific gravity of different substances. What the economist determines is of historical value only; he is in his statistical work a historian, but not an experimenter. The work of the late lamented Henry Schultz[2] was economic history; what we learn from his research is what happened with some commodities in a limited period of the past in the United States and Canada. It tells us nothing about what happened with the same commodities elsewhere or in another period or what will happen in the future.

But there still has remained the belief that it is different with money. I may cite, for example, Professor Fisher's book on the *Purchasing Power of Money*, which is founded on the assumption that the purchasing power of the monetary unit changes in inverse proportion to the quantity of money.[3] I think that this assumption is arbitrary and fallacious.

The second conclusion which we have to draw is the futility of all endeavors to make money stable in purchasing power. It is beyond the scope of my short address to explain the advantages of a sound money policy and the disadvantages of both inflation and deflation. But we should not confuse the political concept of sound money with the theoretical concept of stable money. I do not wish to discuss the inner contradictions of this stability concept. From the point of view of the present subject it is more important to emphasize that all proposals for stabilization, apart from other deficiencies, are based on the idea of money's neutrality. They all suggest methods to undo changes in purchasing power already effected if there has been an inflation they wish to deflate to the same extent and vice versa. They do not realize that by this procedure they do not undo the social consequences of the first change, but simply add to it the social consequences of a new change. If a man has been hurt by being run over by an automobile, it is no remedy to let the car go back over him in the opposition direction.

The popularity of all schemes for stabilization invites us to a philosophical consideration. It is a general weakness of the human mind to regard the state of rest and absence of change as more perfect than the state of motion. The absolute, that old phantom of misguided philosophical speculation, is still with us; its modern name is stability. But stability, i.e., absence of change, is, we have to repeat, absence of life.

2 [In his treatise *Theory and Measurement of Demand* (Chicago: University of Chicago Press, 1938), he set forth his crop theory of cycles. — Ed.]

3 [Irving Fisher, *The Purchasing Power of Money*, 2nd ed. (New York: Macmillan, 1920), p. 157: "there is no possible escape from the conclusion that a change in the quantity of money (M) must normally cause a proportional change in the price level." — Ed.]

The third conclusion which we may draw is the futility of the distinction between statics and dynamics and between short-run and long-run economics. The way in which we have to study monetary changes provides us with the best evidence that every correct economic consideration has to be dynamic and that static concepts are only instrumental. And at the same time we have to realize that all correct economic theorizing is a gradual progress from short-run to long-run effects.

But the most important value of the theory of money's dynamism is its use for the development of the monetary theory of the trade cycle. The old British Currency-Theory was already in a restricted sense a monetary explanation of the cycle. It studied the consequences of credit expansion on the assumption only that there is credit expansion in one country whereas in the rest of the world things are left unchanged. This seemed to be enough for the explanation of the business cycle in Great Britain in the first half of the nineteenth century. But the explanation of an external drain does not provide an answer to the question what may happen in a completely isolated country or in the case of a simultaneous credit expansion all over the world. But only the answer to this second question could be considered satisfactory under the conditions prevailing in the twentieth century. Only the answer to this second question is important, if we have to consider the proposals for eliminating the cyclical changes either by loosening the international ties of the national economy or by making credit expansion international in the way the Bretton Woods Agreement[4] provides. It is the boast of the monetary theory of the trade cycle that it provides us with a satisfactory answer to these and to some other serious problems.

I do not wish to infringe more upon your time and so I wish only to add some remarks on the treatment of the problem by certain younger economists. I myself am not responsible for the term "neutral money." I have developed a theory of the changes in purchasing power and its social consequences. I have demonstrated that money acts as a dynamic agent and that the assumption that the changes in purchasing power are inversely proportional to the changes in the relation of demand for to the supply of money is fallacious. The term "neutral money" was coined by later authors.[5] I do not wish to consider the question of

4 [The Bretton Woods Agreement in 1945 established an international gold exchange standard that valued the dollar at 1/35th of an ounce of gold. — Ed.]
5 [F. A. Hayek, *Prices and Production*, 2nd ed. (New York: Augustus M. Kelley, 1935), pp. 31 and 129–31. — Ed.]

whether it was a happy choice. But in any case I must protest against the belief that it has to be a goal of monetary policy to make money neutral and that it is the duty of the economists to determine a method of doing so. I wish to emphasize that in a living and changing world, in a world of action, there is no room left for a neutral money: Money is non-neutral or it does not exist.

CHAPTER 6

The Suitability of Methods of Ascertaining Changes in Purchasing Power for the Guidance of International Currency and Banking Policy

Introduction

The expressions "fluctuations in the purchasing power of gold" and "measurement of the fluctuations in the purchasing power of gold" cannot be used unless we have, at the same time, a conception of the purpose for the attainment of which it is essential to have an exact definition of these terms. They have been evolved to meet mainly practical requirements, not purely theoretical ones. Being conscious of the undesirable effects of certain changes in prices, we seek ways and means of eliminating their undesirable effects or, even better, the causes which generate them. Consequently, any study referring to these expressions must take as its starting point a consideration of what it is we find undesirable, why we find it undesirable, and what can be done with a view toward its removal without putting something more undesirable in its place.

I The Social Effects of Changes in the Purchasing Power of Gold

There are two distinct reasons why changes in the purchasing power of gold affect income and capital conditions. If it were not for the operation of these factors, changes in purchasing power would be a matter of no more importance, so far as social effects are concerned, than changes in the system of weights and measures or changes in the calendar. If (a) there were no deferred payments, i.e., no debts or claims ex-

[Memorandum prepared for the Gold Delegation of the Financial Committee of the League of Nations, F/Gold/51 (Geneva: October 10, 1930). This memo had been forgotten and only rediscovered when doing research for this volume in the League of Nations Library Archives.—Ed.]

pressed in terms of gold, with all money transactions being cash trans-actions and (b) if changes in the purchasing power of money affected the whole economic system and every particular commodity simulta-neously and to the same extent, we would have no reason to concern ourselves with the effects of changes in the purchasing power of gold.

(a) Changes in Purchasing Power and Indebtedness

Changes in purchasing power affect debt contracts expressed in terms of gold due to the fact that the parties contracting such liabilities do not make allowance for changes in the purchasing power of gold. In general, the world clings to the view that gold is of "stable value," naive as that view may be and as incapable as it may be of withstanding any exact analysis. However, even if this view were not prevalent, in the case of long-term commitments it would not be possible to adjust for changes in the purchasing power of gold; there is no means of making any sort of estimate about either the direction or the extent of future changes in purchasing power over a considerable future time-period. The case of short-term liabilities is different. If it is anticipated that the prices of commodities will rise in the course of the next few weeks or months, the rate of interest for short-term loans correspondingly rises, and it falls if it is expected that commodity prices will fall. Therefore, the problem of the effect of changes in purchasing power arises only in the case of long-term debt contracts, and not in the case of short-term liabilities.

(b) The Second Category of Consequences of Changes in Purchasing Power

English and American writers have investigated the influence of changes in purchasing power on the tenor of debt contracts with excep-tional thoroughness for more than a century, at a time when this prob-lem was almost entirely neglected on the Continent and, especially, in Germany. On the other hand, English and American writers have de-voted very little attention to the second category of consequences that are caused by changes in purchasing power. As a result, the numerous projects and proposals for the elimination of the unfavorable conse-quences of such changes have, as a rule, been concerned exclusively with the effect on debt contracts, while leaving other effects of such changes unaccounted for.

If changes in purchasing power affected all commodities and services simultaneously and to the same extent, the effect on people's incomes and expenditures would be identical, and nobody would be a penny the better or the worse for the change (apart from the case of debt contracts discussed in the previous section). However, this is never the case. Eminent economists, from David Hume and John Stuart Mill downwards, have vainly endeavored to construct a theoretical case in which a change in purchasing power might affect all commodities and services simultaneously and to the same extent. It is impossible to construct such a case.

Changes in purchasing power always make themselves felt, at first, at some particular point of the economic system, and its effects only then spread from there by successive stages. When the volume of money is increased, those into whose hands the additional new money first passes are able—with their increased income—to go on paying the previous market prices for commodities and services, i.e., at prices formed *without* regard, as yet, to the new supply of money. In this case, an increase in money income is tantamount to an increase in real income and may even ultimately result in an increase in capital. On the other hand, those whose incomes are the last to be increased are at a disadvantage, owing to the fact that they are compelled to pay for a large portion of the commodities and services they purchase at prices formed *with* regard to the new supply of money, i.e., before their incomes have risen correspondingly. This process was clearly observed in every country in the inflationary period during and after the war. But it is most conspicuous in the field of international economic relations; Cairnes has an admirable account of its operation in his *Essays in Political Economy*, in which he traces the effects of the discoveries of gold and the progressive course of depreciation to which they gave rise.

Study of the social consequences of changes in purchasing power cannot be restricted to the consideration of their effect on indebtedness. The effects of the time lag, which I have described, also have to be taken into the account.

But it is just when we endeavor to do this that we become aware of the immense difficulties in the way. If we only consider the effect of changes of purchasing power on indebtedness, we are prone to assume that all that is required is to determine an average figure for the purchasing power of money, leaving the rise of one price to be offset by the fall of another. But this is not enough, if we take the second category of consequences of changes in purchasing power into account; for these consequences are due precisely to the fact that some prices have risen while others are still lagging behind. Therefore, if we proceed along the lines of the proposals for the stabilization of purchasing power, i.e., by correcting changes in purchasing power *after they have occurred* in accordance with some system of index numbers, we shall have done nothing to eliminate this particular category of social effects.

II   Analysis of Attempts at Stabilization

Obviously, before we enter upon the task set by our topic, we must understand the object toward which these measures are to be applied.

The serious disturbances which follow in the train of cyclically re-occurring economic depressions have led many in the world to entertain the conceptual ideal of a "stable" economic system. However, this can never mean an economic system in which all prices remain unchanged. All that can be attempted is the establishment of a system which is not exposed to grave shocks from the "money-side."

A number of writers have argued in favor of altering the legal basis of debt contracts in the sense of expressing them, not in terms of gold, but in terms of a definite quantity of commodities. The aim of such proposals is the establishment of what is called a "commodity standard" or a "tabular standard." For a long time it was innocently assumed that such a standard would necessarily be "equitable." I have, I think, sufficiently shown, as have other economists before me, that this assumption is not likely to be universally accepted.[1]

But even if we ignore the objections to the "equitable character" of commodity and tabular standards, we cannot fail to see what has already been pointed out, namely, that the establishment of such a standard can only eliminate a part of the social effects of changes in purchasing power. It will, perhaps, be said that it is much to be able to eliminate the consequences in the case of debt contracts, even if the more difficult problem of the elimination of the second category of consequences would have to be left to the future. This, however, is not a tenable view. No doubt, the problem of a standard of deferred payment is extremely important; but here as in other questions, the

---

1   [Ludwig von Mises, "Monetary Stabilization and Cyclical Policy" [1928], in *On the Manipulation of Money and Credit*, Percy L. Greaves, Jr., ed. (Dobbs Ferry, N.Y.: Free Market Books, 1978), pp. 99ff. — Ed.]

economy "helps itself," certainly in the case of short-term, and possibly even in the case of long-term, debt contracts. The circumstance that in the last few decades those who have lent money at long-term, i.e., bond-holders, have suffered losses has induced a certain caution on the market for long-term obligations. This tendency is apparent today; but it has also been noticeable in earlier periods of depression, even if not to the same extent. The reluctance of those elements which might otherwise be purchasers of bonds—as a result of the unfortunate experiences of the last few decades—is responsible for the very wide margin between the rates for money at short-term and the rates for long-term capital investment. If this cautious attitude persists, those who desire to take up long-term credits will be compelled to pay a premium as a contingency against falls in purchasing power, in addition to the interest on their loans; otherwise, they will have to satisfy their requirements on the short-term market, where (as has already been pointed out) allowance is made for probable changes in purchasing power.[2]

In the case of the second category of social consequences of changes in purchasing power, no similar adjustment mechanism is present. Some people are inclined to ignore this second category on the grounds that its effects are only temporary; this is true only in the sense that the effect on income and capital conditions caused by the irregular and unequal incidence of changes in purchasing power cease to operate when the changes have permeated the entire economic system. The effects on the income and capital conditions, however, remain. One man has gained and another has lost. In this respect, then, the second category of effects does not differ from the first.

All the proposals that have been made for stabilizing the purchasing power of money are vitiated by the fact that they are designed only to eliminate the effect on the tenor of debt contracts. They leave entirely out of account the second effect of such changes, in the belief that it is only, or mainly, the effect on debt contracts that matters. Every one of these proposals for stabilizing the value of money contemplate adjustments *after the event* and according to the changes in purchasing power calculated on the basis of a system of average values.

A distinction should be made between two such systems. The older system is that of the "tabular standard" and makes the adjustments only in the case of deferred payments; that is to say, it merely alters the

2 [The reader should recall this was written in 1930.—Ed.]

nominal amount of the debt contract without touching the monetary system at all. The second system, represented by Irving Fisher's "stabilized dollar" and J. M. Keynes' "manipulated currency," involves an adjustment of the purchasing power of the money in circulation as a whole. Here, again, there is to be no adjustment until *after the change in purchasing power has taken place* and after its unequal and irregular incidence has had its effect. Such *ex post facto* adjustments do nothing either to eliminate or to mitigate the effects of the second category; they can only apply to the effects of the first category. That is the essential point that needs to be made.

In general, therefore, it may be said that all proposals which aim at stabilizing the value of money have regard only to one part of the effects of changes in purchasing power. They can only eliminate those effects touching upon the tenor of long-term debt contracts in terms of gold. They can do nothing to remove the other effects of changes in purchasing power, which are no less acute than those of the first category and, perhaps, maybe are even more important.

If this is borne in mind, it will be realized that radical though these proposals sound, they would by no means be so drastic in practice. They are far from being as superior to the old, more modest, program of the "sound currency" school as one is tempted at first to imagine. This older program did not attempt to stabilize the value of money; it was content to aim at the elimination, as far as possible, of all factors likely to give rise to sudden and excessive changes in purchasing power. It was from this standpoint that the decision was made in favor of the gold standard, because it was felt that the gold standard offered at least relative, if not absolute, stability.

Has anything happened to disappoint the expectations entertained some decades ago by the English and Continental adherents of the classical gold standard?

III   Causes of the Changes in Purchasing Power the Last Few Decades

Since the second half of the last decade of the nineteenth century, the purchasing power of gold has steadily declined. There is no need to go into what has been generally written about the extent of this change or the reasons for it. But one point must be emphasized with special insistence, because, as a rule, it has unfortunately been completely overlooked in recent discussions of the problem. I refer to the fact that the chief cause behind the fall in the purchasing power of gold during the period in question is to be found in the monetary policies of the various governments, rather than in the conditions of gold production. In their monetary policies, the various governments have consciously aimed at an "economizing" of gold, with these efforts leading to a much greater fall in the purchasing power of gold than would have been the case if endeavors had not been made to drive gold out of effective circulation. If we had gold coins in actual daily circulation everywhere in the world, as was the case some decades ago in Germany and England, and if the banks of issue of the smaller and poorer States kept their currency reserves in actual gold and not principally in gold claims on foreign countries, the depreciation of gold either would not have taken place at all, or at least would not have to anything like the extent to which this actually occurred between 1896 and 1920.

It is no doubt true that individual governments did not realize that the consequence of all countries following this same policy would be a general rise in prices. What each State had in view was a cheapening of the costs of circulation in its own country. Above all else, they were influenced by the fallacious idea that it was possible to bring about a decrease in interest rates by various monetary policy measures, including a concentration of the national supplies of gold in the basements of the central banks. But whatever individual governments may have had in view in following this policy, one thing is beyond dispute: the result was bound, other things being equal, to lead to a fall in the purchasing power of gold and an increase of commodity prices in terms of gold. Therefore, it is remarkable that public opinion should have regarded the rise in prices during this period as due solely to the conditions of gold production—quite independent of governmental policies—and have failed to realize that the increase in prices could never have assumed the dimensions it did if a different policy had been followed by their governments.

If governments *had* followed a different policy and the rise in the prices of commodities (in terms of gold) had, for this reason, either not taken place or, at any rate, not taken place to the extent that it did, there would never have been any talk at the time of a failure of the gold standard. And if today, at a time of falling prices, the cry for a departure from the gold standard is even more clamant, it can only be pointed out, once again, that the great collapse of prices—which has been the outstanding economic event of the last few years—represents an inevitable reaction after the previous expansion of credit. Credit policy mistakes may be blamed for many things, but the gold standard is certainly not one of them. It is, therefore, quite unjustified to say that events have shown the inapplicability of the gold standard. It is not the old classical gold standard, with effective gold circulation, which has failed; what *has* failed is the gold "economizing" system and the credit policy of the central banks of issue.

All that can be said is that no conclusions should be drawn for the future. Apprehensions are expressed today that the transition to the gold standard by countries which have so far not adopted it, coupled with a decline in the production of gold, will lead in the future to a fall in the gold prices of commodities (i.e., a rise in the purchasing power of gold). These apprehensions certainly cannot be dismissed offhand, though all prophecy as to the future value of money must be taken with the utmost reserve. But it is just as well to remember that, even if the production of gold in the next few decades should decline, and even if the gold standard should be adopted everywhere (including China and Russia), it need not necessarily involve a fall in prices. This would be the case if the policy of "economizing" gold, which has gradually spread during the last few decades to all the countries in the world, is maintained and, perhaps, even strengthened.

The problem is rendered particularly complex by the fact that it is closely connected with the question of the issue of currency via credit expansion, i.e., bank notes and bank balances without gold cover.

Public opinion, looking upon a low rate of interest as the ideal of economic policy, more or less openly encourages the banks of issue to follow a policy of expanding credit in order to reduce the rates for money below the market rates, i.e., the rate which would prevail on the money market if the banks did not intervene. The fact that this policy must necessarily lead to a rise in prices is not seen as an objection from the businessman's point of view; on the contrary, he regards rising prices as a sign of prosperity. It was not until the interests of classes in the population other than the entrepreneur's began to have increased influence on judgments about general economic conditions that the world began to realize that rising prices were not an unmixed blessing. To the businessman, a period of rising prices is a period of "expansion" and "boom"; to the renter, the civil servant, and, in general, the man with a relatively fixed income, rising prices mean an "increased cost of living."

The businessmen, who want cheap money through the intervention of the banks, pay no attention to the lesson taught by the older economists of the Currency School and, more recently, by Wicksell and all modern adherents of the monetary theory of the trade cycle (or more accurately, the circulation credit theory of the trade cycle). The gist of this lesson is that all efforts by the banks to artificially lower the free-market rates for money by expanding credit may at first lead to increased business, but in the long run must inevitably create a situation of crisis and depression.

Those believing that changes in purchasing power are susceptible to exact measurement are quite consistent in demanding that banking policy should be tied to the results of these measurements in such a way that the banks should be required to make the goal of their credit policy the stability of the purchasing power of the monetary unit. Therefore, before going further, we must consider the question whether the various methods proposed for measuring fluctuations in purchasing power do, in fact, provide an instrument that can profitably be used for the purposes of economic policy.

IV   The Various Methods of Measuring Fluctuations in Purchasing Power and Their Importance for the Problem of Stabilization

The assumption that changes in the purchasing power of money are susceptible to exact measurement is based on the belief that modifications in the exchange relationships of particular commodities and services are sufficiently taken into account when a general average is taken. It is upon this fiction that the conception of a "level" of prices is based; all that appears to be necessary is an ascertainment of whether this "level" has risen or fallen as a whole. The avowed neglect of changes taking place among the prices of particular commodities and services relative to one another has been fostered by the fact that among the effects of changes in purchasing power, those mainly considered are the ones arising out of money's function as a standard of deferred payment; the other social consequences of changes in purchasing power, caused by the fact that all commodities and services do not feel their incidence at the same time or to the same extent, have been almost completely left out of account.

But even on the assumption that it is quite sufficient to calculate changes in the purchasing power of money with reference to an average of the prices of commodities and services, there are a number of fundamental difficulties for which there appears no single solution. In the first place, there is the question of "the average." Is it to be the arithmetical mean, the geometrical mean, the harmonic mean, or any other form of "mean" known to mathematics? There is no categorical answer to this question.

Second, what method is to be followed in the weighting of the individual prices? That is to say, what coefficients of relative importance are to be assigned to the particular commodities and services? Here, again, there is no single solution.

It is just because there *is* no single solution for these two questions, i.e., no solution which can be said to be indubitably the right one and all the others wrong, that we are driven to the conclusion that the index-number method is fundamentally unsuitable for the purpose of an accurate measurement of changes in the purchasing power of money. It is not contested that the majority of the systems proposed are well suited for affording the approximate indication of the changes in purchasing power which have taken place, and that they have, *pro tonto*, much educative value in directing public attention to the fact that changes have taken place. Nor need it be disputed that as a general rule and over relatively short periods of time, the calculated results by the different methods do not diverge very greatly from one another. But it is nonetheless necessary to insist, with all possible emphasis, on the fact that all such calculations are only *approximate* and not exact, and that an exact calculation is fundamentally impossible. It is necessary to emphasize this point, not merely to calm the conscience of theoreticians, but in order to draw attention to the far-reaching effect which it has as regards the practical application of index numbers for currency and banking policy.

As there are various methods for calculating an index of changes in purchasing power—all of which are equally right and wrong, equally correct and incorrect—and as each of these methods gives different results, it is inevitable that, once the index figures cease to be of a purely academic interest and acquire a direct bearing on economic policy, this purely scientific problem will become the field of serious conflicts of interest. Supposing the dollar were stabilized in accordance with the proposals of Irving Fisher, or that a "manipulated currency" was introduced on the lines of Keynes' system, or that the credit policy of the central banks were made dependent on the results of the index measurements, the various interest groups would immediately take sides on behalf of this or that method of calculation, according to whether they were interested in a rise or a fall of prices. The purchasing power of the monetary unit, which under a gold standard is to a certain extent independent of direct political influence and is ultimately based on the profit to be earned from the production of gold, would then become the plaything of political parties and political struggles. A sudden change in the purchasing power policy of the government, or even the anticipation of such a change, would be the occasion for grave disturbances within the individual countries. And the position vis-à-vis international trade would be completely intolerable. Just imagine the consequences if particular States—or all States—were to make an attempt through some joint organization, appointed by the League of Nations perhaps, to pursue a uniform currency policy based on the results of index measurements. The commercial antagonisms of the several countries would be automatically intensified, with an element of quite peculiar bitterness at once introduced into the conflict by the fact that the world is divided into two groups of people—the debtor and creditor countries.

The various writers, who have argued for some kind of tabular standard, have been so convinced of the correctness of their own particular methods of calculation that they have not seen this fundamental defect in their systems. Irving Fisher, again, attaches too much importance to the assertion that the several methods of calculating index numbers do not differ greatly in their results. It is not true that they do not differ; but even if it were so, it must be remembered that in view of the great importance of manipulations in purchasing power, even small differences would be sufficient to give rise to serious conflicts of interest in each country, and even more importantly, conflicts between one country and another.

Even if the fundamental difficulties standing in the way of index calculations could be overcome, the practical difficulties remaining would still be very great. The most correct manner of arriving at the prices of commodities and services would be to consider only commodities and services which are ripe for consumption, i.e., at the point of delivery to the ultimate consumer. Any other system will break down (apart from all other theoretical objections) for the reason that it must be a matter of entirely arbitrary selection as to how many intermediate stages of production are to be included in the calculation. The results are bound to be largely influenced by the number of times a product is treated as a separate commodity in its intermediate stages of production, and included as such in the calculations. The insuperable difficulties which stand in the way of a survey of the final consumer products are due to the impossibility of establishing any unvarying standard for dealing with changes in product quality. In order to eliminate the problem of variations to quality, all index-number systems are compelled to restrict themselves to the not very large number of articles (mainly raw materials) in the case of which the identity of quality can be ascertained beyond dispute. In addition to variations to quality, changes in consumption (due to the consumer including new articles in his consumption "basket") present immense difficulties in the way of statistical measurements. Once again we are led to the conclusion that disputes between the various interests in each country—and still more between nations—are bound to arise as soon as these statistical calculations emerge from the sphere of theory and assume practical economic significance.

The above considerations may be summed up as follows: any economist is able to propose a system for the approximate ascertaining of changes in purchasing power, which he thinks comes nearest to the solution of this insoluble problem. But no economist is able to prove conclusively to an unprejudiced party the necessity of preferring his system to all others. The selection of a method for calculating index numbers is always more or less arbitrary. If far-reaching practical consequences are involved in such selections, as must be the case if they serve as a basis for currency policy, there will be no possibility of agreement on the parts of the various nations—or the various social groups within nations—since the individual interests of each nation and of each social group will be affected.

The above arguments may appear not only as drastic and skeptical, but at first sight to be in conflict with the results of more than a hundred years of industrious research into these problems by a series of the most eminent economists. But, in fact, my comments represent nothing more than the conclusion which inevitably emerges from the entire literature on the subject. What lends them special weight is the fact that they alone explain why the ingenious proposals of eminent economists for the creation of stable currencies based on index numbers have hitherto never been put into effect. Up to the present, it has been more than a purely conservative attitude which has led statesmen and businessmen to stand aloof from these proposals; rather, it has been the recognition of the fundamental defects inherent in them.

These objections are especially weighty when the problem is considered from the international standpoint. It is astonishing that even people who are aware of the importance of the international exchange of commodities and money take the standpoint that the stability of domestic prices is more important than the stability of the international exchanges. The consequence of such proposals, if they were put into force, would be that each separate country would pursue a monetary policy based on the index system it considered best, with the result of exposing the international exchanges (the movements of which, under the gold standard, are confined within narrow limits) to abrupt and extensive fluctuations. No one can fail to see that this would introduce a major factor of instability and uncertainty into international commercial relations and, more importantly, into the conditions of *international indebtedness*.

V   The Pure Gold Standard and the Gold Standard Influenced by the Banks

Before considering the function of international cooperation in the field of currency policy, something must be said about the influence of banking policy on purchasing power.

In view of the disadvantages which arise from manipulations of purchasing power, the principle underlying the pure gold standard is that it is preferable to make the world's supply of money dependent on the accident of gold production. As matters stand today, a pure gold standard would give us a monetary system under which prices of commodities would slowly fall. It is improbable that discoveries of gold will again take place on such a scale as to reduce the purchasing power of gold. But whether it rises or falls, purchasing power under a pure gold standard, at any rate, changes slowly, and the changes continue over a considerable period of time in the same direction. With a pure gold standard, an increase of the world's supply of money (in a wide sense) can only come from new gold being produced and put into circulation in the form of money. A decrease in the supply of money can only come from gold being diverted from monetary to industrial uses.

It is characteristic of the gold standard that the banks are not allowed to increase the amount of notes and bank balances without a gold backing, beyond the total which was in circulation at the time the system was introduced. Peel's Bank Act of 1844 and the various banking laws which are more or less based on it represent attempts to create a pure gold standard of this kind. The attempt was incomplete because its restrictions on circulation included only bank notes, leaving out of account bank balances on which checks could be drawn. The founders of the Currency School failed to recognize the essential similarity between payments by check and payments by bank note. As a result of this oversight, those responsible for this legislation never accomplished their aim.

If this omission had not existed in the bank laws and if, in consequence, all expansion of credit by the banks had been effectively precluded, the world would have had a monetary system in which—even apart from the discoveries of gold in California, Australia, and South Africa—prices would have shown a general tendency to fall. The majority of our contemporaries will find that a sufficient ground for regarding such a monetary system as bad in itself, since they are wedded to the belief that good business and high prices are one and the same thing. But that is a prejudice. If we had had slowly falling prices for eighty years or more, we would have become accustomed to look for improvements in the standard of living and increases in real income through falling prices with stable or falling money income, rather than through increases in money income. At any rate, a solution to the difficult problem of reforming our monetary and credit system must not be rejected offhand merely for the reason that it involves a continuous fall in the price level. Above all, we must not allow ourselves to be influenced by the evil consequences of the recent *rapid* fall in prices. A slow and steady decline of prices cannot in any sense be compared with what is happening under the present system: namely, sudden and big rises in the price level, followed by equally sudden and sharp falls.

As a result of the Currency School's oversight, the world has acquired a monetary system which is affected not only by the fluctuations in the production of gold, but also by fluctuations in banking policy. Spurred on by a public opinion looking for salvation through low interest rates and rising prices, the banks are perpetually endeavoring after periods of depression to give an artificial stimulus to economic activity by means of credit expansion. They create a period of rising prices and continue with their expansionary policy until a point is reached at which they are at last compelled to call a halt; and once more they, then, bring about a decline in prices via restriction of credit.

It is such a period through which we are now passing. Eminent economists look for the cause of the depression in the restrictive measures of the banks. But the root cause of the evil is not in the restrictions, but in the expansion which preceded them. The policy of the banks does not deserve criticism for having at last called a halt to the expansion of credit, but, rather, for ever having allowed it to begin.

Consider what would happen if the banks were to perpetually continue a policy of credit expansion once it had begun. To maintain the artificially induced situation they would be compelled to have recourse to continually increasing the expansion of credit, the result of which would be an ever sharper and more rapid rise of prices. But once the business world realizes that there is no end in sight to the progressive expansion of credit, i.e., that prices are going to rise uninterruptedly, it will at once speculatively discount the price increases in advance by applying to the banks for more and more credit—since every purchase on credit will be a profitable transaction—and the end result becomes a progressive inflation. But inflation cannot last forever without leading to a panic and a collapse of the entire monetary system; this is a truth on which it is no longer necessary to expatiate, since it is amply confirmed by the experiences of the inflationary period of the last decade and a half and been explained in numerous works on the subject.

Therefore, when it is argued in various quarters that the recent fall in prices is due to the change in the policy of the banks, it is, literally speaking, true. A closer scrutiny of the facts, however, will show that sooner or later the policy of expanding credits must come to an end and that the evil consequences for which it is responsible will be the more serious the longer it has been pursued. The evil is not in the restrictions, but in the expansionist policy which preceded them. One ultimate reason for the present drop in prices is the circumstance that the banks—with the assent of public opinion, and indeed at the direct instigation of the press, the business world, and the governments— have made use of their power to issue additional circulation, i.e., to increase credit artificially. If the banks were to make no use of this power—which could only be the case either if the Central Banks were explicitly prohibited in their reserve-issuing privileges or if public opinion rigorously condemned the practice—we should have no economic fluctuations. We would probably have slowly falling prices, since the purchasing power of money would depend exclusively on the production of gold. But we should certainly not have the abrupt transitions from a sharp rise in prices to an equally sharp fall in prices, such as we have been through twice during the last ten years.

VI   Attainable Reform Objectives

From the outset any systematic policy of influencing the purchasing power of money should be kept within narrow limits, if it is not to do more harm than would result from leaving events to take their own course. To begin with, it is necessary to completely get away from the attempt, as unscientific as it is impracticable, to maintain the purchasing power of money "stable." Furthermore, we have to rid ourselves of the notion that a decline in purchasing power is in some way better than an increase in purchasing power. Lastly, we have to realize that theories based on the idea that the rate of interest can be lowered by banking policy are wrong; all endeavors in this direction may, indeed, at first provoke an expansion of business, but in the end it can only lead to crisis and depression owing to the diversion of capital into wrong channels.

It also has to be borne in mind that proposals for a radical transformation of the constitutions of the banks of the various nations of the world have no prospect of being put into effect now or for a number of years to come. All that can be done is to take mitigating action during periods when the tendency for purchasing power to continuously increase is clearly marked and to take contrary action in periods showing an equally well established tendency toward a continuous fall in purchasing power. In neither case should action be taken to the point of interfering with the normal tendency conditioned by gold production, either to the extent of arresting or actually reversing its operation.

Whether taken by each country separately or as part of a program of international cooperation, the extent of such action will have to be exercised with great caution. To prevent a policy that influences purchasing power from becoming the plaything of the various economic interests—because of the impossibility of finding any one method of calculating index numbers which by itself is correct—it is essential to restrict that interference to those changes in purchasing power, in one direction or the other, which are admitted without question by all parties. That implies that action to increase the purchasing power of money should only be taken when the decline in purchasing power is unquestionably established by all the different possible methods, and should, again, be suspended the moment any one of the methods yields divergent results; the same applies to measures to bring about a decrease in the purchasing power of money.

Any other policy followed by a single country would lead to serious conflicts between internal interests; and if followed by some common international organization it would lead to serious conflicts between nations. In all probability, at the first appearance of such conflicts all attempts at uniform international treatment of questions concerning currency and banking policy would have to be abandoned.

It is not the object of this memorandum to investigate the measures which should be taken for the attainment of these aims. Its objective is merely to consider which method of ascertaining changes in purchasing power is the best. The above explanatory digression was necessary in order to answer this question. We can now proceed to give a concrete reply.

VII   The Measurement of Changes in Purchasing Power as a Standard for Currency and Banking Policy

The considerations set forth above considerably restrict the functions which an instrument for the measurement of changes in purchasing power would perform. The problem is no longer that of satisfying the impossible demand for an exact standard for measuring changes in the purchasing power of money: the question is only one of forming an approximate estimate of the direction which those changes are taking. Up to the present, nearly all the proposals that have been made have been aiming at a correct standard—the one "correct" standard, the one "scientific" standard—of measurement. We must realize, however, that all we are looking for is a conventional standard, which means an arbitrarily selected standard. That is not a reproach to our proposal, since any and every standard is open to weighty objections and whatever standard *is* decided upon, the decision must always be an arbitrary one. The justification for our proposal is simply the fact that, at the outset, we set up much narrower aims for the currency and banking policy which would be guided by our standard, as opposed to the schemes which aim at stabilization. Our policy only comes into operation when the change in purchasing power has been ascertained over a considerable period with such unquestionable certainty that no one can dispute it; it ceases to operate as soon as it has been successful in bringing purchasing power back to a point at which it is possible for doubts to arise as to whether the tendency which it is desired to combat still exists or not. Under these circumstances, there is no need to criticize particular proposals which have been made for the measurement of changes in purchasing power. Dozens of volumes have been written on the subject, and the acutest economists have dealt with it. It would be altogether a mistake to attempt to add a new proposal to those which have already been made. But what must be realized is that any proposal of this kind is inevitably defective.

The advantage of the suggestion put forward here is to be found in the fact that it makes possible, to a certain extent, a general conspectus of changes in purchasing power, which can serve as a basis for currency and banking policy without provoking conflicts and antagonisms of interest. That a number of proposals which have been made for the measurement of changes in purchasing power are impracticable at the outset—irrespective of their theoretical advantages—is clear. This is especially the case with proposals to base the calculation of changes in purchasing power on wages and retail prices. The only practical proposals are those which take wholesale prices as their primary foundation; even in this case it will be necessary, in order to get around the difficulties connected with variations of quality, to make a selection and confine the calculation to articles whose constancy of quality can be indisputably established.

Systematic attempts to regulate purchasing power can only be made through international agreement. If separate countries were to take such action, they would find themselves in a position of monetary isolation; as a result, one of the most important achievements facilitating international trade, namely, the monetary unification ensured by the gold standard, and its corollary of relatively stable exchanges, would be lost. But international action in this field can only be attempted if conflicts of interest are avoided from the outset. The attenuation of sharp changes in the purchasing power of money in one direction or the other is an object on which all nations will readily agree, and for such a purpose the methods which we have at our disposal are sufficient for the measurement of changes in purchasing power. To attempt anything more than this would be asking an international organization to assume a heavier burden that it is able to carry.

With the adoption of such a policy as has been indicated above, the problem of the measurement of changes in purchasing power is relatively easy to solve. But with a policy pursuing more far-reaching aims, the problem would be altogether insoluble.

CHAPTER 7

The Great German Inflation

I

All the misfortunes from which Europe has suffered in the last two decades have been the inevitable result of the application of the theories which have dominated the social and economic philosophy of the last fifty years. Our troubles are the upshot of much laborious thought. The German inflation, above all, was the outcome of the monetary and banking theory which for many years had obsessed the men who occupied the chairs of economics at the Universities, the men who governed the financial policy of the Reich, and the editors of the most influential newspaper and periodicals.

The central feature of these erroneous theories was a total rejection of the Quantity Theory[1] and of all the teachings of the Currency School.[2] The *empirisch-realistische Volkswirt*,[3] who distrusted every "theory" — especially theories imported from abroad — was firmly convinced that both the Quantity Theory and the Theories of the Currency School were nothing but an inexplicable blunder committed by Ricardo and his followers. The German *Kathedersozialisten*[4] did not

[This is a review article of Frank D. Graham's book *Exchange, Prices, and Production in Hyper-Inflation: Germany, 1920–1923* (Princeton, N.J.: Princeton University Press, 1930). The review is reprinted here from *Economica* (May 1932).—Ed.]

1 [The Quantity Theory says that the general price level is primarily a function of the money supply.—Ed.]

2 [As Mises understood it both the British Currency School and the British Banking School, broadly speaking, were advocates of central banking. The Currency School, however, advocated rules for the expansion of money and credit, with some theorists even favoring 100 percent specie reserves. The Banking School advocated a discretionary central banking policy with few or no rules concerning money and credit expansion.—Ed.]

3 [Translated as empiricist-relativist political economist.—Ed.]

4 [Members of the "Younger" German Historical School who used their university positions as vehicles to advocate political intervention and reform in the economy. These professors were called "academic socialists" or "socialists of the chair."—Ed.]

waste their time on the study of English political economy. Hence they were unaware of the problems which were the subject of the long-lasting controversy between the Banking School and the Currency School. The only source of their knowledge of the matter was the book published in 1862 by Adolph Wagner under the title *Theorie der Peel'schen Bankakte*. Wagner lacked absolutely the gift of economic ratiocination. He accepted without any criticism all the statements of the Banking School; from his book it was utterly impossible to gather what objections the Currency School had had against the theories of the Banking School.

The other leading authority on monetary and banking problems, Wilhelm Lexis, was still less endowed with the power of economic reasoning. He, like Wagner, was entirely innocent of any understanding of the Ricardian theory of the foreign exchanges — the "purchasing power parity" theory. Each firmly believed that the foreign exchanges are governed by the balance of payments.

Hence would-be economists who owed their education to the teachings of such men were prepared to accept without criticism the doctrines of Knapp and Bendixen, who in the years immediately preceding the outbreak of the war dominated German monetary and banking theory. Knapp, Professor of Political Science at the University of Strasburg, was a trained statistician and had devoted much time in archives to the study of Prussian policy concerning the peasantry. There is not the slightest indication in his writings that he had ever glanced at Ricardo or any other of the British monetary economists. The occasional allusions to Ricardo's ideas, which one finds in Knapp's writings, impute to Ricardo opinions which are rather the contrary of what we read in Ricardo's books and pamphlets. Knapp ignored absolutely the problem of prices. In his view the task of monetary theory is nothing else than the purely formal classification of the various kinds of currency. He had not the slightest idea that government interference in the mechanism of price-making is subject to certain conditions which cannot be controlled simply by governmental decree.

Not less fatal for the formation of German views on monetary theory was the influence of Bendixen, the manager of a mortgage corporation, who, inspired by Knapp, wrote some booklets, which expounded the principles of the Banking School. The most striking feature of Bendixen's contribution was that, being unfamiliar with monetary literature, he honestly believed he was enunciating something entirely new!

In passing under review the German monetary and banking policy from the outbreak of the war to the catastrophe of 1923, the most startling thing is the absolute ignorance even of the most elementary principles of monetary science on the part of literally all German statesmen, politicians, bankers, journalists, and would-be economists. It is impossible for any foreigner even to realize how boundless this ignorance was. For this reason, in the last three years of the German inflation, some foreigners came to believe that the Germans ruined their own currency of set purpose in order to involve other countries in their own ruin, and to evade the payment of reparations. Such imputation of secret satanism to German policy does it wrong. The only secret of German policy was Germany's total lack of any acquaintance with economic theory.

Thus Herr Havenstein, the governor of the Reichsbank, honestly believed that the continuous issue of new notes had nothing to do with the rise of commodity prices, wages, and foreign exchanges. This rise he attributed to the machinations of speculators and profiteers and to intrigues on the part of external and internal foes. Such indeed was the general belief. Nobody durst venture to oppose it without incurring the risk of being denounced both as a traitor to his country and as an abettor of profiteering. In the eyes both of the public and of the rulers the only reason why monetary conditions were not healthy was the lamentable indulgence of the government in regard to profiteering. For the restoration of sound currency nothing else seemed to be necessary than a powerful suppression of the egotistic aims of unpatriotic people.

It would be very interesting to show that this attitude was the necessary sequel to the whole system of social and economic philosophy as taught by the school of Schmoller. According to the *étatiste* outlook of this school, power *(Macht)* is the deciding factor in social life. That even the most powerful government is not free to do everything and that there exist certain unalterable conditions of human existence insusceptible to the influence of the most powerful intervention are propositions which it never admitted. The study of economic theory, it said, was useless, for the various systems of theoretical economics all overlooked the fact that governments had the power to alter all conditions. It was ready to admit that the Ricardian system was a faithful description of the state of England at his time, but it denied its applicability to Germany. In the realm of the Electors of Brandenburg and the Kings of Prussia everything was different. It therefore replaced the study of economic theory by the history of Prussian administration in the academic curriculum. It taught that there is nothing important in social life but power, and its notion of power was very materialistic. Power in its eyes was soldiers and guns. It had never understood Hume's discovery that all government is founded on opinion.

But to trace this evolution would involve writing the entire history of the transition of the German mind from the liberal thought of Goethe, Schiller, and Humboldt to the militarist ideas of Treitschke, Schmoller, and Houston Stewart Chamberlain. It would involve writing the history of the Prussian hegemony of the nation which has been styled the nation of poets and thinkers, and the history of the Reich founded by Bismarck and lost by Wilhelm II. It is obvious that this would exceed the purpose of these lines.

II

In these circumstances it is easy to understand that the German books dealing with the history of the Inflation Period are for the greater part of little value. They are so full of prejudices, and are often so entirely lacking in the theoretical insight which must necessarily precede all historical description that they cannot even give an adequate picture of the great historical event. For this reason this work by a learned American is all the more welcome. In his *Exchange, Prices, and Production in Hyper-Inflation: Germany, 1920–1923*, Professor F. D. Graham of Princeton University has taken great pains to provide a reliable narrative.

In judging this valuable book we must bear in mind that all the experience of the German inflation brought nothing that could puzzle the theoretical economist. There were many things which were quite inexplicable to the *étatiste Volkswirt*[5] of the Schmoller type; nay, the whole thing was quite inexplicable to them, but there was nothing that had not been observed and satisfactorily explained by the theorist in previous inflations.

In reading Professor Graham's historical survey even those who were witnesses of the inflation must again and again be amazed at the incredible incapacity evinced in regard to the monetary problem by all

5 [Translated as a political economist who advocates total control of all economic planning as a function of the government. — Ed.]

sections of the German nation. For the economist the most astonishing fact is the inadequacy of the Reichsbank's discount policy. This is Professor Graham's verdict: "From the early days of the war till the end of June 1922 the Reichsbank rate remained unchanged at 4 per cent.; it was raised to 6 per cent. in July, to 7 per cent. in August, 8 per cent. in September and 10 per cent. in November 1922, to 12 per cent. in January 1923, 19 per cent. in April, 30 per cent. in August and 90 per cent. in September. But these increases were as nothing when measured alongside the progressive lightening in the burden of a loan during the time for which it ran. Though, after September 1923, a bank or private individual had to pay at the rate of 900 per cent. per annum for a loan from the Reichsbank, this was no deterrent to borrowing. It would have been profitable to pay a so-called interest, in reality an insurance, charge, of thousands or even millions of per cents. per annum, since the money in which the loan would be repaid was depreciating at a speed which would have left even rates like these far in the rear. With a 900 per cent. interest rate in September 1923 the Reichsbank was practically giving money away and the same is true of the lower rates in the preceding months when the course of depreciation was not quite so headlong. The policy of the Reichsbank authorities in encouraging the discount of commercial bills that they might thus mitigate the scarcity of credit was but further evidence of the Alice-in-Wonderland determination of the directors of that institution to run ever faster in order to keep up with themselves. The scarcity of credit was due solely to currency depreciation and the cure prescribed was to increase the volume of means of payment!"[6]

But one should not forget that the Reichsbank was not alone in this folly. The private banks, too, lent money to every speculator who furnished collateral security. It was very easy to get rich by buying shares with the money borrowed from the banks. In this way some acquired big fortunes in a very short time and painlessly. Since then all these much-admired and envied profiteers have lost all that they won, and in many cases even much more—a proof that they were not gifted with great business ability. Indeed, no great business ability was needed to outwit any one of the big German banks. That their managers and directors were really incompetent has been proved by the subsequent failure of the institutions which they governed.

6 Cf. p. 65 of Graham's book.

It took years for German businessmen to understand that the Mark was no longer a suitable unit for economic calculations. For a very long time they really believed that the profits, which an account of profit and loss reckoned in Marks showed, were genuine earnings. They did not understand that a computation made in a more stable currency would lead to quite a different result. Of course the businessmen discovered this truth somewhat earlier than the general public. They then replaced the *Markrechnung* [calculation in Marks] by the *Goldrechnung* [calculation in gold]. This was the beginning of the end. The Mark-currency had perforce to break down when its unrestrainable depreciation could no longer be overlooked.

As long as the inflation was working, socialist labor leaders and the socialists of the chair were all in its favor and taught that not the increase in quantity of money but the unpatriotic behavior of the profiteers was the cause of the depreciation of the Mark. After inflation was over they changed their minds. Now they accuse the "capitalists" of having of set purpose made the inflation to enrich themselves. For the German public mind every misfortune is due to the machinations of the "exploiter class."

III

For the economist the German inflation brought some interesting illustrations of his theoretical principles, but no experience which did not conform to them. In this instance monetary and economic theory had nothing new to learn. Of course, the German politico-economic science of the Schmoller-Knapp type had everything to learn from it. But in fact, with the exception of some of the younger men, they have declined to draw the conclusion. Unteachable as they are, they still believe in the theory which attributes changes in the value of a national currency to variations in the national balance of payments. The failure of the policy of inflation they attribute to lack of energy on the part of the government and to lack of patriotism on the part of the people.

Nor has the German politician learned a whit more from the inflation. The government and the Reichsbank both believe that monetary troubles arise from an unfavorable balance of payments, from speculation, and from unpatriotic behavior of the capitalist class. They therefore attempt to fight the menace of depreciation of the Reichsmark by controlling dealings in foreign currency and by confiscating German holdings of foreign assets. They do not understand that the only safe-guard against the fall of a currency's value is a policy of rigid restriction. But though the government and the professors have learned nothing, the people have. When the war inflation came nobody in Germany understood what a change in the value of the money unit meant. The businessman and the worker both believed that a rising income in Marks was a real rise of income. They continued to reckon in Marks without any regard to their falling value. The rise of commodity prices they attributed to the scarcity of goods due to the blockade. When the government issued additional notes, it could buy with these notes com-modities and pay salaries because there was a time lag between this issue and the corresponding rise of prices. The public was ready to ac-cept notes and to keep them because they had not yet realized that they were constantly losing purchasing power. This went on for years. But as they learned that the government was determined not to stop with the further issue of notes and that the increase of their quantity must needs lead to a progressive rise of prices, their conduct changed. Every-body became anxious not to keep the money in his pocket. The service which money renders consists in its being the commodity which is saleable at the best terms. By keeping money in his purse everybody is enabled to buy in the most convenient way any commodity he may want one day. But when money loses purchasing power from day to day its retention involves a loss. Whoever gets money, therefore, spends it immediately—even by buying something for which he has no present use and maybe even no future use. In the last days of the inflation the employees got their payment daily. At once they handed it over to their wives and these hurried to spend it as quickly as possible by buying at any rate something or other. Nobody wished to retain money; every-body dropped it like a live coal. When this tendency, which on the Stock Exchange was called *Flucht in die Sachwerte*—flight into invest-ments in goods—became general, so that even the least businesslike people adopted it, the end was at hand. The Mark broke down. The gov-ernment gained no further advantage by issuing notes, because the de-preciation then outran the increase.

A nation which has experienced inflation till its final breakdown will not submit to a second experiment of this type until the memory of the previous one has faded. No German government could succeed in the attempt to inflate the currency by issues in favor of the Treasury as long as the men and women are still alive who have been the witnesses and victims of the 1923 inflation. Made overcautious by what they suffered, at the very outset of the inflation they would start a panic. The rise of prices would be out of all proportion to the increase in the quantity of paper money; it would anticipate the expected increase of notes. The more money the government issued, the less it would be able to buy. The higher the salaries the civil servants and the soldiers drew, the fewer the goods would they be able to purchase. So the government would fail in the endeavor to ameliorate its financial position by issuing notes. From the point of view of officialdom, inflation would be nugatory.

The economist might urge that this lesson could have been learned at a lower cost from theory than from experience. Had the German people paid more attention to the teachings of economic theory they could have learned all these things without having to pay so dearly. This is a melancholy comment to have to make after the event.

But in any case the monetary history of the last three lustrums in Germany and many other European countries proves that no nation can afford to treat economic theory with contempt.

CHAPTER 8

Senior's Lectures on Monetary Problems

Nassau William Senior's famous lectures on money and international trade have been newly issued by the London School of Economics and Political Science in their series of reprints.[1] On re-reading these classic treatises one is led to the conclusion that the practical application of economic reasoning seems to meet with very great difficulties. We are living in a world where trade barriers become more and more insurmountable. In defending the system of protection and prohibition, every day the same arguments are heard again which Senior and his fellow economists have refuted and which Ricardo had already refuted years before. Why could this acute criticism of the Mercantile Theory of Wealth[2] not succeed in convincing public opinion? Is there a weak point in the demonstration of the futility of the protection doctrine?

The foremost argument in the protectionist's reasoning today is again, as in the days of the Mercantile Theory, the monetary standpoint. Restriction of imports is said to be indispensable for the maintenance of a country's monetary equilibrium. It is true: one no longer speaks of the danger of losing the circulating stock of coined precious metals to foreign countries. But the only reason for this is the fact that practically no country maintains today an effective circulation of gold coins as most of them did till the outbreak of the War. The modern pro-

---

[This review article is reprinted from the *Economic Journal* (September 1933). — Ed.]

1 Nassau W. Senior:
   1 Three Lectures on the "Transmission of the Precious Metals from Country to Country and the Mercantile Theory of Wealth."
   2 Three Lectures on the "Value of Money."
   3 Three Lectures on the "Cost of Obtaining Money and on Some Effects of Private and Government Paper Money."

Numbers 3, 4, and 5 in the *Series of Reprints of Scarce Tracts in Economic and Political Science* (London: London School of Economics and Political Science, 1931).

2 [The Mercantilists believed that gold and other precious metals embodied true wealth; thus they advocated maximizing a country's exports while minimizing its imports. — Ed.]

tectionist insists rather upon the necessity to secure the exchange ratio between the national and the foreign currency. What he does not wish to admit is that the exchange ratio does not ultimately depend on the balance of payments and that there is no danger of its being impaired so long as there is no over-issue of notes at home.

The question to be answered today is exactly the same as is expounded in Senior's lectures on the "Transmission of the Precious Metals from Country to Country." The difference lies only in the formulation, not in the substance. The problem is whether there is an automatic readjustment of the balance of payments or whether government is bound to interfere lest disastrous consequences follow. The chain of reasoning by which Senior proves that governmental interference is superfluous for this purpose considers a state of things where imports and exports of commodities dominate international business relations. For the present situation it seems necessary to keep in view the importance of credits, and accordingly to lay stress not only on the prices of commodities but also on the rates of interest. This, of course, does not in any way alter the essence of the problem, but it does seriously affect the political and ethical aspect of the question.

Considerations of this nature play in the eyes of public opinion a bigger role than is generally supposed. In discussing the problem of trade restrictions primarily with reference to the prices of goods, one imagines a selfish producer who demands higher prices from the poor consumer. In this case sympathy is on the side of the consumer. But in regard to rates of interest sympathy is given to the lender. Whereas in the question of commodity prices public opinion splits into two parties so that against the friends of higher prices stand always friends of lower prices; in the problem of interest there is but one opinion, i.e., in favor of low interest. As the matter of controversy seems to lie in the dilemma whether to maintain at home a lower rate of discount at the cost of import restrictions or to let the price of money rise under free trade, the scale goes down in favor of import restrictions. There is in every country a considerable opposition against import duties which one tries to justify by the necessity of raising the home price level in favor of home production. The opposition is very weak when import duties are apologized for by the expediency of maintaining a low rate of interest.

There is no doubt that in countries where capital is very abundant the rate of interest would be much lower were there not opportunities of exporting capital to countries with a higher rate of interest. Had the United Kingdom or had France in the fifty or sixty years preceding the

War not invested a large amount of money abroad, the money rate at London and Paris would have been much lower than it actually was. If at this time someone in England had demanded a restriction of foreign investments from the labor point of view, as the Liberal Industrial Report did after the War, it would have been intelligible at least from the point of view of a short-sighted class policy. But the strange thing was that at this time, not the capital-exporting countries, but the capital-importing countries complained more about the consequences of the international capital movements, assuming that it must lead to higher interest, whereas its effect for them was the contrary. Strange to say, in the 'seventies of the nineteenth century in Austria the theory was evolved that the Austrian paper currency isolated the country from the solidarity of international money markets and so enabled the bank of issue to expand credit and maintain a comparatively low rate of interest without any disadvantages. This false theory was duly refuted by Wilhelm Luccam, the then manager of the Austrian Central Bank. But nevertheless it survived in Austria and had from year to year more success in the whole of Europe, especially in Germany, and even in America.

When people today generally assert that things have so radically changed since the time in which the classical theory of money and foreign exchanges was expounded, that one cannot apply their results to modern conditions, they unfortunately do not give any proof. It is totally wrong to pretend that raising the rate of discount would not have any effect today on the flow of gold and on the exchange rate, or an insufficient effect. There is no proof that discount policy of the old type is inapplicable to the present situation. The fact is that the ruling parties prefer the consequences of a depreciation of the national currency to the consequences resulting from non-interference in the market's money rate.

Let us consider separately the different recent cases of departure from the old gold parity. There was the case of England in 1931. Britain had to choose between a policy of defending the gold standard by raising the rate of discount, as has been done over and over again, and a policy of depreciation. She decided for the second because it made it possible to maintain unchanged the British level of prices and wages in the midst of a world of falling gold prices. Opinions differ on the soundness of this policy, and there is no doubt that it was very unsound from the point of view of Senior's ideas. But there was nothing in the situation which could not be explained from the point of view of Senior's theoretical teaching. It is true that his decision would have been very different from that of Great Britain's rulers in 1931. He would have believed that nominal wages had to fall *pari passu* with prices, and that there was nothing alarming in a situation where the prices of raw materials which England buys fall more rapidly than the prices of the manufactures which England exports. But Senior in discussing these problems with Mr. Norman and Mr. Keynes would at the end of the conversation have said: "I see, gentlemen, that you follow other aims." But he would have had no reason to say: "You have to cope with a situation which my theory does not cover."

Yet in another respect a radical change in the financial situation has been accomplished. In the modern banking system the short-term debts play a dominating role. The banks of the lending countries have lent enormous sums to the banks of the borrowing countries. Literally they had the right to withdraw this money at short notice. But in fact such withdrawals could not be effected at once, as the borrowing banks had lent this money to business which could not pay it back at all or at least only after some delay. The international credit relations were based on a fallacious assumption of liquidity. The moment the lenders tried to exert their right of withdrawal there were only two alternatives: open declaration of bankruptcy by the debtor banks or intervention of the government which suspended payments to foreign countries. The introduction of foreign exchange control in some continental countries in the summer of 1931 was a makeshift for a formal moratorium.

Banking today is not sounder when considered from the point of view of the home situation. Deposits subject to checks and saving deposits are two entirely different things. The saver wishes to entrust his money for a longer period; he wishes to get interest. The bank which receives his money has to lend it to business. A withdrawal of the money entrusted to it by the saver can only take place in the same measure as the bank is able to get back the money it has lent. As the total amount of the saving deposits is working in the country's business, a total withdrawal is not possible. The individual saver can get back his money from the bank, but not all savers can do so at the same time. That does not mean that banking is unsound. It does not become unsound until the banks explicitly or tacitly promise what they cannot perform: to pay back the savings at call or at short notice.

The deposits subject to checks have a different purpose. They are the businessman's cash like coins and bank notes. The depositor intends to dispose of them day by day. He does not demand interest, or at least he would entrust the money to the bank even without interest. The bank, to be sure, could not earn anything if it were to hold the whole amount of these deposits available. It has to lend the money at short notice to business. If all depositors simultaneously were to ask their deposits back, it could not meet the demand. This fact, that a bank which issues notes or receives deposits subject to check cannot hold the total amount corresponding to the notes in circulation and to the deposits in its vaults, and therefore can never redeem at once the total amount of its liabilities of this kind, is the knotty problem of banking policy. It is the consideration of this difficulty which has to govern the credit policy of the banks which issue notes or receive deposits subject to check. It is this consideration that led to the legislation which limits the issue of bank notes and imposes on the central banks the retention of a reserve fund of a certain magnitude.

But the case of the saving deposits is different. Since the saver does not need the deposited sum at call or short notice it is not necessary that the saving banks and the other banks which take over such deposits should promise repayment at call or at short notice. Nevertheless, this is what they did. And so they became exposed to the dangers of a panic. They would not have run this danger, if they had accepted the saving deposits only on condition that withdrawal must be notified some months ahead.

Public opinion assumes that the real danger to maintenance of monetary stability lies in the flight of capital. This assumption is not correct. Capital invested in real estate or in industrial plants or in shares of companies holding property of this nature cannot fly. You can sell such property and leave the country with the proceeds. But—unless there is no expansion of credit—the buyer simply replaces you. If he is a foreigner, then the capital flight of the native is compensated by the immigration of capital from abroad. If the buyer is another native, then he can provide the means—when additional credit is not granted by credit expansion—merely by selling his property, and so the case with him is the same. One person or another can withdraw his capital from a country, but this can never be a mass movement. There is only one apparent exception, i.e., the saving deposit which can be withdrawn from the bank at once or at short notice. When the saving deposits are subject to instant withdrawal and the bank of issue renders the immediate withdrawal possible by advancing credits for these savings to be withdrawn, then credit expansion and inflation cause the exchange ratio to rise. It is obvious that not the flight of capital but the credit expansion in favor of the saving banks is the root of the evil.

The pith of the problem lies in the deposit policy. Banks which promise no more than they can fulfill without extraordinary assistance from the central bank, never jeopardize the stability of the country's currency. And even the other banks that have been imprudent enough to assume liabilities which they cannot meet are only a danger when the central bank tries to assist them. If the Central Bank were to leave them to their fate, their peculiar embarrassment would not have any effect on foreign exchanges. That the additional issue of great amounts of bank notes for the sake of the repayment of the total amount or of a great portion of the country's saving deposits makes the foreign exchange go up is easy to understand. It is not simply the wish of the capitalists to fly with their capital, but the expansion of the circulation, that imperils monetary stability.

Had the central banks not believed that it was their duty to cover up the consequences of the deposit banks' wrong policy they would have not only maintained without artificial and, at the same time, ineffective measures of the stability of the exchange ratio, but would have forced the deposit banks to make agreements with their clients concerning the payments due. By such agreements they would have adjusted the payments due to the payments receivable. The Standstill Agreements would have been made definitively and for all debts, foreign and domestic.

To sum up, we are not entitled to say that Senior in his writings on money and monetary subjects had to deal with problems other than those which we have today. The task of monetary and banking theory is in principle not different today from Senior's time. Different, of course, are the conditions of our banking organization, the institutions, and the considerations which politicians keep in mind. Different are the data, but not the mechanism of exchange and social cooperation. All the questions of principles which Senior had to face are identical with those which our theory has to answer. We may differ from Senior in regard to the treatment of the fundamental items of value and exchange, but we have still the same problems to solve. And notwithstanding all changes in economic thought and reasoning, in social conditions and political aspects, in banking organization, and in business life generally, no one can read these old pamphlets without profit.

☙ Trade

CHAPTER 9

The Disintegration of the International Division of Labor

Introduction

The international division of labor was an achievement of the spirit of Liberalism. International trade has to some extent existed from the oldest times. There was a regular commerce in some commodities the production of which was limited to special geographical conditions. There was occasional trade when some extraordinary event offered unusual opportunities. But however important the civilizatory consequences of this international traffic were and however important its amount was when compared with the technical difficulties that transport had to overcome, the role played by it in supplying the wants of the markets was negligible. A very small part only of the common man's daily consumption was dependent on foreign produce. The commodities imported might for the most part be regarded as luxury goods, as people could do without them without suffering too great privation. At the beginning of the nineteenth century Napoleon's continental blockade even if it had been strictly enforced would not have had any noteworthy consequences on the daily consumption of the masses in Central Europe. In those days for the ordinary man's supply of even sugar (of course, in those days cane sugar only) and cotton were luxuries.

The growth of international trade was due to the abolition of the greater part of the trade barriers which misguided fiscalism and the errors of mercantilist policy had erected. Liberalism broke them down and thus paved the way to unparalleled intensification of international trade relations. When Cobden and Bastiat were at the zenith of their prestige it was the universally accepted belief that trade barriers were

[Extract from *The World Crisis*, Symposium of Studies published on the occasion of the Tenth Anniversary of the Graduate Institute of International Studies (London, New York, Toronto: Longmans Green, 1938).—Ed.]

doomed to disappear forever like the other remnants of a dark past, such as absolutism, superstition, intolerance, ignorance, and wars.

The theory of foreign trade as stated by Ricardo has proved in an irrefutable way that free trade only ensures the highest productivity of the economic efforts and that every kind of protectionism must necessarily result in a reduction of the output of capital and labor. For a hundred and twenty years a flood of books and pamphlets has endeavored to invalidate the teachings of this theory and to show that some good might be reaped from protection. They have all failed. They could not disprove that as far as the supply of the consumer with commodities and services is concerned free trade is more efficient than any other system. Never has any proposition been brought forward that could shake the foundations of the free trade doctrine.

The most famous objection once was the infant industry argument. But everything that could be said about the inability of newly established industries successfully competing with old and well-established producers holds good in both cases whether the competitors are of the same or of different nations. That nobody likewise ventured to demand protection for new firms starting a new business against the overwhelming competition of older firms working in the same town, district, or country can already be considered as a proof that the argument is not economic but political. Of course, every new plant has to meet difficulties of different kinds until it runs smoothly. There are drawbacks which make the business bad for a longer or shorter period of initiation. If there is no prospect that these losses will be over-compensated by later success, then the foundation of the new plant is not a paying concern. Then it is a waste to add new firms or plants to those already existing. In this respect it makes no difference whether the new center of production is working in the same or in another country. Many historical examples prove that industries have been shifted in the same country from a center of less-favorable to a center of more-favorable conditions, although no protective measures sheltered the infancy of the new establishment. In these cases in the calculus of the entrepreneur the losses of the beginning were outweighed by the later prospective gains. Protection was not necessary for the impulse. Nor is it more wanted if the shifting has to take place between different countries. Examined more closely, the infant industry argument reveals its purely political character. It cannot be considered as a sound economic argument in favor of protection.

The infant industry argument played an important role both in economic writings and in policies. But economic history does not give us a single example of protection in infant industries that did not turn into lasting and enduring protection. The industries of America, of Australia, and of the Eastern countries of Europe in their infancy amply enjoyed the blessings resulting from the infant industry protection argument. Now grown-up, they are still protected and even much more efficiently, and there is no question of declaring them of age by abolishing their protection.

The infant industry argument is today a thing of the past. In the present world other arguments have to be credited with the responsibility of protectionism and its logical outcome: the aim of self-sufficiency. These arguments are: the argument of national prestige, the war argument, the wages argument, the over-population argument, and the monetary or foreign exchange argument.

I The Argument of National Prestige

According to List,[1] every nation has to go through different stages of economic evolution. At the highest stage the nation has not only developed agriculture but trade and industry too. Until a nation has reached this last and highest stage it cannot harmoniously evolve all its productive forces. From this philosophy all the nations of the world which were backward in industrial production inferred that not to have a modern industry and modern big-scale production was a sign of inferiority. Whereas the Romantics in the industrial countries wish to bring back the bygone days of a more agricultural age, the Romantics of the agricultural countries yearn for the industrialization of their own country. They think that a nation whose wealth is based on agriculture and the production of raw materials only can never attain the level of moral and intellectual civilization peculiar to the leading nations of the Western world. They long for industry because they desire the perfections of modern culture.

This Romanticism is accountable for the fact that in the more agricultural countries the programs of the nationalistic parties always include protection for industry and put much less stress on the wants of agriculture.

In pre-war days, when immigration into the industrial countries of

1 [Friedrich List, a German economist in the 1820s and 1830s, favored free trade accompanied by tariff protection to stimulate the growth of infant industries as a country progresses through the various stages of economic evolution. —Ed.]

Europe and overseas was still free, the foremost reason for this policy in many European countries was the aim to make emigration superfluous. Conditions for industrial production were in every respect more favorable in Central and Western Europe than for instance in the Balkans. With a policy of laissez faire the excess population of these nations which could not find employment in agricultural production had to emigrate to Central and Western Europe and to the New World. When the governments of these Eastern nations encouraged industrial production by strict protectionism, they wished to reduce emigration figures. They considered emigration as prejudicial to the greatness and to the political and military power of their State. They were afraid of the fact that the emigrants would in their new settlements in the course of the years lose their attachment to their old mother-country, its habits and language, and its civilization. The policy of protection for industrial production was a policy of national and racial self-preservation. Its aim was to keep the citizens away from the melting pot of the European West, the United States, and other American countries. Today this argument has lost its meaning. Immigration is no longer free; the excess population cannot emigrate, because there are hardly any countries where immigration is possible.

In pre-war days the migration argument was valid not only in the agricultural countries of Europe, but even in one of the most industrialized countries, in Germany. When the German agriculture, especially of the Eastern provinces of Prussia, could no longer compete on an unsheltered market with the agricultural production of more fertile countries like Russia, Rumania, the United States, Canada, and Argentina, Germany step by step progressed on the way to protectionism, because it wished as far as possible to reduce emigration losses. But we have not to dwell on this point any longer as today international migrations on a big scale are impossible.

In the opposite way in which the regard for population figures influenced the commercial policy of the countries which were relatively over-populated and therefore countries of emigration, the population argument influenced the relatively under-populated countries. These nations—in the first line the countries of Latin America—wished to increase their population figures by more immigration; protection was, in their eyes, one of the means of attracting more hands. But this too now belongs to the past.

Under present conditions, where migrations are reduced to a minimum and where no important country is ready to open its doors to newcomers, such considerations no longer play any role at all. We shall speak of the part played by the immigration barriers later in the essay.

II The War Argument

The foremost reason for protection and the drive toward self-sufficiency in the world today is the war motive. For the militarist countries the readiness to make war is the primary goal of their policy, and war itself the regular means of attaining their objects. They therefore consider peace nothing but the time to prepare for the coming war. The economic activities of the country have already in peacetime been organized in such a way that they may later serve the interests of war. This scheme includes self-sufficiency for all kinds of produce necessary to a war-making nation.

When the Liberals recommended free trade and international division of labor they did so because peace among all civilized nations was the cornerstone of their political creed. We have to realize that the *conditio sine qua non* of international free trade is goodwill and peace among nations. Division of labor and war are incompatible. The division of labor within a country presupposes peace between its different parts and districts. In the Middle Ages and even later, when the division of labor was hardly developed, it was possible for single towns and countries to go to war with each other. As every part of the country produced everything which was needed in wartime, war-making did not present problems of supply of food, equipment, and arms. The belligerent parties wanted money with which to conduct the war; but if they had it, they could buy what they required.

Things are entirely different in the modern world of international division of labor. The European countries rely more or less on foodstuffs and raw materials imported from abroad. The manufacture of modern arms and war material is only possible in highly specialized big-scale enterprises which must have been working already in peacetime in order to run smoothly in wartime. A nation which does not produce all the raw materials and foodstuffs and all kinds of arms and military equipment within its borders would in time of war lack them.

When, since the nineties of the last century, Germany started its preparations for a decisive war, its economic provisions were limited to the supply of food. Protection for agriculture was among other reasons actuated by the necessity of making the country independent of foreign supply in wartime. But nobody realized that a belligerent country could suffer from the lack of materials other than foodstuffs. It was the experience of the World War[2] that taught this lesson.

Today these Powers who regard war as the means of satisfying their "dynamic" aspirations aim at self-sufficiency in order to be independent of foreign supply in a coming conflagration. It is these Powers which have in a systematic way evolved the theory and practice of self-sufficiency for the purposes of war-making. Their endeavors have been intensified by the consideration of Article 16 of the Covenant[3] providing economic sanctions against a nation going to war.

To attain self-sufficiency in wartime these nations wish to become as far as possible independent of raw materials which have to be imported. They desire to replace the imported raw materials and food-stuffs by home production. They further the expansion of the production of food and raw materials which can be produced within their own borders by the most strict means of protectionism. They try to replace those raw materials which they cannot produce at home by substitutes manufactured in the country. In these efforts there is no regard for the cost of production. In the eyes of the supporters of this policy it is immaterial whether the cost of production of these succedanea is many times higher than the price which has to be paid for the imported commodity. What matters only is that it can be produced at home. It was in this spirit that they proceeded to produce synthetic rubber, synthetic petrol, synthetic wool, etc.

In the reasoning of this militarist argument in favor of self-sufficiency there is nevertheless a striking error. Whenever modern technique succeeds in replacing a raw material hitherto used by a synthetic article which is at least not less efficient, and regard being had to its efficiency not more expensive than the natural product, it is obvious that the new article more or less drives the old article off the market. In this way madder was replaced by aniline. In this way silk and cotton have lost

2 [Bear in mind that this paper was written in 1938 and that the World War that Mises refers to here and throughout this piece is World War I. — Ed.]
3 [The Covenant was a short concise document of twenty-six articles stating the purpose and intentions of the League of Nations. Article 16 said that all members promised to join in common action against any other which made war in violation of the Covenant; i.e., the breaking off of all economic transactions and other benefits with the Covenant-breaking state, and, if this were not successful, then of military action. This article also empowered the League's council to expel any member violating the Covenant. — Ed.]

ground to artificial silk. Under such conditions the new article can no longer be called a substitute in the same way as a motor-car is not a substitute for a carriage, or a gun not a substitute for a bow and arrow. But this is not the problem we have to deal with. The substitutes under consideration are poor substitutes and do not render better and cheaper services than the commodity they have to replace but are less efficient and more expensive. In the endeavors to find such substitutes one may one day invent something new which will give more satisfaction than the materials now in use. But for the moment we have not to reckon with vague expectations but with the present situation. We have to face the fact that nations wish to attain self-sufficiency by replacing some imported raw materials and foodstuffs by a home production which brings them a more expensive and less efficient substitute than the material they wish to avoid importing. But they believe that these disadvantages are compensated by the fact that the country becomes independent of foreign supply and will therefore not suffer from its lack in wartime. They think that if problems of national defense occur, cost of production is negligible. What counts is only independence.

But this reasoning is fallacious. It is not true that it does not play any role whether the production of a material wanted for war-making is more or less expensive. Higher costs of production mean that the same amount of capital and labor produces less. If a belligerent country has to employ more capital and labor to obtain a given quantity of material they will not be so well supplied as their adversaries. Especially the fact that they will have to employ more hands for the production of the same amount of goods is a calamity. Those surplus hands will be lacking in the trenches, as men cannot fight and work at the same time. Already in the World War it was felt as a hindrance by the Central Powers that the production of war equipment absorbed too many younger men.

Then there is a second great inconvenience. The substitutes are less suitable than the materials they have to replace. If they were not less suitable they would not be succedanea but the right material, and the adversary too would use them. The fact that one party is forced to use less appropriate material is a heavy handicap. The better equipped party will reap from its better equipment both a moral and a material advantage. It demoralizes even the best army to realize that their adversaries are better fed, better armed, and better protected against every evil than they themselves. Nothing in the World War discouraged the soldiers of the Central Powers so much as when, capturing trenches of the Allies, they discovered that their adversaries were better armed, equipped, and fed than they were. Nobody can deny that the victory of the Allies was to a great extent due to the superiority of their material.

Then there is to consider that for the production of the substitutes some raw materials too are required. In very rare cases only these raw materials are available in the home market in sufficient quantities. Mostly they too have to be imported, because they are not produced at all in the country, or not in sufficient quantity. For the production of the textile by which Germany wishes to replace cloth, wool is wanted also, and it is doubtful whether it may be possible to expand the German wool production to such a degree that it could produce the whole quantity needed. In any case, the expansion of the wool production can only be effected by restricting other agricultural production, as it requires soil which is scarce in Germany. If Germany and Italy try to produce substitutes out of wood, they have to face the fact that their wood production does not suffice. When Italy under the sanctions planned to produce cloth from dairy produce, it had to face the fact that its milk production too was limited and could not be expanded except by the use of imported fodder. The production of substitutes does not do away with the problem of raw materials; it merely shifts it to other branches of production.

It is the economic characteristic of the modern industrial communities that they cannot do without the import of raw materials which they buy by exporting manufactured goods. These modern industrial countries are thus in relation to the rest of the world in the same position as the centers of industry are in relation to the agricultural and raw material producing districts of their own country. Just as it is impossible for a town to wage a war against the country district which supplies it with food and raw materials, so it is impossible for an industrial country to wage a war against the rest of the world. This is the situation in which the industrial countries of Europe are today.

The Liberal economist deduces from this fact the necessity of international peace. He is of the opinion that war is incompatible with the present state of international division of labor. But the militarist, who considers war-making as the highest and noblest activity of a nation, believes that this international division of labor imposes slavery on his nation by preventing it from making war. His idea of independence is to attain a state of things for his country in which it could wage war against all other nations or against a group of nations without being dependent on foreign countries for supplies. Both Germany and Italy wish to be able to withstand a war against France and nations allied to France without suffering from the lack of a supply of food and raw material. This does not mean that they really wish to attack France or that they think that France will attack them. We have not to discuss this problem. But they consider a state of things in which they are unable to have recourse to war as *ultima ratio* as an unbearable handicap. Freedom as they understand it is the readiness to go to war when the national leader thinks it necessary.

It is obvious that this conception of freedom is limited to big nations only. A small nation could never dare to formulate its claim for independence in this way. Hitler and Mussolini emphasize that their revendication is justified, because a big nation cannot live in conditions which may content a smaller one. They demand territories where they may produce raw materials on their own soil, and when they declare that their nations are not satisfied they bear out this statement by demonstrating the unfair distribution of colonies and raw materials. It is especially in respect of coming negotiations concerning a redistribution of raw materials and colonies that they wish to be provided with self-sufficiency because they wish to throw the sharpened sword into the scale.

Now we may better understand the role played by self-sufficiency in the plans of these two Powers. They do not consider self-sufficiency of their nation within the actual boundaries of the national territory as a lasting but only as a temporary provision for the preparation of the coming war for supremacy. This is the war frequently alluded to by Hitler in his book *Mein Kampf.*[4]

Of course, the policy of self-sufficiency does not seem any more reasonable if considered as a preparation for the next war only than if considered as a lasting military institution.

Some military experts consider the coming war as absolutely different from the past World War. They assume that the aggressor will succeed very quickly if he attacks unexpectedly a country which is not aware of this danger and is therefore not prepared to resist. With one stroke such an "Überfallskrieg" could bring the deciding victory. But

4 Cf. Adolf Hitler, *Mein Kampf,* 42nd ed. (Munich: F. Eher Nachtfolger, 1933), pp.726–43, 757, and 766.

whether such a surprise attack would be more successful in a coming war than it was in past wars is very doubtful. The sudden attack overthrew Saxony in 1756, and Belgium in 1914, but in both cases it neither decided nor ended the struggle, but on the contrary it kindled it only. There is no reason to think that it would be different in a hypothetical new world war. On the other hand, in a war in which the aggressor puts all his trust in a rapid success of his attack, the superiority of his equipment and armament plays a still greater role than in any other war-making. For the success of such a plan inferior quality of the arms due to the use of substitutes for the proper materials may prove fatal.

From the military point of view the substitution of succedanea for the proper raw materials seems therefore in every respect unfavorable. When the Central Powers went to war in 1914 without having made any provisions for the supply of foreign raw materials, they could rely on the great stores of those goods which represented the normal stocks of business. These stocks were sufficient for the needs of the first two years of the War. The result of the policy of self-sufficiency and economic preparation for war will be that in a new campaign such stores will hardly exist.

It is the paradox of self-sufficiency as economic preparation for war that it weakens the military potential of the nation by rendering its arms less efficient. The present state of international division of labor puts to every nation which ventures to wage war a dilemma to which there is no solution. They have to face on the one hand the fact that they cannot fight without a continuous import of raw materials and food, and on the other hand the fact that the replacement of these imported goods by home production of substitutes diminishes their military force.

In time of peace every nation can buy all the raw materials and foodstuffs it requires and is ready to pay for. Of course, this makes the nation depend on foreign supplies and involves it in the international division of labor. But to consider this as a drawback because it renders warmaking impossible is an atavistic view.

III   The War Argument in Neutral Countries

There are fortunate countries which have decided to remain neutral in all wars. For such a country the war argument for self-sufficiency as advanced by the militarists is nil. They do not intend to make conquests and they wish nothing but to live in peace and to have business always undisturbed. But even if they succeed in this policy and if they continue to be a peaceful island in an ocean of blood, they may suffer from the consequences of war. Typical in this respect was Switzerland's situation during the World War. Its supply of imported foodstuffs and raw materials was at the mercy of the belligerents. But for the agreements with the belligerents, the Swiss would have had neither fuel nor food and would have starved.

In such a country a policy in favor of self-sufficiency to provide for the dangers of a new world war seems more reasonable than for countries which wish to attack. The Swiss Confederation cannot hinder its neighbors from going to war. It has simply to protect its own interests. This includes not only armaments, but also provisions for the feeding in wartime. Many measures of the Swiss economic policy which should be regarded as completely unsound in a peaceful and reasonable world are justified by the international situation which the nation has to face. The conditions for some other nations are not very different, although none of the others is in such an unhappy geographical position as Switzerland.

The trend for self-sufficiency is in these cases too the consequence of the warlike spirit which is now infecting the world. The menace of coming wars endangers the maintenance of the international division of labor and every government, even the most peaceful and internationally minded, has to provide for the event.

IV   The Wages Argument

It is one of the effects of the international division of labor that it creates an interdependency of wages all over the world.

With perfect mobility of labor, capital, and commodities all over the earth's surface there would be a tendency for an equalization both in the rate of profit and in wages for labor of the same kind. Capital and labor would be shifted from the areas where the natural conditions of production are less favorable to areas where they are more favorable until this equalization has been reached. Under the actual state of things where there are very effective institutional barriers against the transfer both of capital and labor from country to country, there exist conspicuous differences in the rate of profit and in the level of wages. But the interdependency of both is nevertheless a fact.

One of the factors determining wages in Japan is the circumstance that the Japanese are not free to emigrate, because no country tolerates such an immigration. One of the factors determining wages in the United States is the fact that immigration to that country is restricted. Labor is not free to move from Japan to the United States. But there is nevertheless a connection between the heights of wages in both countries. This connection is effected by the movability of the produce of labor. The commodities produced by either nation enter into competition. In a world of free trade for commodities they would have to be sold at the same price notwithstanding the allowance made for transport. The faculty of a country's trade unions to raise the level of wages seems therefore limited by the competition of goods produced abroad by cheaper labor. The trade unions of the countries with more-favorable conditions for production and higher wages would like to see the wages in the less-favored countries rise. But that could not be attained otherwise than by shifting hands from the less-favored to the more-favored countries. It is precisely this that the trade unions of the better-endowed countries wish to avoid. But without a change in the distribution of workers over the earth's surface equality of wages is impossible.

Under the existing system of immigration restrictions equilibrium wages are different from the level they would attain in a world where labor is free to migrate; they are higher in some countries and lower in others. But there is for every area, within which there are no barriers for the transfer of labor from one place to another, a uniform equilibrium rate of wages for every kind of labor. As long as effective wages do not exceed this equilibrium level, employment and unemployment are normal. It is in the nature of the equilibrium rate to make supply and demand on the labor market coincide.

If the trade unions of the countries endowed with more-favorable conditions for production were to limit their activities to checking immigration, and if they were satisfied with the rise of equilibrium wages due to these restrictions, they would not increase unemployment figures. But if the trade unions try, as they really do, to raise the wages above this equilibrium rate, they bring about lasting unemployment of a great part of the working class. Of course this is in a market economy the unavoidable consequence of a wage rate exceeding the equilibrium rate.

Entrepreneurs ascribe their inability to employ more hands at the rates fixed by collective bargaining to the pressure of foreign competition. Public opinion therefore considers barriers erected against imports from abroad as an effective measure of fighting unemployment without lowering the level of wages. One of the most popular arguments in favor of protection is to defend the national standard of living against the dumping of goods produced by cheap labor.

Now people call dumping, the import of goods produced by cheap labor and regard the exclusion of such goods as quite justified. That means for the countries which on the one hand are endowed by nature and by the plenitude of their capital with the most favorable conditions for production, and on the other hand keep out foreign immigrants, that they consider high import duties, quotas, and even complete self-sufficiency as justified.

If a country neither tolerates the immigration of labor, nor the imports of goods produced abroad by cheap labor, nor the export of capital, it is on the way to complete economic isolation.

The Anglo-Saxon and some other Western countries are doubly responsible for the low rate of wages and for the low standard of living in the over-populated areas: first, by making immigration practically impossible, and secondly, by fighting the import of manufactured goods. In their endeavor to maintain their own higher standard of living they exert a pressure on the standard of living in other countries, especially in Central, Eastern, and Southern Europe, and in Japan. They reduce their imports of manufactured goods but at the same time increase their exports of food, raw materials, and manufactured goods; the consequence is a fall in the total volume of international trade.

The trend to make trade barriers more effective and to isolate the countries economically more and more is therefore an outcome of a policy which wishes to fight unemployment by protection for home production. The idea underlying this policy is misleading. The low wages abroad become still lower, and the country's own selling abroad decreases in the same proportion as imports are reduced.

It is hopeless to try to do away with unemployment by a policy of trade barriers. That wages higher than the equilibrium rate can only be maintained when a considerable part of the labor supply is unemployed is for an isolated country no less the case than for a country buying and selling abroad. It is a fallacy to think that in the long run unemployment can be caused by foreign competition. Foreign competition, or more correctly the fact that the home market forms a part only of the international market, is one of the factors determining the height of the equilibrium wage rate. At the equilibrium wage rate, unemployment is only a transitory phenomenon. Foreign competition may make equilibrium wages lower but cannot directly cause lasting large-scale unemployment.

If a country tries to keep out the influence of the foreign labor markets from its home market, it has to withdraw from the international division of labor. But then it deprives its people of all the advantages of international economic cooperation. That means that in the long run, commodity wages have to go down. The policy of economic isolation is in no way the right means of improving a nation's standard of living.

V   The Over-Population Argument

The over-population argument for protection is nothing but the wages argument as seen from the point of view of the over-populated countries. In these countries wages are low, and there is under the present conditions of migration barriers no hope of making the wages higher by emigration.

Equilibrium wages are low in these countries. But as long as actual wages do not exceed the equilibrium rate, there is no lasting large-scale unemployment. Equilibrium wages of course may fall extremely low as compared with foreign wages.

Low wages are very unsatisfactory, and both governments and trade unions are in search of a remedy. Unfortunately, the only effective remedy—emigration—cannot be taken into consideration. Minimum wages, whether imposed by government interference or by collective bargaining, only increase unemployment. To fight unemployment an effort is then made to protect home production. But this raises commodity prices and lowers the standard of living still more.

The recriminations of the over-populated countries against the more fortunate countries are justified. The countries where equilibrium wages are higher harm them in a twofold way: by making immigration impossible and by closing their markets to the import of their produce. Nevertheless, these over-populated countries themselves make their own conditions only worse by closing themselves to their own markets. In doing so they effect nothing else than a further lowering of their standard of living.[5]

5 [Cf. Ludwig von Mises, "The Freedom to Move as an International Problem" [1935], in *The Clash of Group Interests and Other Essays*, Richard M. Ebeling, ed. (New York: Center for Libertarian Studies, 1978), pp. 11–20.—Ed.]

In this case, too, protection and self-sufficiency are remedies that only increase the evil.

VI   The Monetary or Foreign Exchange Argument

The monetary or foreign exchange argument in favor of protection differs from most other arguments in that it is purely economic. Unfortunately, it is like the other arguments a fallacious one.

The maintenance of a sound currency has nothing to do with foreign trade. It is the old and fundamental error of all types of Mercantilism that an unfavorable balance of trade drives money out of the country. But the balance of trade is one item only in the balance of payments. An excess of imports over exports is compensated or over-compensated by assets from other items. The balance of payments always balances. If both sides of the balance of payments equalize only by an export of gold, prices have to fall. The low prices increase exports and check imports. In countries where the currency is not purely metallic, the outflow of gold forces the Bank to restrict credit. Then the adjustment is effected by the inflow of foreign short-term loans attracted by the higher rate of interest. Thus, under both conditions, the equilibrium is re-established automatically. In the long run a country which has not embarked on inflation and credit expansion can never be in danger of seeing its monetary stocks go out of the country. On the contrary, if there is inflation and if as a consequence of the excess of currency prices rise and the national monetary unit depreciates, nothing can prevent the working of the mechanism described by Gresham's law. If the government attributes the same legal tender quality to the depreciated paper money as to the gold coins the latter disappear from circulation. As under the conditions of inflation and credit expansion the automatic readjustment cannot take place, the gold standard is replaced by a paper currency, which depreciates more and more with the advance of inflation.

It is in vain that governments try to stop the course of depreciation by restricting imports. If the government prevents the citizens from buying foreign goods they will buy more home products. The price of these home products will then go up and their export will decrease. Thus the interference of the government, which is directed to an improvement of the balance of trade by restricting imports, results in bringing down both sides of the balance. It cuts simultaneously both imports and exports. The effect is a reduction in the total volume of foreign trade.

If the government wishes to succeed in its policy it would have to take away from the hands of the citizens the excess of their cash holdings. The government would have to tax the citizens or to issue a loan on the home market and then to withdraw from circulation the money received. This means a policy of deflation. Of course deflation is the only efficacious means of bringing down the rate of foreign exchange and of re-establishing the former purchasing power of the monetary unit. But if the government does not wish to deflate, it has no means of reducing the prices paid for foreign exchange.

The foreign exchange regulations as they exist in many countries are of two different types. There are countries which wish to maintain simply the market rates of the foreign exchanges. They believe that something should be done to prevent a further depreciation and that foreign exchange regulation is the right way. But they do not intend to force the citizens to buy and sell foreign exchange at a price lower than the market price. Under such conditions the effects of foreign exchange regulations are not very harmful. As there are no endeavors to impose on the market a lower price for foreign exchange, as foreign exchange is bought and sold at the market price, it does not matter whether the dealings are free, or the privilege of an institution like the Central Bank, or a Foreign Exchange Equalization Account. Of course, if the government or this institution for the management of foreign exchange dealings hinders some imports for the sake of economizing foreign exchange, it restricts imports too and thereby the volume of foreign trade. But there is under these conditions no urgent cause to take very drastic measures in this respect, as the foreign exchange regulations do not directly restrict the available amount of foreign exchange.

It is different, where the aim of the foreign exchange regulations is to impose on the market a lower price for foreign exchange than that which would be formed on a free market. If every citizen is bound to sell all foreign exchange to the Exchange Equalization Account at this legal or official price, which is lower than the market price, things are exactly the same as if there were a duty on exports. The amount of exports falls, and therefore the amount of foreign exchange offered to and bought by the Exchange Equalization Account. A scarcity of foreign exchange is the unavoidable consequence of a policy which imposes on the market too low a price for gold and foreign currency. The more these regulations are enforced, the greater the scarcity becomes. Exports would cease completely but for export premiums paid by the government to compensate losses which the exporter suffers by the compulsion to sell the foreign exchange at a price below the market value.

If a country which has adopted this regime complains of a shortage of foreign exchange it has to realize that the evil is due to its own policy only. But for the consequences of foreign exchange regulations, there is no difference for the citizens whether they buy home or foreign produce. There is no such thing as a problem of transfer. Whether a German wishes to buy cotton or some home produce, let us say coal, does not make any difference either for him or for the country's monetary system. In both cases he has to abstain from buying something else. He has to spend fewer Marks for other purposes than he would have done if he had not bought the cotton or the coal. The problem is whether he is rich enough to buy cotton or coal, whether he disposes of the amount of Marks necessary. If he buys more imported goods he has to abstain from buying home-made goods. These goods therefore then become cheaper and can more easily be exported, thus compensating the outflow of money by an inflow. If for some reason exports cannot be expanded, the greater demand for foreign exchange makes the prices of foreign exchange and therefore those of the imported goods rise, and this upward movement of prices forces the citizens to restrict their buying of imported goods. Here too the automatism of the market works smoothly.

Let us assume that by a redistribution of the areas producing raw materials some part of Australia and of the South of the United States became German possessions. Nothing in the economic and monetary sphere would be changed by such an arrangement. The German consumer would have to pay just the same for cotton and wool as he has to pay now. It would not be easier for him or more difficult for the British or the Americans to buy in these newly ceded territories. Of course, under present conditions too, trade between Great Britain and Australia is not conducted in any other way than the trade between Great Britain and Germany, or between Germany and Australia. It is not any advantage for the British buyer of wool that his King is at the same time the ruler of Australia, or that the citizens of Australia speak English and are the offspring of British ancestors. The German buyer on the wool market competes under equal conditions with the British or Danish or Polish buyer.

Let us, on the other hand, assume that Bavaria were separated from the Reich. But for government interference in the currency system and for foreign exchange regulations, the trade between Bavaria and the rest of the Reich could not be affected by such a change. What Saxonians buy in Bavaria has to be paid either by direct exports or by triangular trade, whether Bavaria is a part of the Reich or not.

It is misleading to think that the buying of imported goods absorbs a quantity out of the Devisen-stock [foreign exchange] of the nation. It is an error to say to a man: you must not buy this foreign commodity because for this purchase a part of the nation's hoard of foreign exchange is wanted. There is no such thing as a fund of foreign exchange. Foreign exchange holdings are in a continuous flux and reflux; they are daily filled up and daily depleted. In buying foreign goods the consumer creates at the same time, by reducing his buying at home, the amount of foreign exchange necessary for his buying.

The fact that there are trade barriers does not alter the working of this mechanism. Trade barriers of course make it more difficult to export and to get foreign exchange. But the fall in exports and in the inflow of foreign exchange automatically leads to a restriction of buying abroad. When prices, wages, and profits in the export industries fall, the groups affected have to reduce either their buying of foreign goods or their buying of home-produced goods. In the first case the demand for foreign exchange falls; in the second case the prices of these goods sold on the home market in lesser quantities fall, and it is easier to export them.

If a country wishes to enjoy the advantages of a sound currency and stability of foreign exchanges, it has but to avoid inflation and credit expansion. If it prefers the pretended advantages of depreciation, then it has to let the market fix the value of its currency unit. In both cases it would not find any monetary difficulty in dealing with foreign countries. It is but the aim to fix foreign exchanges below the market price by means of foreign exchange regulations which creates the shortage of foreign exchange.

Germany's position in the world's economic system, like the position of many other European nations, was and is based on industry. They import mostly raw materials and food and export mostly manufactured products. By restricting the purchases of raw materials, the German government restricts the exports of manufactured goods too. By using the imported raw materials for rearmament purposes instead of the production in the exporting plants, it reduces the amount of foreign exchange available. But Germany is only the most outstanding case of a policy followed today by many other countries too.

In an economic system based on barter and direct exchange between two parties only, nobody would doubt that satisfaction is given to both parties. The function of money is to provide the same facilities in triangular trade. This clearing function of money is not limited to local trade only; it works in the same way in inter-local, inter-regional, and international trade. The most efficient clearing system and the most simple too is the monetary system. If a nation replaces the use of money in international trade by bilateral clearings, it deprives itself of the advantages of triangular trade. It loses thereby the faculty of buying on the cheapest market and of selling where it may obtain the highest prices. It has to buy notwithstanding the height of the prices where it has something to sell, and it has to sell notwithstanding the low level of prices where it wishes to buy something.

The gold standard was and is still the best and even the only practical solution to an international organization of triangular trade. That it no longer works is not due to inherent defects or to a change in the conditions it presupposes. It is simply the consequence of the fact that governments no longer wish to let its mechanism work. They combat the international division of labor, and they therefore intend to destroy the most important tool of international trade. It is not the breakdown of the gold standard, and it is not the unsatisfactory state of the world's monetary system which necessitate a policy of trade restrictions for monetary reasons. On the contrary. The gold standard and the world's monetary system collapsed because the governments destroyed them purposely for the sake of doing away with international trade.

VII   Protection from the Point of View of Home Policy

The nations went in for protection because they believed that in trade the national interests were in conflict with the interests of other nations and that it was therefore necessary to protect the home market against foreign commodities. But even if these erroneous considerations of national interests as contrasted with the international point of view had not worked, considerations of home policy only would have brought about the same effect.

In many countries of the world today it is commonly assumed that it is the duty of the State to protect the less efficient producer against the competition of the more efficient. In this way the government prevents the more efficient producer from using his full superiority. It restricts the sphere of action of big stores for the benefit of the shopkeepers. It forces upon a whole industry a proportional reduction of output instead of letting the market eliminate the marginal producers. It makes it more difficult for the motor-car to compete with the railway. It tries to create by interference a better marketing for commodities which are produced in greater quantities than public demand.

The strong governments of the authoritarian States, who emphasize their mission to lead and not to be led and to force their subjects to obey their orders, act under the rule of the theories of government interference and interventionism not differently than the democratic governments whom they reproach with their weakness. Every government, whether parliamentary or dictatorial, is today ready to interfere for the particular interests of groups on whom they wish to rely. Even small groups are sometimes considered as very important for the political concept of the ruler, whether he is democratic or dictatorial. The case of silver in the United States is an excellent example of how a special strategic position may even to a small group give the possibility of influencing a big country's policy. In a similar way, in every country small groups of entrepreneurs and trade union members back particular measures of protection and restriction.

It seems to our contemporaries justified that our fellow citizens who find it difficult to stand foreign competition should be protected. It is the belief that a government which did not try to help a less efficient producer would neglect its first duty.

But it would be too simple an explanation to say that at the bottom of protection is the selfishness of particular interests as contrasted with the general interest. These particular interests are always the interests of minority groups. The producers—both entrepreneurs and workers—of every single commodity are always a minority if compared with the bulk of the consumers. They succeed in getting their particular interests protected against the greater interest of the majority only because they are supported by public opinion, which considers such protection as beneficial for the nation. A hundred years ago the coachmen and the postilions did not find protection against the overwhelming competition of the steam engine and the railway, because in those days the Liberal spirit was opposed to privilege which benefited a small group to the disadvantage of the public. Today, the claim of the railways for safeguard against the motor-car seems justified to the legislator. Today every particular interest is sure to find support in public opinion. It is this attitude of public opinion which is responsible for the privileges and not the desire of those who wish to enjoy a privilege. Seen from the point of view of home policy, protection is but a category of measures in the system of government interference.

VIII   The International Conflict of Economic Interests

In our world of migration barriers there are very grave conflicts of economic interests between nations. In restricting immigration figures some nations succeed in making wages for their citizens higher, but only at the expense of the citizens of other nations. The international clash of economic interests is due to this fact. There are no serious conflicts about raw materials or colonies in a world of peace and peaceful trade, where everybody has the right to buy on the same terms as everybody else. But there is a conflict when the citizens of some countries of Europe and Asia are prevented from moving to the countries where they may earn more than in their own country. The high standard of living in the United States and in the British Dominions has its corollary in the low standard of living in Eastern, Central, and Southern Europe, in India, China, and Japan.

The people of the United States and the British Dominions defend their higher standard by closing their doors to newcomers. The result is that within their boundaries many millions of acres lie barren, whereas much poorer soil in other countries has to be cultivated. Any account of the world's present economic and political situation which does not stress this fact is inadequate.

There are three reasons why this vital problem is generally overlooked in present public discussion. First of all, our economic and political considerations are prejudiced by the Marxian doctrine. According to Marxism, the interests of the proletarians all over the world are identical. The conflicts between nations and States are only the outcome of the prevailing particular class interests of the bourgeoisie. Nationalism, hatred between nations, and imperialistic and militaristic tendencies in international relations are peculiar to the rule of capitalists. A world of popular regime would be peaceful and adverse to international conflict. The proletarians are all brothers and friends. Biased by this dogma, the Marxians ignore that the poverty of the great mass of the proletarians in Europe and Asia, which they deplore, is due to the fact that they have to dwell, live, and work in areas where the natural conditions of production are less favorable because the proletarians of better-blessed areas refuse them the right to enter their countries. A consistent application of the Marxian "superstructure" theory would have to say: the proletarians of Europe and Asia are exploited by the proletarians of the New World; modern imperialism and militarism are the "superstructure" of the conflict of economic interests between the proletarians of the more-favored with those of the less-favored nations. But the Marxians intentionally keep silent over these conflicts. It is very characteristic how scarce the writings about the migration restrictions are when compared with the abundance of publications on all other measures of present economic policy. It is even more characteristic how eager the Marxians are to develop highly artificial and futile hypotheses to explain imperialism out of alleged difficulties of the capitalist order.

Nor are the opponents of Marxism on our political stage, the fascists and nationalists, more ready to discuss the migration barriers. Their philosophy is against emigration. They want all their men for the coming war. They wish to conquer the richer countries and to annex them; they do not wish to send their sons as emigrants to foreign lands. Their remedy for the *Volke ohne Raum* (people without room) is conquest. The population pressure in Italy, highly aggravated by the post-war migration checks, does not make Mussolini criticize the policy of the countries not allowing Italian immigration. On the list of his grievances no mention is made of immigration barriers. On the contrary, desirous of increasing his military strength, he himself is against emigration and wishes to raise the birthrate.

There is still a third reason for the underrating of the importance of the migration barriers. The most eminent upholders of international mind today are the intellectuals of the English-speaking nations. Without their noble attitude the case for peace and international collaboration would be hopeless. But these intellectuals sympathize with trade unions, which in the English-speaking countries are the champions of immigration barriers.

The drawbacks of the immigration barriers are further increased by the obstacles raised against the transfer of capital. It is difficult to decide whether it was more the policy of the debtor countries or the policy of the creditor countries which was responsible for the abolition of the movability of capital. The countries which had imported capital destroyed the internationality of capital transactions by open repudiations and by foreign exchange regulations. But the capital-exporting countries too had their share in limiting the outflow of capital. The result is that the populations, which by the immigration restrictions are forced to work in areas where the natural conditions for production are less favorable and where in consequence wages have to be low, find their existence made even worse by a shortage of capital, which lowers the marginal productivity of labor and thereby wages still more.

It may seem striking that public opinion is more concerned today with the apparent problem of raw materials and does not deal with the most serious problem of contemporary international relations: with the problem of the movability of labor.

But whether we consider the raw material question or the migration question as the crucial point of internationalism, in any case we have to realize that neither the suppression of international trade nor war can be considered as appropriate remedies. Even a nation handicapped by the poverty of its territory, which cannot yield enough raw materials, and whose citizens are prevented from emigrating cannot draw any advantage from protection. It is noteworthy to realize that Ricardo's irrefutable proof of the superiority of free trade policy is precisely based on an argumentation which assumes that capital and labor do not move freely from country to country as they do within a country. This assumption of the immovability of capital and labor was true for the days of Ricardo. It was not true for the late nineteenth century and for the beginning of the twentieth century; it is true again for our days. It is therefore a mistake to say that Ricardo's arguments are no longer valid for our days as conditions have changed. On the contrary, conditions are again the same.

But neither is war a solution for the present conflicts. Given the geographical and political conditions of our world, it seems hopeless for the over-populated European countries to force by war upon the countries closed to immigration a change in their policy. That is why Hitler in *Mein Kampf* does not propose as the goal of German policy the conquest of overseas territories, but only of European territories. But these European neighboring countries of Germany, apart from the fact that they are already now over-crowded, could not give the German emigrant what he wants.

It would be ostrich policy to deny the existence of very grave con-

flicts between the nations of our world. But we have to realize that neither war nor protectionism and self-sufficiency can provide a solution
for the problems involved.

Conclusion

Liberalism is a philosophy of peace and international cooperation. It
is the basic point of its social and economic theory that, rightly conceived, the interests of all individuals and of all nations are harmonious in a society of private ownership and free trade. For the Liberal,
democracy and peace are the outcome of his ideas on life, work, and
human cooperation.

But Liberalism is for the time being the privilege of a small and uninfluential minority. The world is ruled by other ideas. These ideas lead
to armaments and to protectionism, to barriers against the movability
of commodities, labor and capital, to militarism, and to dictatorship.

It is a mistake to assume that as long as such conceptions prevail
any endeavors to lower the obstacles to international trade could be
successful. If the theories in favor of protection and self-sufficiency are
considered as right, then there is no reason to bring down trade barriers; only the conviction that these theories are wrong and that free
trade is the best policy can shake them. It is inconsistent to support a
policy of *low* trade barriers. Either trade barriers are useful—then they
cannot be high enough; or they are harmful—then they have to disappear completely. The pre-war policy of moderate protectionism was
the result of a labile equilibrium between two conflicting theories; now
when the theory of protectionism has driven the theory of free trade off
the field of public opinion there is no more limit to trade barriers.

It is hopeless to expect a change by an international agreement. If a
country thinks that more free trade is to its own advantage, then it may
always open its frontiers. But if it views free trade as a disadvantage to
its own interests it will not be more willing to grant it in an international treaty. Every nation is today anxious to expand the volume of
exports, but no nation is prepared to sacrifice the particular interests of
an existing industry or even of an industry which has still to be created.
It is this tendency that is continually reducing the volume of international trade.

The poor results obtained by the League of Nations and the failure
of the World Economic Conferences and of the more special confer-

ences and negotiations between smaller groups of nations are due to the fact that the world lacks today the mentality of peaceful cooperation. Under the rule of militarist ideas the efforts at international collaboration are doomed.

What the world needs is not more conferences and conventions but a radical change of mentality.

CHAPTER 10

Autarky and Its Consequences

I Terminological Remarks

There is considerable ambiguity concerning the terminology to be used in dealing with the problems of international economic relations. It seems therefore expedient to start with a clear definition of some terms.

Chauvinism is the overvaluation of one's own nation's achievements and qualities and the disparagement of the other nation's. As such it does not result in any political action.

Patriotism is the zeal for one's own nation's welfare, flowering, and freedom. But the patriots disagree with regard to the means to be applied for the attainment of this end.

The *free traders* (liberals in the old sense attached to the term liberalism, today mostly disparaged by the self-styled "progressives" as orthodox, reactionaries or economic royalists, as Manchestermen[1] or as supporters of laissez faire) want to make their own nation prosperous by free trade and by its peaceful incorporation into the world-embracing commonwealth of the international division of labor. They recommend free trade not for the sake of other nations, but from the viewpoint of the rightly understood or long-term interests of their own nation. They are convinced that even if all other nations cling to protection, a nation best serves its own welfare by free trade.

The *nationalists*, on the contrary, believe that a nation cannot further its own well-being but by inflicting harm upon other nations. *Aggressive* or *militaristic nationalism* aims at conquest and at the subjugation of other nations by arms. *Economic nationalism* aims at furthering

[Previously unpublished manuscript, dated May 5, 1943. —Ed.]
1 [The Manchestermen, along with the British liberals of the nineteenth century, thought that the best way to insure peace was by an unlimited laissez-faire economy. Free trade was both domestically and internationally a necessary prerequisite to preserve a lasting peace. —Ed.]

the well-being of one's own nation or of some of its groups through inflicting harm upon foreigners by economic measures, for instance: trade and migration barriers, expropriation of foreign investments, repudiation of foreign debts, currency devaluation, and foreign exchange control.

Economic nationalism results in war if some nations believe that they are powerful enough to brush away, by military action, the measures of foreign countries which they consider as detrimental to their own interests.

The free traders want to make peace durable by the elimination of the root causes of conflict. If everybody is free to live and to work where he wants; if there are no barriers for the mobility of labor, capital, and commodities; and if the administration, the laws, and the courts do not discriminate between citizens and foreigners, the individual citizens are not interested in the question where the political frontiers are drawn and whether their own country is bigger or smaller. They cannot derive any profit from the conquest of a province. In such an ideal—Jeffersonian—world of democracy and free trade war does not pay.

The nationalists, on the contrary, assert that peace itself is an evil and that war is, as the English writer John Ruskin said, "the foundation of the arts and of all the high virtues and faculties of man." Consequently the Nazis considered it as the most desirable state for a nation "to be always at war," and Mussolini exalted "the dangerous life." The Japanese clung to the same tenets.

Pacifism is the belief that all that is required for the abolition of war is the building up of an international organization and the establishment of an international world court whose rulings should be enforced by a world police force.

The noble-minded founders of the League of Nations were guided by this type of pacifism. They were right in their idea that autocratic governments are warlike, while democratic nations cannot derive any profit from conquest and therefore cling to peace. But what President Wilson and his collaborators did not see was that this is valid only within a system of private ownership of the means of production, free enterprise, and unhampered market economy. Where there is no economic freedom things are entirely different. In our age of statism and socialism, in which every nation is eager to insulate itself and to strive toward autarky it is quite wrong to assert that no man can derive any gain from conquest. Every citizen has a material interest in the nullification of measures by which foreign governments injure his economic interests.

Autarky, or *economic self-sufficiency,* is a state of affairs where there is no foreign trade at all; every nation consumes only goods produced within its own borders. No contemporary nation is ready to admit openly that it strives toward autarky. But as every nation is anxious to restrict imports and as exports must needs fall concomitantly, we can characterize the economic policies of the last decade preceding the present war as autarkic.

II The Rise of Modern Protectionism

In the 'sixties of the nineteenth century, public opinion was almost unanimous in the assumption that the world was on the eve of an age of everlasting free trade and peace. True, there was only one big nation which had unconditionally espoused the principle of free trade: Great Britain. But there seemed to prevail a general tendency all over Europe toward a step-by-step abolition of trade barriers. Every new commercial treaty between civilized and politically advanced nations brought a reduction in tariffs and included the most favored nation clause. The teachings of Ricardo and John Stuart Mill, of Cobden and Bastiat, met with general approval. People were optimistic enough to expect that trade barriers and war were doomed to disappear with other remnants of the dark ages like despotism, intolerance, slavery and serfdom, superstition, and torture.

However, the greater part of the world still had tariffs. There were two groups of protectionist countries.

There were, on the one hand, the countries of the European continent which had long since embarked upon a Mercantilist[2] policy of protection. People were convinced that these nations would soon learn that protectionism does not further but seriously checks their own material well-being and would turn to free trade.

There were, on the other hand, the former colonies, the countries peopled by the descendants of European settlers. These countries had in earlier days considered import duties as the most expedient means

---

2 [The seventeenth-century Mercantilists thought that hoarding precious metals was the best way to accumulate wealth. They advocated political intervention in foreign trade to increase exports — to bring money (metals) into the country—while hampering imports. They called this form of hoarding a favorable balance of payments. — Ed.]

for taxing their citizens. Their tariffs had originally only fiscal purposes. With the progressive evolution of economic civilization and the increase of population figures these tariffs changed their character and provided ample protection to the growing domestic industries. In the middle of the nineteenth century they were, especially in the United States, already more effective in this regard than those of the then most protectionist European powers, Austria and Russia. However, the optimists hoped that at least the United States would outgrow what they qualified as the remnants of its colonial past.

The optimists were entirely wrong. The protectionist nations did not abandon protection, but raised their tariffs; furthermore, the free trade countries themselves turned toward protection. Great Britain and Switzerland, once the champions of free trade, are today fanatically devoted to the most radical methods of economic nationalism.

III   Remarks on the Theory of Foreign Trade

The return to protectionism, the progressive aggravation of trade restrictions through the multiplication of import duties and through the application of new methods for prevention of imports, and the evolution of the tariff system into a system under which all kinds of commercial transactions with foreigners (even tourism, the consultation of foreign doctors, and education at foreign schools) require a special license on the part of the authorities—all these are not the outcome of a change in the theory of foreign trade. The desperate attempts of the advocates of protection to refute the statements of the classical economists concerning the consequences of free trade and protection failed lamentably. All they could demonstrate was that under special conditions the interests of some groups of the population can derive temporary benefits from protection. But the economists have never denied this. What they asserted was:

1. If protection is granted to one branch of production or to a few branches only, those privileged are benefited at the expense of the rest of the nation.

2. If protection is granted to the same extent to all branches of domestic production (*"lückenloser Schutz der nationalen Arbeit,"* as the Germans call it), nobody can possibly derive any net profit. What a man profits on the one hand *qua* producer, he loses on the other hand *qua* consumer. Moreover, everybody is hurt by the fact that produc-

tion is diverted from those lines in which its physical productivity is highest; all nations and every individual are injured by the fact that less-favorable conditions of production are exploited, while some more favorable remain unused.

3. It is vain to try to "improve" the balance of trade by import restrictions. But for capital transactions (foreign investments and foreign loans and the payments resulting therefrom), gifts and tributes, the total value of the commodities sold and the services rendered to foreigners exactly equals the value of the goods and services received.

4. The advantage derived from foreign trade lies entirely in importing. The exports are only the payment for the imports. If it were possible to import without exporting at all, the importing country would not suffer, but enjoy prosperity.

It has been asserted again and again that conditions have changed since the days of Ricardo and that his conclusions are no longer valid under present conditions. This, however, is a fallacy too.

Ricardo assumes that there is no mobility of capital and labor, but that on the other hand there is some mobility for commodities. (If there is no mobility at all for commodities either, then every nation lives in perfect autarky and there is no question of any foreign trade.) The conditions assumed by Ricardo changed in the course of the nineteenth century. Millions of workers emigrated from the comparatively over-populated countries and immigrated into the comparatively under-populated countries offering more-favorable conditions for labor and consequently higher wage rates. Today things have changed and the state of affairs is by and large the same as in the time of Ricardo. Migration is almost impossible. The international capital market is disintegrated. The capitalists shun foreign investment because discriminatory taxation, expropriation and confiscation, foreign exchange control and repudiation of debts make them too risky. The governments of those countries whose capitalists could consider foreign investment are ready to put an embargo upon capital export because they view it as contrary to the interests of the most influential domestic pressure groups, labor, and farming.

In a world of perfect mobility of capital, labor, and products there prevails a tendency toward an equalization of the material conditions of all countries. Those parts of the earth's surface which offer more favorable natural conditions of production attract more capital and men than those offering less propitious ones. There are areas more densely populated and areas less densely populated. Freedom of migration and capital transfer tend to make the difference of comparative overpopulation and comparative underpopulation disappear. They tend toward an equalization of wage rates and rates of interest and concomitantly of standards of living.

In a world of immobility of men, some countries are comparatively overpopulated, others comparatively underpopulated. There are conspicuous differences in wage rates and in standards of living. The restrictions imposed upon the mobility of capital intensify this outcome.

Ricardo has demonstrated what the consequences of free trade in such a world are. His law of comparative cost has never been disproved. Even if all other countries cling to protection, every nation best serves its own interests by free trade.

IV Big Business and Protection

For the self-styled "progressives" big business is the scapegoat for all evils. The selfish class interests of the capitalists and entrepreneurs, they say, have pushed the nations toward hyper-protectionism. Modern nationalism is but the ideological disguise of the class interests of the exploiters.

However, big business is not afraid of foreign competition. The American motor-car producers and the German electric companies do not fear that any foreign competitor could supersede them on their domestic market.[3] Neither do they ask for protective duties in those foreign countries into which they want to export; indeed their interests are considerably hurt by the import duties of these countries. If they are not ready to lose these markets, they are forced to build subsidiary plants in protected countries and to produce at a higher cost. Instead of supplying the consumers with merchandise manufactured in big-scale plants located at the sites offering the most advantageous opportunities, they are compelled to produce a good deal of their output in smaller plants located in less appropriate places. But for protectionism it would never have occurred to Mr. Ford to fabricate cars in Canada, in France, in Germany, and in some other countries. The characteristic feature

3 [The reader should keep in mind that these passages were written in 1943. — Ed.]

of present-day big business is that the enterprises own subsidiaries in many countries. They are not interested in the continuation of production of the subsidiaries. They would, in the absence of protection, concentrate their whole production in those plants in which costs are lowest.

If it were true that big business is favored by protection, there would be no protection in this age of violent anti-capitalism. It can hardly be denied that the general trend of the economic policies of all countries in the last decades was to inflict as much harm as possible on big business.

The present structure of business and the location and the size of the single plants are adjusted to the conditions brought about by protectionism. A transition to free trade would cause a general reshuffling, as many plants are now located in places where production costs are so high that they cannot, when unprotected, compete with industries operating in places offering more propitious opportunities. The vested interests of many enterprises are therefore opposed to free trade. But this is not the cause of protection; it is rather its outcome. If there had not been any protection at all, the capitalists would not have invested their funds in places in which profit can only be expected under protection.

While some enterprises are menaced by free trade, the interests of the bulk of industry and of the whole nation are not. On the contrary! Everybody would be benefited if production were discontinued where the physical input needed for the attainment of one unit of output is higher, and were to expand where the input required is lower.

Under free trade for products and capital and under immigration barriers for labor, there would prevail in America a tendency to prefer those branches of manufacturing in which wages form a smaller part of the total costs of production. The country would favor more the expansion of the heavy industries and less those branches which require comparatively more labor. The resulting imports would bring about neither bad business nor unemployment. They would be compensated by an increase in the export of goods which can be produced to the highest advantage in this country. They would raise the standard of living both in America and abroad.

American processing industries do not need any protection. They are, but for some special branches, like Paris dressmaking and English cloth, paramount in the world. Natural conditions of production are extremely favorable in this country, the supply of capital is more abundant than anywhere else, the ingenuity of the entrepreneurs, the efficiency of the inventors and the designers, and the skill of the workers are unsurpassed. The technical equipment of the plants and the methods of business management are unparalleled.

The main argument advanced in favor of American protectionism is the wage-rate argument. The American standard of living, people say, has to be protected against the "dumping" of industries producing at lower labor costs.

Real wages are higher in this country than in almost all other countries because America is comparatively underpopulated, while most of the other countries are comparatively overpopulated. As immigration is restricted, there does not prevail a tendency toward an equalization of wage rates. In those countries in which physical conditions of production are less favorable than in America, wage rates must needs be lower. There would be but one means to raise the extremely low standard of living in China: to let the Chinese freely emigrate to countries in which natural conditions of production are more favorable, capital is more abundant, and population is comparatively less dense.

The comparatively high state of market real wage rates, i.e., wage rates as they would be in the absence of any trade union pressure and compulsion, in this country is not an outcome of protectionism and does not need to be safeguarded by tariffs. The abolition of protection would not lower the American standard of living, but raise it. American processing industries would concentrate their efforts upon those branches in which their superiority is highest. Their products would buy on the world market a greater amount of those products whose production would be discontinued in this country because American superiority is lower in those fields. The total amount of American consumption would increase, not decrease.

Money wage rates may drop. But they would drop less than the prices of consumers' goods, now artificially raised by protection.

V   Protection and Defense

It has been asserted that the nations strive after autarky because they are warlike and want to be independent of foreign supply.

The truth is that Germany strove after autarky and therefore wanted to conquer more *Lebensraum,* i.e., a territory so large and so rich in natural resources that the Germans would live in economic self-sufficiency at a standard not lower than that of any other nation.

Moreover, economic nationalism is not a phenomenon peculiar to aggressive nations. Peace-loving nations are no less imbued by the spirit of economic nationalism than militaristic peoples.

It may be reasonable to explain the protection (operated by a government wheat monopoly) which Switzerland grants to its domestic wheat production as a defense measure. But it is impossible to apply the same explanation to the Swiss import restrictions upon china, glassware, and silver plates. The country applies the quota system to passenger cars although there is no domestic production and no hope that such a production could be bolstered up!

VI Protection and Government Control of Business

A nation's policy forms an integral whole. Foreign policy and domestic policy are closely linked together; they are but one system. Economic nationalism is the corollary of the present-day domestic policies of government interference with business and of national planning as free trade was the complement of domestic economic freedom. There can be protectionism in a country with domestic free trade, but where there is no domestic free trade, protectionism is indispensable. A national government's might is limited to the territory subject to its sovereignty. It does not have the power to interfere directly with conditions abroad. Where there is free trade, foreign competition would in the short run already frustrate the aims sought by the various measures of government intervention with domestic business. When the domestic market is not to some extent insulated from the foreign markets, there can be no question of government control. The farther a nation goes on the way toward public regulation and regimentation, the more it is pushed toward economic isolation.

We do not have to deal with the problem whether economic interventionism, i.e., government interference with business, can attain the ends aimed at by the government and by the "progressives" who endorse this system. Its champions — the German *"Sozialpolitiker,"* the right wing of the British Fabians, the American Institutionalists, the moderates among the New Dealers, and many other groups — have contended that interventionism is feasible and workable as a permanent form of social economic organization. They have claimed that it is as far from socialism as it is from capitalism, that it stands as a third solution of the problem of society's economic organization midway between communism and laissez faire, and that while retaining the advantages of both it avoids the disadvantages inherent in both of them. However, modern economic theory has demonstrated in an irrefutable way that this alleged third method is contrary to purpose, and that the various measures of government interference with business not only do not attain the ends sought but, on the contrary, must needs result in a state of affairs which—from the viewpoint of the government and the supporters of its policy—is even much more unsatisfactory than the conditions which they wanted to alter.

Neither do we have to deal with the lessons to be learned from historical experience. For more than sixty years all governments of civilized nations have experimented with various modes of economic interventionism. The outcome was always the same: manifest failure. The *Sozialpolitik* of the German Reich, inaugurated at the end of the 'seventies of the nineteenth century and solemnly publicized by the old Kaiser's imperial message of November 17, 1881,[4] and the American New Deal are the outstanding examples.

From the viewpoint of the subject with which this paper deals we have to stress another point. Every act of government interference with business raises the domestic costs of production and thus disarranges the conditions for competition. Under free trade it would immediately result in a drop of sales on the part of domestic producers, in restriction of output and in discharging of workers. People would quickly realize that the system of interventionism does not work and that it causes unemployment and bad business. They would ask for a return to the conditions prevailing before the government interfered, i.e., for repeal of the detrimental measure.

But things are different if there is protection preventing foreign business from competing on the domestic market or at least rendering such competition more expensive. Then the domestic entrepreneur can react to the increase of costs through raising prices. The government and the supporters of its policy triumph; they are convinced that their

4 [This scheme was the blueprint of modern state welfare. Its aims were to increase the income of the average worker to gain a better standard of living. This was obtained through political intervention and legislation favoring the working man. Labor unions thrived during this time, and social security was instituted for the first time. — Ed.]

methods of improving the material well-being of the workers have succeeded. What they do not see is that the public has to pay the bill and that the workers are burdened with higher prices. The same is valid with regard to wage raises brought about by the trade union compulsion and pressure. Wage rates on the unhampered labor market are higher in the United States than—with the exception of New Zealand—in any other country. Natural conditions of labor are more favorable, and capital is more abundant in this country; on the other hand immigration is restricted. If the American trade unions try to raise wage rates above this market level—a high level indeed, when compared with that of the rest of the world—the same problems present themselves. The immediate manifest failure of the trade union methods can only be avoided by a rise of prices which requires protection.

If there were free trade in the United States, prices—due allowance being made for transportation costs—could not rise above world market levels. An employer whom the unions have forced to pay wages higher than his business can afford would have to restrict output and to discharge workers.

If the industry concerned exports a part of its products, it is in a special position. It is not free to raise the prices of the exported commodities. But protectionism provides another way out. The domestic producers form a cartel, charge monopoly prices on the domestic market, and compensate for the losses incurred in selling abroad at low prices by a part of the monopoly profit. This was especially the case with Germany. Germany, which is forced to export a great part of its manufactures, was, from the end of the 'seventies of the nineteenth century to the outbreak of the First World War, far ahead of all other nations in matters of *Sozialpolitik* and trade unionism. Its much admired and glorified system of *Arbeiterschutz*, social insurance and collective bargaining, could work only because German industries, sheltered by all-round protection, built up cartels and sold on the world market much more cheaply than at home. The alleged success of the "*soziales Königtum der Hohenzollern*" and of the German Social Democrat party was apparent. In their capacity as consumers, the workers themselves had to bear the burden. Cartel and monopoly were necessary complements of German interventionism.

Popular legends have misrepresented the fact. They teach that the trend toward monopoly is inherent in capitalism. The German champions of government control of business have repeated again and again that private enterprise, if left free and not restrained by government control, must result in monopolization and that this inextricable tendency makes nationalization of business necessary. They passed over in silence the fact that cartelization was only possible because government and parliament had decreed import duties; that the law itself ordered the entrepreneurs to form a cartel if they refused to so do of their own accord, as was, for instance, the case with potash; that the Prussian government itself in its capacity as owner and operator of coal mines joined the coal cartel.

It is a characteristic feature of present-day governments and political parties that they promise in the same breath low prices to the consumers and high prices to the producers. But as it is beyond the power of any government to make prices lower than they would be on the competitive market unhampered by government interference, what results is always only a policy of raising prices. The governments pretend to fight monopoly, but they never take recourse to the measure which would render vain in most of the branches of industry all attempts to bolster up a monopoly, namely the abolition of import duties.

That the governments and the parliaments favor monopoly prices is clearly evidenced by their actions with regard to international monopolistic schemes. If the protective tariffs result in the formation of national cartels in various countries, international cartelization can in many cases be attained by mutual agreements between the national cartels. Such agreements are often very well served by another pro-monopoly activity of governments, the patents and other privileges granted to new inventions. However, where technical obstacles prevent the construction of a national cartel—as is almost always the case with agricultural production—no such international agreements can be built up. Then the governments interfere again. The history between the two world wars is an open record of state intervention to foster restriction and monopoly by international conventions. There were schemes for wheat pools, rubber, tin and sugar restrictions, and so on. Of course most of them collapsed soon. But this failure was rather an outcome of government inefficiency than of government preference for competitive business.

We have to realize that even protectionism cannot make government interference with business work and achieve the ends sought. All that it can bring about is to delay for a shorter or longer time the appearance of the undesired consequences of interventionism. Its failure must finally become manifest. The schemes to raise by decree or by trade union pressure the income of the wage earners above the height fixed by the unhampered market must necessarily sooner or later result in mass unemployment prolonged year after year; protection can only postpone this effect, but does not brush it away. But it is exactly this temporary adjournment which the supporters of interventionism aim at. It disguises the futility and ineptitude of their cherished policies. If the detrimental effects of their measures were to appear immediately, the public would more quickly understand their vanity. But as they are delayed, the champions of government control and trade unionism have in the meantime the opportunity to boast that the employers were wrong in predicting that the artificially raised wage rates and the burdens imposed upon business by discriminatory taxation and by labor legislation would make their plants unprofitable and hamper production.

Economic nationalism is the necessary complement of the endeavors to interfere with domestic business conditions.

VII   Protectionism on the Part of Creditor Nations

The tariff barriers against imports are especially nonsensical when erected by creditor nations. If the debtor nations in accordance with the terms stipulated pay interest and repay the principal of the debts and if they do not hinder the foreign investors taking out the business profits earned, their balance of trade must show an excess over imports, i.e., become favorable. Concomitantly the balance of trade of the creditor nations becomes unfavorable. The terms "favorable" and "unfavorable" are, of course, misleading. It is not unfavorable to be a rich nation and to receive large payments of interest, dividends, and profits from abroad. Great Britain was in the past century the world's richest nation, not although, but because it had a very "unfavorable" balance of trade.

The United States, in the years of its glorious geographic and economic expansion, had offered very propitious investment opportunities for foreign capital. The capitalists of Western Europe provided a part of the capital needed for the construction of American railroads and for the building up of American mining and American processing industries. Then later the Americans began to repatriate the stocks and bonds owned by foreigners; these operations made the nation's balance of trade active. With the First World War things changed. America became a creditor nation, the greatest capital exporting nation. Its favorable balance of trade—in the years 1916 to 1940 the excess of exports over imports was about 30 billion dollars—had now another significance; it was the outcome of the loans granted abroad and of investments in foreign countries.

But at the same time, American tariff policy made the payment of interest and the transfer of dividends more burdensome to the debtor nations. The same policy was applied by the other creditor nations, for instance Great Britain, France, the Netherlands, Belgium, and Switzerland. The debtor nations were, it is true, not very enthusiastic about the payments they had to make; debtors mostly are not very anxious to keep to the terms of the contract. But the conduct of the creditor nations, which sensibly prejudiced their interests, provided them with an opportune pretext for refusal to pay. They took recourse to currency devaluation, foreign exchange control, moratoriums, and some of them even to open repudiation and bankruptcy.

The policy of the creditor nations was especially paradoxical in the case of the German reparations and the inter-Allied debts. If Germany had really paid reparations out of her own funds—and not out of foreign, mostly American, credits granted to her—these payments would have rendered necessarily the receiving countries' balance of trade "unfavorable"; their imports would have exceeded their exports *because* they collected reparations. But this effect appeared, from the viewpoint of mercantilist fallacies, as a tremendous mischief. The Allies were at the same time anxious to make Germany pay and not to get the payments. They simply did not know what they wanted. But the Germans knew very well what they themselves aimed at. They did not wish to pay. They succeeded.

The same holds true with regard to the inter-Allied debts.

VIII Totalitarianism and Autarky

Ferdinand Lassalle, the founder of the German Social Democrat Party and the eloquent champion of government control of business, is credited with the dictum: "The State is God." Eminent scholars, for instance, Ambassador Carlton Hayes, call nationalism a new religion, the creed of our day.

People distinguish between the parties of the Left and the parties

of the Right. The former, they say, are the "progressives," the supporters of government control of business, the socialists and the communists; the latter the "reactionaires," the nationalists. This classification
is spurious. The socio-economic tenets of both groups differ only in
minor points. They both aim at full government control of business. It
is difficult to decide to which of these two totalitarian groups the most
eminent intellectual harbingers of present-day "unorthodoxy" are to
be assigned. There is no doubt that Lassalle was also the forerunner of
German National Socialism and the first German who aimed at the
Führer position. The Frenchman Georges Sorel, the advocate of the
"action directe," i.e., violent trade union activities and general strike,
was the preceptor both of Lenin and Mussolini. The socio-economic
program of Italian Fascism, the *stato corporativo*, is an exact replica
of the schemes of British Guild Socialism; its most lucid exposition is
the book of the English Fabians and enthusiastic pro-Soviet writers,
Sidney and Beatrice Webb: A *Constitution for a Socialist Commonwealth of Great Britain* (1920). Not only Mussolini, but many outstanding French collaborationists and German Nazis (for instance, Werner
Sombart) were Marxian readers before they turned to the "Right."

The truth is that modern nationalism is a corollary of the domestic
policy of government control of business. It has been demonstrated
that government control of business would manifestly fail already in
the short run if the country is not isolated from the rest of the world.
A government aiming at full regimentation of business must aim at
autarky too. Every kind of international economic relations impairs its
power to interfere with domestic business and limits the exercise of its
sovereignty. The state cannot pretend to be an omnipotent god if it has
to bother about its citizens' ability to compete with foreign business.
The outcome of government interference with business is totalitarianism, and totalitarianism requires economic self-sufficiency.

The same is valid with regard to self-proclaimed socialist states, that
is, states which have openly nationalized all economic enterprises and
boast of this achievement. Socialism, when not operated on a world
scale, is imperfect, if the socialist country depends on imports from
abroad and therefore still has to produce commodities for sale on a
market. It does not matter whether these foreign countries to which it
has to sell and from which it has to buy are socialist or not. Socialism
must always aim at autarky.

Protectionism and autarky mean discrimination against foreign labor and capital. They not only lower the productivity of human effort and thereby the standard of living for all nations; they create moreover international conflict.

There are nations which for lack of adequate resources cannot feed and clothe their population out of domestic resources. These nations cannot aim at autarky, but by embarking upon a policy of conquest. With them bellicosity and lust of aggression are the outcome of their adherence to the principles of government control of business. This was the case with Germany, Italy, and Japan. They said that they wanted to get a fair share of the earth's resources, thus they aimed at a new distribution of the areas producing raw materials. But these other countries were not empty; their inhabitants were not prepared to consider themselves as an appurtenance of their mines and plantations. They did not long for German or Italian rule. Thus there originated conflicts.

IX Sovereignty in the Present World

The principle of national sovereignty does not stand in the way of international division of labor and of peaceful collaboration of all nations within the framework of the world-embracing Great Society, provided that every nation unswervingly clings to the policies of democracy and capitalism. In the socio-economic setting of market society (laissez faire, laissez passer) the state is not an omnipotent God, but—as Lassalle used to say disparagingly—just a "night-watchman." The state is not an end, much less the only and supreme end, but simply a means for the promotion of the citizens' welfare. The acknowledgment of the indispensableness of private ownership of the means of production and of unhampered market exchange restricts the exercise of sovereignty. Although formally free in the exercise of their powers, the individual governments are subject to the supremacy of a principle which prevents the rise of international conflicts.

If the state administered in accordance with the ideas of economic interventionism, statism, and socialism, sovereignty becomes unlimited and absolute. The totalitarian state pretends to be omnipotent, supreme and above any principle, law, rule, or consideration for anybody and for anything. Nothing counts but its "sacred egoism." Right is what the state declares to be such.

This excessive notion of national sovereignty is incompatible with the present state of economic evolution. It cannot coexist with international division of labor. It wrongs all other nations and must result in strife.

Mankind is not free to return from a higher state of division of labor to a lower state. Autarky of every nation would impair very sensibly the standard of living of all peoples. There are today no such things as domestic affairs of an individual nation which do not affect the well-being of the rest of the world. Every nation has a material interest in the other nations' economic well-being because maladministration of one country hurts all other nations too.

If a national government hinders the most productive use of its country's resources, it hurts the interests of all other nations. Economic backwardness of a country with rich natural resources challenges all those whose conditions could be improved by a more efficient exploitation of this natural wealth.

Protectionism and autarky result in a state of affairs in which a country's resources are not used to the extent that they would be under free trade. For instance, the fact that the tariffs of those nations whose soil offers the most favorable physical opportunities for the production of wheat — the United States, Canada, and Argentina — hinder the import of manufactures would, even in the absence of European tariffs on wheat, compel Europeans to grow wheat on a soil which is less fertile than millions of acres of untilled soil in those countries better endowed by nature.

A country's economic insulation impairs not only the material well-being of its own citizens. It is no less detrimental to the economic interests of foreigners. This is why, in the middle of the past century, Great Britain and France induced China to open its harbors and why the United States applied a similar policy with regard to Japan.

X   The United States and World Affairs

Not only economic isolation, but political isolation too is unfeasible in the present world.

The Western Hemisphere was once safe against aggression. Thousands of miles of ocean separated it from possible invaders. The airplane has radically changed this state of things. The American isolationists have not yet realized this fact.

They argue this way: "It is a very deplorable fact that the peoples of Europe are fighting one another, that they have wrecked their glorious civilization, and that they are consequently doomed to starvation and misery. It is no less deplorable that similar things happen in Asia. Unfortunately we cannot save them from disaster. They themselves have to learn that peaceful cooperation would be more beneficial to them than war and mutual extermination. We cannot police the whole world. All we can do is to look out for ourselves and to preserve the Western Hemisphere's independence. We will keep neutral, will not interfere with other continents' affairs, and thus preserve our American way of life."

But it is not without concern for America what happens in the rest of the world. The establishment of two big totalitarian empires, one on the other side of the Atlantic, one on the other side of the Pacific, would have been a tremendous menace to America's political independence. The German nationalists had always emphasized that the last goal of their ambitions was the conquest of a large colonial domain on the American continent. The present writer is not familiar with the Japanese language and does not know whether Japanese economists and publicists were equally frank in their printed utterances. But he knows from conversations with many Japanese professors and students that they considered the Americans and not the Chinese their main enemies.

For the sake of its own vital interests America cannot remain neutral in world affairs and cannot live in political isolation. It has to realize that every international conflict will sooner or later involve America too and that it must be its main concern to establish a post-war order which will make the peace last.

There have been suggested various plans for such a scheme for a durable peace. Nobody can foretell today which of them will be put into execution.[5] However, all these proposals must needs imply a close and permanent cooperation either among all nations or at least among one group of nations, those united today in the war. If conflicts are not eliminated, there can be no question of a durable political alliance. But protectionism and still more autarky provoke conflicts.

The Second World War was not caused by Nazism alone. The failure of all other nations to erect in time a barrier against a possible aggression was no less instrumental in bringing about the disaster than the plans of the Nazis and the other Axis powers. If the Nazis had expected

---

5 [This was written before the United Nations Charter was drafted on January 1, 1942.—Ed.]

to encounter on the first day of hostilities a united and adequately armed front of all those nations which later came united in fighting them, they would never have ventured an assault. But collective security is unrealizable among nations bitterly fighting one another in the economic sphere. Economic nationalism has divided the peace-loving nations. If the United Nations does not succeed in brushing away economic nationalism, post-war conditions will not differ from those prevailing in the years between the two world wars. Then a third and much more dreadful war is unavoidable.

Every nation has to choose. The United States too. The alternatives are unity among the peace-loving nations or return to the chaos out of which new conflict will originate. But unity is incompatible with protection. Every day experiences anew that the good-neighbor policy among the American republics comes into collision with economic nationalism. How should Latin America and the European democracies enter into a close political collaboration with the United States if their citizens suffer from American foreign trade policies?

If economic nationalism is not abandoned, the most radical disarmament will not prevent the defeated aggressors from entering anew the scene of diplomatic intrigues, from building up new blocks and spheres of interest, from playing off one nation against the others, from rearming, and finally from plotting new attacks. Economic nationalism is the main obstacle to lasting peace.

CHAPTER 11

Economic Nationalism and Peaceful Economic Cooperation

The task of one privileged to address an audience of serious and conscientious citizens on problems of international relations is thankless indeed. If he is anxious to do his duty and to show things as they really are, he cannot help dispelling illusions, unmasking fallacies, and exhibiting the intricacy of the problems involved.

The instigators of the ordeal through which mankind is going today are gangs of rascals. There have always been bad people and there always will be. But it is the main goal of social organization to prevent them from doing harm. The fact that our age has failed in this respect is the proof that something is fundamentally wrong with our institutions and policies. If Messrs. Hitler and Mussolini had been born fifty years earlier, they would probably never have acquired fame. They did not bring about the chaos. It was the chaotic conditions which placed them at the head of two great nations and gave them power to inflict harm upon millions of peace-loving people.

Looking backwards on the history of the last hundred years we have to realize the sad fact that eminent writers have preached the gospel of war, violence, and usurpation, and have disparaged the endeavors to promote peace and good will among the nations. This phenomenon was not limited to Germany only. There was, for instance, the Scotchman Thomas Carlyle who glorified the Prussian King Frederick II, the ruthless tyrant and aggressor. There was the Englishman John Ruskin, the fanatical lover of art, who declared that "war is the foundation of the arts and of all the high virtues and faculties of man." There was the Frenchman Georges Sorel, the father of French syndicalism and master both of Lenin and of Mussolini, who advocated violence, brutality, and cruelty. There were finally German professors who asserted that the most desirable thing for a nation is to be always at war.

[This article is from a talk given in 1943; previously unpublished. —Ed.]

These are hard facts. However, world wars are not fought in order to abide by the teachings of distinguished authors. *La trahison des clercs,* the treason of the intellectuals, as the Frenchman Julien Benda stigmatized these attitudes of many literati, is a deplorable historical phenomenon.[1] But it is not responsible for the terrible events of our day. It has not produced the conflicts which have caused these wars.

Many people confuse chauvinism with nationalism and consider chauvinism as the main cause of the clash of nations. Chauvinism consists in a conceited overestimation of one's own nation's qualities and achievements and in a prejudicial disparagement of all other peoples. It is a disposition of mind not more conspicuous among narrow-minded philistines than personal conceit and arrogance. It is surely not a virtue. But it does not result in action and political ventures. The Germans do not embark upon conquest because, as the Frenchman Count Arthur Gobineau and the Englishman Houston Stewart Chamberlain told them, they are the only really human race, while all other peoples are simply trash and underdogs. They are aggressive because they believe that aggressive nationalism is the best, is the only way to promote their own material well-being.

Mr. Carlton Hayes, formerly of Columbia University and today American Ambassador in Spain, and Professor Walter Sulzbach, formerly of the University of Frankfurt, today at Pomona College, California, have provided us with brilliant analyses of chauvinism.[2] But they both are mistaken in confusing chauvinism with nationalism. Nor has chauvinism begotten nationalism. Its only function in the scheme of nationalist policies is that it adorns nationalism's shows and festivals. People overflow with joy and pride when the official speakers hail them as the elite of mankind, praise the immortal deeds of their ancestors, and the invincibility of their armed forces. But when the words fade away and the celebration reaches its end, the participants return home and go to bed. They do not mount the battle horse.

Nationalism cannot be explained or excused by chauvinist intoxication. It is a policy of cool-minded Machiavellian politicians; it is the outcome of reasoning, of course of misguided reasoning. Scholarly books, full of thoughts, of course of erroneous thoughts, have carefully

---

1 [Julien Benda, *The Treason of the Intellectuals* [1928] (New York: W. W. Norton, 1969).—Ed.]

2 [Carlton J. H. Hayes, *The Historical Evolution of Modern Nationalism* (New York: Richard R. Smith, 1931); Walter Sulzbach, *National Consciousness* (Washington, D.C.: American Council on Public Affairs, 1943).—Ed.]

elaborated the doctrines, whose application has led to the clash of nations, to bloody wars and destruction.

About eighty years ago public opinion all over the world was almost unanimous in the belief that mankind is on the threshold of an age of undisturbed peaceful cooperation of all nations. There was no organized pacifist movement in those days. People did not base their conviction that wars will disappear on the working of pacifist societies but on the fact that liberalism was on the point of abolishing the root causes of war. Within a world of popular government and perfect free trade there are, they said, no conflicts among the various nations. War will become obsolete because it will be useless to fight and to conquer.

Princes and kings, they argued, are eager for conquest because they can increase their power and their personal income by the annexation of a province. But a democratic nation cannot derive any profit from the enlargement of its territory. All that is needed to make for eternal peace is to remove the tyrants who oppose democratic government. Some wars and revolutions are still unavoidable in order to accomplish this task. But once the world is safe for democracy, it will be safe for peace too.

Such were the tenets of President Wilson. To make the world safe for democracy and to make it safe for peace was in the eyes of this great humanitarian one thing. Eliminate the Kaiser and his Junkers[3] and you have established everlasting peace. The war against the Hohenzollern, not against the German people, is the war for the abolition of all wars, is the last war.

But unfortunately President Wilson and his noble-minded collaborators did not realize that their main thesis is only correct if there prevails perfect free trade. If the laws, the administration, and the courts do not discriminate between citizens and foreigners, if everybody is free to live and to work unmolested where he wants, if the transfer of labor, capital, and commodities from country to country is not subject to any regimentation or taxation, then of course it is without any concern for the individual citizen whether his country is bigger or smaller and where the political frontiers are drawn. No citizen can expect any profit from the incorporation into his own country of a piece of land previously owned by another nation. Wars no longer pay, they are useless.

The reality in which we have to live and to settle our political issues

3 [The Junkers were members of the Prussian aristocracy owing allegiance to the Kaiser.—Ed.]

is very different from this liberal utopia as depicted and aimed at by Frédérick Bastiat and Richard Cobden. Ours is not an age of laissez faire, laissez passer, but an age of economic nationalism. All governments are eager to promote the well-being of their citizens or of some groups of their citizens by inflicting harm upon foreigners. Foreign goods are excluded from the domestic market or only permitted after the payment of an import duty. Foreign labor is barred from competition on the domestic labor market. Foreign capital is liable to confiscation. This economic nationalism must needs result in war, whenever those injured believe that they are strong enough to brush away, by armed violent action, the measures detrimental to their own welfare.

A nation's policy forms an integral whole. Foreign policy and domestic policy are closely linked together; they condition each other. Economic nationalism is the corollary of the present-day domestic policies of government interference with business and of national planning as free trade was the complement of domestic economic freedom. There can be protectionism in a country with domestic free trade, but where there is no domestic free trade, protectionism is indispensable. A national government's might is limited to the territory subject to its sovereignty. It does not have the power to interfere *directly* with conditions abroad. Where there is external free trade, foreign competition would even in the short run frustrate the aims sought by the various measures of government intervention with domestic business. When the domestic market is not to some extent insulated from the foreign markets, there can be no question of government control. The further a nation goes on the way toward public regulation and regimentation, the more it is pushed toward economic isolation. International division of labor becomes suspect because it hinders the full use of national sovereignty. The trend toward autarky is essentially a trend of domestic economic policies; it is the outcome of the endeavors to make the state paramount in economic matters.

In such a world of economic nationalism every citizen has a material interest in the nullification of measures by which foreign governments injure his interests. Every citizen is therefore eager to see his own country mighty and powerful, because he expects personal advantage of its military might. Small nations cannot help being victimized by other nations' economic nationalism. But big nations place confidence in the valor of their armed forces. Present-day bellicosity is not the outcome of the greediness of princes and of Junker oligarchies; it is a pressure group policy whose distinctive mark lies in the methods applied but not in the incentives and motives.

It is therefore of no use to tell the aggressors, as the pacifists do: Do not fight; even a victorious war does not pay; you cannot derive any profit from conquest. These aggressors are convinced that victory pays. The Japanese argue: If we conquer Australia and make it consequently possible for 20 million Japanese to settle down in Australia, we will raise wage rates and standards of living for all Japanese, both for the emigrants and for those staying at home. There is only one counter-argument which they accept as valid: the victory of those assaulted. In our age of economic nationalism the only method to prevent war is armaments. Watch your borders day and night!

The Geneva experiment did not fail because America did not join the League or because the Covenant[4] was unsatisfactory. It failed because it is vain to aim at peaceful cooperation among nations fighting one another unswervingly in the economic sphere.

This war was not caused by Nazism and the Japanese alone. The failure of all other nations to stop in time the rise of Nazism and to erect a barrier against a new German aggression was not less instrumental in bringing about the disaster than were events of Germany's domestic evolution. There was no secrecy about the ambitions of the Nazis and their Italian and Japanese friends. The Nazis themselves advertised them in innumerable books and pamphlets and in their newspapers and periodicals. Nobody can reproach the aggressors with having concocted their plots clandestinely. It was easy indeed to know all about their plans. This Second World War would never have broken out if the Nazis expected that they would have to encounter on the first day of hostilities a united and adequately armed front of all the nations which are today united in fighting them. But such a union could not be organized in time among nations waging a permanent economic war against one another.

4 [The League of Nations' Covenant was signed on April 28, 1919, and was composed of twenty-six articles that proposed an agreement to collectively maintain peaceful settlements of disputes in an effort to obtain economic and social cooperation worldwide. Keep in mind that World War I had just ceased in Europe prior to this attempt. As long as there are restrictions on import and export markets and government intervention to protect industries there will inevitably be clashes leading to disputes. —Ed.]

It is not my task to dwell upon the events of the past. I have mentioned all these facts only in order to demonstrate what has to be achieved for the future.

It is not difficult to draft seemingly excellent proposals for a post-war reconstruction and for a durable peace if one is prepared to abstract from stark reality and to indulge in daydreams. If there were no economic nationalism, if there were perfect free trade, it would not even be necessary to plan special institutions and provisions for the safeguarding of peace. In the absence of conflicting interests there is no war. But we cannot hope that economic nationalism will disappear in a not too distant future as all nations are firmly resolved not to return to what they call domestic laissez faire.

This is my main objection against the pacifist platform as represented by the distinguished English scholar Sir Norman Angell. Sir Norman's reasoning would be quite correct if there were no clash of economic interests. But this assumption is unfortunately illusory.

The pacifists suggest a world authority, a world court for the settlement of disputes and an international police force for the enforcement of the rulings of the world authority and the finds of the world court. But how should this world government be organized?

The League of Nations was not a world government, but rather a social club of nations. You are free to join a club and you are not less free to walk out. The majority has not the right to impose its own will upon a dissenting minority. Such articles of association are, of course, incompatible with government. The essence of government is compulsion and coercion applied against people not ready to obey spontaneously. Under a democratic constitution the majority has the power to enforce its will upon dissenting minorities. The first step required for the transformation of the impotent League of Nations into a more efficient institution is to establish a procedure for voting and for the determination of the will of the majority.

But how should voting be done? If to every nation one vote is assigned, Luxemburg and Estonia together would have two votes, Great Britain one vote only. The twenty republics of Central and Southern America would get twenty votes against one vote of the United States.

Another solution would be to assign to every nation as many votes as correspond to its population figures. This would be really democratic. But then the peoples of Asia and of Africa will by far outnumber the most advanced peoples, those which have created Western civilization.

What will happen if the majority declares that migration barriers are contrary to the fundamental principles of international cooperation and have to be abolished? Will the citizens of Australia and New Zealand surrender to such a ruling?

Let us not indulge in illusions. There exist differences in civilization and in standards of living which render futile all plans for the immediate establishment of a democratic world government. There are not more than 600 million Christians in the world and more than 1500 million members of other religious groups. Almost two-thirds of the world's population are virtually illiterate. There are conflicts of economic interests. The citizens of the comparatively underpopulated countries are not willing to admit immigration from the comparatively overpopulated countries. No country is ready to open its borders to foreign products.

The fathers of the League of Nations and the champions of all plans for a world-embracing commonwealth of nations did not take into account that our contemporaries lack entirely the mentality which alone can make for peaceful international cooperation. They were eager to build up institutions, offices, and courts, and to draft articles of covenants and pacts. But what is needed is to change public opinion and to substitute for the spirit of mutual hatred and rivalry a spirit of mutual cooperation. The pacifists are quite right in asserting that our civilization is based on international division of labor and that it is doomed if we do not succeed in eliminating war. But our contemporaries are possessed by the idea that to bar access to foreign products and to immigrants serves best their own nation's interest. A return to free trade, to laissez faire, laissez passer is for them out of the question.

Thus we must first try to change this mentality. A small group of economists are intent on demonstrating that economic nationalism is detrimental to the rightly understood selfish interests of all men and all nations and that everybody should aim at free trade, not for the sake of foreigners, but for the sake of his own people. Even if all other nations cling to protectionism, every nation serves best its own well-being by free trade. I do hope that these endeavors will succeed. But a radical change of ideologies takes a long time. Years must elapse, generations must pass away, new ages must rise before such a change can be expected even in the most favorable case. We must not abandon the idea of a commonwealth of nations, but we have to provide for the transitional period. We must not neglect the task of our time, merely because a more distant future will bring a perfect solution. We have today to face an urgent problem. We have to prevent a third world war. On the eve of victory we have to plan for a system which will make it hopeless for militarist nations to embark upon a new aggression.

Such are the aims of various proposals suggested by distinguished authors. These men do not reject the idea of a universal League of Nations or of such statutes as the Kellogg-Briand pact.[5] Only they are realistic enough to comprehend that, in the absence of an adequate ideology, a universal scheme can work only after a long period of transition. They take account of the fact that the aggressive mentality of the 250 million Germans, Italians, Japanese, Hungarians, Rumanians, and Slovaks cannot be changed overnight. They are looking for an expedient and emergency measure, as it were, for the impending day.

It is not my intention to make propaganda for any patent-medicine. On the contrary, I am rather skeptical with regard to these proposals. But I believe that it is the duty of every serious and conscientious man to examine them carefully. Mr. Clarence Streit has rendered a great service to mankind, even if the examination of his project proves that it is under present ideological conditions unfeasible. He has tried to find a way out of the dilemma: return to perfect free trade or endless wars.

The basic idea of Mr. Streit is this: in order to avoid a new aggression it is necessary to make the cooperation of the Western democracies, today united in the struggle against Germany and Japan, lasting and permanent. The present-day military and political alliance has to be transformed into a permanent union, into a solid block, which no foreign intrigues could disintegrate. Such a powerful union could prevent the rearmament of the defeated aggressors and thus preserve peace. On the other hand it is quite obvious that a return to the state of affairs which prevailed in the period between the two wars would finally result in a new war.

The nations which have to form this union have to abandon essential features of their national sovereignty for the benefit of the supernational authority. They have to pool their foreign policies and their

---

5 [A treaty renouncing war as an instrument of national policy and an agreement by signatory members not to seek settlement of any conflict except by peaceful means. There existed loopholes for the use of military action in cases of self-defense and fulfillment of treaty obligations. The treaty did not contain sanctions for breaches of the agreement; thus the sixty-three nations that signed it on July 24, 1929, did so as a formality. — Ed.]

armed forces and they have to stop fighting one another in the economic field. They have to enter into a permanent customs union and monetary union. In short: they have to form a new federation.

It is not necessary to dwell upon more details either of Mr. Streit's project or of similar projects brought forward for other parts of the world, for instance, for the whole of Europe—Paneurope of Count Coudenhove-Kaleigi—or for Eastern Europe or the Danubian area. The distinctive mark of all these plans is that they suggest the formation of a new super-national federation.

Now we are back where we started from. Not only is a world-embracing commonwealth of nations incompatible with the preservation of economic nationalism but even a federal union among a smaller group of nations. What renders all schemes for a better post-war order futile is the present-day doctrine of government interference with business. In every country there are powerful pressure groups opposed to every infringement of their vested privileges.

I have not at all exaggerated the detrimental consequences of economic nationalism. On the contrary. I was anxious not to allude to the delicate problem of migration barriers. I am optimistic enough to believe that migration barriers alone would not necessarily frustrate endeavors for international cooperation. But protectionism does. And protectionism is indispensable if there is government interference with business.

I do not refer to the problem of the warlike nations like Germany, Japan, and Italy. Whatever their aspirations may be, they could never embark upon a new war if all American republics, Great Britain, and the British Dominions and the smaller democracies of Europe are welded together into a solid bloc of peace-loving peoples. But such a bloc cannot last if there is protectionism. If the Argentinean cattle-breeders feel injured by the policy of the United States regarding the imports of beef and if the Paris dressmakers suffer from the British measures concerning imports of garments, they will not cling to the union. But on the other hand, they are not ready to see almost all the powers which are now vested in their own national governments shifted to a super-national authority. They already resent the concentration of more and more powers in their own national capitals; they would be much more shocked by the establishment of the hundred times larger bureaucratic body of the new super-national authority.

Peaceful coexistence of sovereign nations is possible if every individual nation is convinced that it would be contrary to its own selfish interests to hinder the mobility of capital, labor, and products. Such a policy of free trade presupposes domestic free trade, today generally disparaged as laissez faire. Government control of business results in conflicts of national interests for which up to now no peaceful solution has been discovered.

It is an illusion to believe that such conflicts could be settled by arbitration on the part of impartial courts. A court can administer justice only according to the articles of a code. But it is exactly these prescriptions and rules which are contested. Let us abstract from the problem of migration barriers and restrict our discussion to the problem of trade barriers only. The peoples of the comparatively overpopulated areas of Europe and Asia, the immense majority of the earth's population, consider trade barriers of the comparatively underpopulated areas as the main obstacle for their material improvement. They say that they have not free access to the raw materials and the trade of the world. I do not want to quote the formulation of this grievance by the representatives of the aggressor nations. There is in the present world an authority which is above the parties. The Pope is not a party in a conflict. There are Catholics on both sides and the Pope does not side only with one party. It is therefore of great importance what the ideas of the highest dignitary of the Roman Church are with regard to the future world order. Says the Pope in his Christmas Eve broadcast of December 24, 1941, only a few days after the entry of the paramount Catholic country into the War:

> Within the limits of a new order founded on moral principles, there is no place for that cold and calculating egoism which tends to hoard the economic resources and materials destined for the use of all to such an extent that the nations less favored by nature are not permitted access to them.
>
> In this regard, it is for us a source of great consolation to see admitted the necessity of a participation of all in the natural riches of the earth, even on the part of those nations which in the fulfillment of this principle belong to the category of "givers" and not to that of "receivers."

The Pope was not mistaken in asserting that these principles are acknowledged by all nations, by those which he calls the "givers" not less than by those which he calls the "receivers." The proof is provided by Point Four of the Atlantic Charter:[6] It reads: They, i.e., the governments of the United States and of the United Kingdom, will endeavor with due respect for their existing obligations, to further the enjoyment by all States, great or small, victor or vanquished, of access on equal terms, to the trade and to the raw materials of the world which are needed for their economic prosperity.

The Pope, of course, is not an economist. If he were an economist he would not consider free trade as a concession granted on the part of one group of nations to the exclusive benefit of other nations. He would emphasize that free trade serves best both parties and that it is inappropriate to speak with regard to free trade of givers and of receivers.

But be this as it may, the main issue is that the governments of the world's two paramount powers and the head of the world's most numerous religious community agree with regard to the importance of the trade problem. It is still a far cry from this academic recognition of the problem to a satisfactory solution. The obstacles to be overcome are enormous, and nothing less than a radical change in the generally accepted economic doctrines is required. But if there is anything which justifies optimism, then it is the fact that people are beginning to realize that free trade is the indispensable condition of lasting peace.

6 [The Atlantic Charter was the result of several meetings—held on board warships in the North Atlantic—between President Franklin D. Roosevelt and British Prime Minister Winston Churchill in August 1941. The thrust of the Charter was an eight-point program seeking to secure a "better future for mankind" by not seeking new territories; the right of self-determination and self-government for all peoples; access to trade and raw materials; and once peace is established all nations must abandon the use of force. The Charter was later incorporated into the Declaration of the United Nations, January 1, 1942.—Ed.]

CHAPTER 12

The Plight of the
Underdeveloped Nations

I

Foreign investment was an achievement of laissez-faire capitalism. It developed step by step only in the nineteenth century. Writing in 1817, Ricardo could still assert that most men of property are "satisfied with a low rate of profits in their own country, rather than seek a more advantageous employment for their wealth in foreign nations."[1]

What impelled entrepreneurs and capitalists toward foreign investment was, of course not "altruism," but the eagerness to earn profits by supplying the domestic consumers in the best possible and cheapest way with those commodities they demanded most urgently. They went into foreign countries in order to supply the home market directly or indirectly (i.e., by triangular trade) with raw materials and foodstuffs which could otherwise not have been obtained at all or only at higher costs. If the consumers had been more eager for the acquisition of a greater quantity of goods that could be produced at home without the aid of foreign resources than for imported food and raw materials, it would have been more profitable to expand domestic production further than to invest abroad.

But foreign investment benefited the receiving nations no less than the investing nations. These receiving nations were backward and underdeveloped insofar as they had been slow in developing those ideological and institutional conditions which are the indispensable prerequisite of large-scale capital accumulation. While amply endowed by nature, they lacked the capital needed for the exploitation of their

[This article is from 1952; previously unpublished. —Ed.]

1 [David Ricardo, *On the Principles of Political Economy and Taxation*, vol. 1 of *The Works and Correspondence of David Ricardo*, Piero Sraffa, ed. (Cambridge: Cambridge University Press, 1951–1973), p. 137. —Ed.]

dormant resources. On account of the paucity of capital available, the marginal productivity of labor and thereby wage rates were low when compared with the state of affairs in the capitalistic countries. The inflow of foreign capital raised wage rates and improved the masses' average standard of living.

The socialists provide a different interpretation of the problems involved. As they see it, a business enterprise is a contrivance to exploit unfairly the workers employed. Its very existence and operation are contrary to the external laws of morality. There is but one means to put an end to this exploitation, namely, socialization, i.e., the expropriation of the private capitalists and entrepreneurs and the transfer of their plants, mines, and farms to the hands of the state. This is what the labor government is anxious to achieve in the United Kingdom and what the Iranian government, imbued with a truly Fabian spirit, is just doing in its own country. If it is right for the British to nationalize the British coal mines, it cannot be wrong for the Iranians to nationalize the Iranian oil industry. If Mr. Attlee[2] were consistent, he would have congratulated the Iranians on their great socialist achievement. But no socialist can be or ever was consistent.

It is hopeless for the British to dissuade the Iranians from nationalizing the British-owned wells, refineries, and pipelines by pointing out the disadvantages that will certainly result for the people of Iran. They themselves did not pay heed to such "reactionary" talk when the problem of nationalizing various British industries was at issue.

Under the present state of international law every sovereign nation is free to deal as it pleases with all property situated within its boundaries. A foreign government may diplomatically protest and support claims of its citizens for an indemnification. But if the government of the nationalizing nation is not prepared to yield to such diplomatic overtures, that settles the matter. It is enough to refer to such precedents as the case of Russia in 1917 or the case of the Mexican expropriation of the oil industry.

The foreign government may submit the case to the International Court of Justice. But the decisions of this Court are practically unenforceable.

If the foreign government resorts to the *ultima ratio regum,* to mili-

2 [Lord Clement Attlee was leader of the British Labor Party from 1935 to 1955 and a committed socialist. He was prime minister of England from 1945 to 1951. — Ed.]

tary intervention, this would under the charter of the United Nations represent a clear case of aggression.

The pundits of international law and the lawyers of the United Nations will certainly write very profound reports and treatises about the legal aspect of the Anglo-Iranian conflict. Such utterances are not worth the paper on which they are printed. The simple truth is that if the government of Iran does not of its own accord change its mind because it may expect some immediate political and material gain from such a change, nothing can prevent it from expropriating the oil industry. For it is obvious that Great Britain cannot win anything by military measures. Even in the unlikely event of a British success, the British would discover that bayonets are very uncomfortable to sit upon in a business office. Besides there is the specter of a Russian occupation of the greater part of Iran and the still more threatening danger of a new world war.

II

The immediate consequences of the Iranian oil expropriation are very sad indeed. It seriously affects the military plans of the Western powers and revolutionizes conditions on the world oil market.

Still more important are the remoter consequences of the affair. Foreign investment of private enterprises and citizens already came to an almost complete standstill years ago. The private investor has learned from experience that investing abroad is virtually tantamount to throwing away one's own wealth. It is true, not all receiving countries resorted to undisguised expropriation of property and repudiation of loans. But many of the "good" countries too have effectively robbed the foreign investors and creditors by foreign exchange control and discriminatory taxation. It is of little use for an American or a Swiss to own a blocked balance with a Ruritanian bank, especially if he notices that the purchasing power and the equivalent in hard currency of the Ruritanian monetary unit is dropping more and more.

The American Administration recommends as an adequate substitute for private investment abroad public investment and loans either granted directly by the governmental (national or international) banks or guaranteed by such banks. The idea is that the governments, first of all the American government, should fill the gap that the anti-capitalistic policies of the underdeveloped countries have willfully created. But the example of Iran shows that such governmental investments and loans are also not safe against predatory ventures. Why should the American government pump American funds into Ruritania if the Ruritanian parliament is free to deal with them as it pleases? Are there no investment opportunities left within the United States? It is rather unrealistic to assume that Congress will continue to tolerate a policy that subsidizes foreign countries at the expense of the American taxpayer. There is no use in fooling ourselves. The hopes that the much talked about Point Four[3] may work as a satisfactory substitute for the disintegrated international capital market have proved fallacious.

III

It is this disintegration of the international capital market that creates the plight of the underdeveloped countries.

These countries were in the last decades benefited by the modern methods of fighting epidemics and other diseases which the capitalistic West has developed. Mortality rates dropped and the average length of life was prolonged. Population increased considerably. But the economic policies of these nations are preventing an expansion of the insufficient amount of domestic saving and capital accumulation; sometimes they even directly induce capital de-accumulation. As there is no longer any importation of foreign capital worth mentioning, the per-head quota of capital invested decreases. The outcome is a drop in the marginal productivity of labor. But at the same time the governments and the labor unions try to enforce wage rates which exceed the marginal productivity of labor. The result is spreading unemployment.

Unaware of the causes of unemployment the governments try to remove it by various measures which, although entirely futile, are so costly that they by far exceed the public revenue and are financed by the issuance of additional fiat money. Inflation still more discourages domestic saving and capital formation.

The governments of all these underdeveloped countries indefatigably talk of the necessity to "industrialize" and to modernize the outdated methods of agricultural production. But their own policies are the main obstacle to any improvement and economic progress. There

3 [Point Four of the Atlantic Charter was concerned with equality of access to trade and raw materials of the world and to securing for all nations an improved labor standard, economic adjustment, and social security. — Ed.]

cannot be any question of imitating the technological procedures of the capitalistic countries if there is no capital available. Whence should this capital come if domestic capital formation as well as the inflow of foreign capital is sabotaged?

About two hundred years ago conditions in England were hardly better, perhaps even worse than they are today in India and China. The then prevailing system of production was lamentably inadequate. In its frame there was no room left for an ever increasing part of the population. Masses of destitute paupers were barely living on the verge of starvation. The ruling landed aristocracy did not know of any means to cope with these wretched people other than the poorhouse, the workhouse, and the prison. But then came the "Industrial Revolution." Laissez-faire capitalism converted the starving beggars into self-supporting breadwinners. It improved conditions step by step until, at the end of the Victorian age, the average standard of living of the common man was the highest in Europe, much higher than that of people whom earlier ages had considered as sufficiently well-to-do.

What the underdeveloped nations must do if they sincerely want to eradicate penury and to improve the economic conditions of their destitute masses is to adopt those policies of "rugged individualism" which have created the welfare of Western Europe and the United States. They must resort to laissez faire; they must remove all obstacles fettering the spirit of enterprise and stunting domestic capital accumulation and the inflow of capital from abroad.

But what the governments of these countries are really doing today is just the contrary. Instead of emulating the policies that created the comparative wealth and welfare of the capitalistic nations, they are choosing those contemporary policies of the West which slow down the further accumulation of capital and lay stress on what they consider to be a fairer distribution of wealth and income. Leaving aside the problem whether or not these policies are beneficial to the economically advanced nations, it must be emphasized that they are patently nonsensical when resorted to in the economically backward countries. Where there is very little to be distributed, a policy of an allegedly "fairer" redistribution is of no use at all.

IV

In the second part of the nineteenth century the shrewdest among the patriots of the underdeveloped nations began to contrast the unsatisfactory conditions of their own countries with the prosperity of the West. They could not help realizing that the Europeans and Americans have better succeeded in fighting penury and starvation than their own peoples. To make their own peoples as prosperous as those of the West became their foremost aim. So they sent the elite of their youth to the universities of Europe and America to study economics and thus to learn the secret of raising the standard of living. Hindus, Chinese, Africans, and members of other backward nations thronged the lecture halls, eagerly listening to the words of the famous British, American, and German professors.

This is what these professors — Marxians, Fabians, Veblenians, socialists of the chair, champions of government omnipotence and all-round planning, peacemakers of inflation, deficit spending and confiscatory taxation — taught their students: rugged individualism, the policy of laissez faire, and private enterprise are the worst evils that ever befell mankind. They enriched a few robber barons and condemned the masses of decent people to ever-increasing poverty and degradation. But fortunately the black age of capitalism is approaching its end. People will no longer let themselves be fooled by the spurious doctrines of the sycophants of the bourgeoisie, the depraved apologists of a manifestly unfair social order. We, the adamant advocates of justice and riches for all, have forever exploded the fallacies and paralogisms of the orthodox authors. The Welfare State will bring prosperity and security to everybody. The economics of abundance and plenty will be substituted for the economics of scarcity. Production for use will be substituted for production for profit. There will be freedom from want; i.e., everybody will get all he wants.

Never did these professors mention the — in their opinion manifestly absurd — truism that there is no means to improve the conditions of any nation or the whole of mankind other than to increase the per-head quota of capital invested. On the contrary. They indulged in expounding the Keynesian dogma of the dangers of saving and accumulating capital. Never did they refer to the fact that nature — not the capitalists — has made the means of human sustenance scarce. As they saw it, the State had inexhaustible funds at its disposal that enabled the government to spend without any limits. They have even today not yet realized that progressive taxation has already exhausted this alleged surplus in all other countries and will have exhausted it even in the United States very soon.

Indoctrinated with these principles the graduates of the Western universities returned to their countries and tried to put into effect what they had learned. They were sincerely convinced that to create prosperity for all, nothing else was needed than to apply the formulas of Occidental pseudo-progressivism. They thought that industrialization means labor unions, minimum wage rates, and unemployment doles and that trade and commerce means controls of every kind. They wanted to nationalize before they had permitted business to build plants and enterprises which could be expropriated. They wanted to establish a new fair deal in countries whose distress consisted precisely in the fact that they had not known what is today disparaged as the old and unfair deal.

All these radical intellectuals of the underdeveloped countries blame Europe and America for the backwardness and poverty of their own peoples. They are right, but for reasons which are very different from those they themselves have in mind. Europe and America did not cause the plight of the underdeveloped nations, but they have prolonged its duration by implanting in their intellectuals the ideologies which are the most serious obstacle to any improvement of conditions. The socialists and interventionists of the West have poisoned the mind of the East. They are responsible for the anti-capitalistic bias of the East and for the sympathies with which those Eastern intellectuals look upon the Soviet system as the most intransigent realization of Marxian ideas.

All underdeveloped countries are flooded with translations of the writings of Marx, Lenin, and Stalin and of the books of all shades of non-Marxian socialism and anti-capitalism. But only very rarely have books expounding the operation of the market economy and critically analyzing the dogmas of the socialist creed been published in one of the languages of these nations. Little wonder that their reading public believes that the description of capitalism as provided by the *Communist Manifesto* exactly fits present-day American conditions, that, for instance, the laborer "sinks deeper and deeper" with the progress of industry and that "the bourgeoisie is incompetent to assure an existence to its slave within his slavery." Little wonder that they look upon the Soviet system as the model of a better future.

We must comprehend that it is impossible to improve the economic conditions of the underdeveloped nations by grants in aid. If we send them foodstuffs to fight famines, we merely relieve their governments from the necessity of abandoning their disastrous agricultural policies. In the past, for instance, Yugoslavia's main problem was how to find foreign markets for its considerable surplus of cereals, pigs, fruits, and lumber. Today the country that includes the most fertile land of Europe outside Russia and Romania is famine stricken. If we send to the poor countries manufactures or "lend" them dollars, we virtually pay for the deficits of their nationalized transportation and communication systems and their socialized mines and processing industries. The truth is that the United States is subsidizing all over the world the worst failure of history: socialism. But for these lavish subsidies the continuation of the socialist schemes would have become long since unfeasible.

The problem of rendering the underdeveloped nations more prosperous cannot be solved by material aid. It is a spiritual and intellectual problem. Prosperity is not simply a matter of capital investment. It is an ideological issue. What the underdeveloped countries need first is the ideology of economic freedom and private enterprise and initiative that makes for the accumulation and maintenance of capital as well as for the employment of the available capital for the best possible and cheapest satisfaction of the most urgent wants of the consumers.

In no other way can the United States contribute to the improvement of the economic conditions of the underdeveloped countries than by transmitting to them the ideas of economic freedom.

~ Comparative Economic Systems

CHAPTER 13

Capitalism versus Socialism

I

Most of our contemporaries are highly critical of what they call "the unequal distribution of wealth." As they see it, justice would require a state of affairs under which nobody enjoys what are to be considered superfluous luxuries as long as other people lack things necessary for the preservation of life, health, and cheerfulness. The ideal condition of mankind, they pretend, would be an equal distribution of all consumers' goods available. As the most practical method to achieve this end, they advocate the radical expropriation of all material factors of production and the conduct of all production activities by society, that is to say, by the social apparatus of coercion and compulsion, commonly called government or state.

The supporters of this program of socialism or communism reject the economic system of capitalism for a number of reasons. Their critique emphasizes the alleged fact that the system as such is not only unjust, a violation of the perennial God-given natural law, but also inherently inefficient and thus the ultimate cause of all the misery and poverty that plague mankind. Once the wicked institution of private ownership of the material factors of production will have been replaced by public ownership, human conditions will become blissful. Everybody will receive what he needs. All that separates mankind from this perfect state of earthly affairs is the unfairness in the distribution of wealth.

The essential viciousness of this method of dealing with the fundamental problems of mankind's material and spiritual welfare is to be seen in its preoccupation with the concept of distribution. As these authors and doctrinaires see it, the economic and social problem is to

[Reprinted from *The Intercollegiate Review* 5 (Spring 1969).—Ed.]

give to everybody his due, his fair share in the endowment that God or nature has destined for the use of all men. They do not see that poverty is "the primitive condition of the human race."[1] They do not realize that all that enables man to elevate his standard of living above the level of the animals is the fruit of his planned activity. Man's economic task is not the distribution of gifts dispensed by a benevolent donor, but production. He tries to alter the state of his environment in such a way that conditions become more favorable to the preservation and development of his vital forces. He works.

Precisely, say the superficial among the critics of social conditions. Labor and nothing but labor brings forth all the goods the utilization of which elevates the condition of men above the level of the animals. As all products are the output of labor, only those who labor should have the right to enjoy them.

This may sound rather plausible as far as it refers to the conditions and circumstances of some fabulous non-human beings. But it turns into the most fateful of all popular delusions when applied to *Homo sapiens*. Man's eminence manifests itself in his being fully aware of the flux of time. Man lives consciously in a changing universe; he distinguishes, sooner and later, between past, present,[2] and future; he makes plans to influence the future state of affairs and tries to convert these plans into fact. Conscious planning for the future is the specifically human characteristic. Timely provision for future wants is what distinguishes human action from the hunting drives of beasts and of savages. Premeditation, early attention to future needs, leads to production for deferred consumption, to the intercalation of time between exertion and the enjoyment of its outcome, to the adoption of what Böhm-Bawerk called roundabout methods of production. To the nature-given factors of production, man-made factors are added by the deferment of consumption. Man's material environment and his style of life are radically transformed. There emerges what is called human civilization.

This civilization is not an achievement of kings, generals, or other *Führers*. Neither is it the result of the labors of "common" men. It is the fruit of the cooperation of two types of men: of those whose saving, i.e., deferment of consumption, makes entering upon time-absorbing,

1 Jeremy Bentham, "Principles of the Civil Code," vol. 1, in *Works*, J. Bowring, ed. (London: Simpkin, Marshall, 1843), p. 309.
2 About the praxeological concept of "present," see *Human Action*, 3rd ed. (Chicago: Henry Regnery, 1966), pp. 100f.

roundabout methods of production possible, and of those who know how to direct the application of such methods. Without saving and successful endeavors to use the accumulated savings wisely, there cannot be any question of a standard of living worthy of the qualification human.

Simple saving, that is, the abstention from immediate consumption in order to make more abundant consumption at a later date possible, is not a specifically human contrivance. There are also animals that practice it. Driven by instinctive urges, some species of animals are also committed to what we would have to call capitalistic saving if it were done in full consciousness of its effects. But man alone has elevated intentional deferment of consumption to a fundamental principle of action. He abstains temporally from consumption in order to enjoy later the continuous services of appliances that could not have been produced without such a postponement.

Saving is always the abstention from some kind of immediate consumption for the sake of making an increase or improvement in later consumption possible. It is saving that accumulates capital, dissaving that makes the available supply of capital shrink. In acting, man chooses between increasing his competence by additional saving or reducing the amount of his capital by keeping his consumption above the rate correct accountancy considers as his income.

Additional saving as well as the non-consumption of already previously accumulated savings is never "automatic," but always the result of an intentional abstention from instantaneous consumption. In abstaining from instantaneous consumption, the saver expects to be fully rewarded either by keeping something for later consumption or by acquiring the *property* of a capital good.

Where there is no saving, no capital goods come into existence. And there is no saving without purpose. A man defers consumption for the sake of an improvement of later conditions. He may want to improve his own conditions or those of definite other people. He does not abstain from consumption simply for the pleasure of somebody unknown.

There cannot be any such thing as a capital good that is not owned by a definite owner. Capital goods come into existence as the property of the individual or the group of individuals who were in the position to consume definite things but abstained from this consumption for the sake of later utilization. The way in which capital goods come into existence as private property determines the institutions of the capitalistic system.

Of course, today's heirs of the capitalistic civilization also construct the scheme of a world-embracing socialist body that forces every human being to submit meekly to all its orders. In such a socialist universe everything will be planned by the supreme authority, and to the individual "comrades" no other sphere of action will be left than unconditional surrender to the will of their masters. The comrades will drudge, but all the yield of their endeavors will be at the disposal of the high authority. Such is the ideal of socialism or communism, nowadays also called planning. The individual comrade will enjoy what the supreme authority assigns to him for his consumption and enjoyment. Everything else, all material factors of production, will be owned by the authority.

Such is the alternative. Mankind has to choose: on the one side—private property in the material factors of production. Then the demand of the consumers on the market determines what has to be produced, of what quality, and in what quantity. On the other side—all the material factors of production are owned by the central authority, and thus every individual entirely depends on its will and has to obey its orders. This authority alone determines what has to be produced and what and how much each comrade should be permitted to use or consume.

If one does not permit individuals to keep as their property the things produced for temporally deferred utilization, one removes any incentive to create such things and thus makes it impossible for acting man to raise his condition above the level of non-human animals. Thus the anti-property (i.e., socialist or communist) authors had to construct the design of a society in which all men are forced to obey unconditionally the orders issued from a central authority, from the great god called state, society, or mankind.

II

The social meaning and the economic function of private property have been widely misunderstood and misinterpreted, because people confuse conditions of the market economy with those of the militaristic systems vaguely labeled feudalism. The feudal lord was a conqueror or a conqueror's accomplice. He was anxious to deprive all those who did not belong to his own cluster of any opportunity to make a living otherwise than by humbly serving him or one of his class comrades. All the land—and this means in a primitive society virtually all the material factors of production—was owned by members of the proprietary caste and to the others, to those disdainfully called the "villains," nothing was left but unconditional surrender to the armed hereditary nobility. Those not belonging to this aristocracy were serfs or slaves; they had to obey and to drudge while the products of their toil were consumed by their masters.

The eminence of the inhabitants of Europe and their descendants who have settled in other continents consists in the fact that they have abolished this system and substituted for it a state of freedom and civic rights for every human being. It was a long and slow evolution, again and again interrupted by reactionary episodes, and great parts of our globe are even today only superficially affected by it. At the end of the eighteenth century the triumphal progress of this new social system was accelerated. Its most spectacular manifestation in the moral and intellectual sphere is known as the Enlightenment, its political and constitutional reforms as the liberal movement, while its economic and social effects are commonly referred to as the Industrial Revolution and the emergence of modern capitalism.

The historians dealing with the various phases of this up-to-now most momentous and weighty period of mankind's evolution tend to confine their investigations to special aspects of the course of affairs. They mostly neglect to show how the events in the various fields of human activity were connected with one another and determined by the same ideological and material factors. Unimportant detail sometimes engrosses their attention and prevents them from seeing the most consequential facts in the right light.

The most unfortunate outcome of this methodological confusion is to be seen in the current fateful misinterpretation of the recent political and economic developments of the civilized nations.

The great liberal movement of the eighteenth and nineteenth centuries aimed at the abolition of the rule of hereditary princes and aristocracies, and the establishment of the rule of elected representatives of the people. All kinds of slavery and serfdom ought to be abolished. All members of the nation should enjoy the full rights and privileges of citizenship. The laws and the practice of the administrative officers should not discriminate among the citizens.

This liberal revolutionary program clashed very soon with another program that was derived from the postulates of old communist sects. These sects, many of them inspired by religious ideas, had advocated confiscation and redistribution of land or some other forms of egalitarianism and of primitive communism. Now their successors proclaimed that a fully satisfactory state of human conditions could be attained only where all material factors of production are owned and operated by "society," and the fruits of economic endeavors are evenly distributed among all human beings.

Most of these communist[3] authors and revolutionaries were convinced that what they were aiming at was not only fully compatible with the customary program of the friends of representative government and freedom for all, but was its logical continuation, the very completion of all endeavors to give to mankind perfect happiness. Public opinion was by and large prepared to endorse this interpretation. As it was usual to call the adversaries of the liberal[4] demand for representative government the parties of the "right," and the liberal groups the parties of the "left," the communist (and later also the socialist) groups were considered as "more to the left" than the liberals. Popular opinion began to believe that while the liberal parties represent only the selfish class interests of the "exploiting" bourgeoisie, the socialist parties were fighting for the true interests of the immense majority, the proletariat.

But while these reformers were merely talking and drafting spurious plans for political action, one of the greatest and most beneficial events of mankind's history was going on—the Industrial Revolution. Its new business principle—that transformed human affairs more radically than any religious, ethical, legal, or technological innovation had done before—was mass production destined for consumption by the masses, not merely for consumption by members of the well-to-do classes. This new principle was not invented by statesmen and politicians; it was for a long time even not noticed by the members of the aristocracy, the gentry, and the urban patricians. Yet, it was the very beginning of a new and better age of human affairs when some people in Hanoverian En-

3 The term "socialism" was fashioned only many decades later and did not come into general use before the 1850s.
4 "Liberal" is here used in its nineteenth-century meaning that still prevails in European usage. In America "liberal" is nowadays used by and large as synonymous with socialism or "moderate" socialism.

gland started to import cotton from the American colonies; some took charge of its transformation to cotton goods for customers of modest income; while still others exported such goods to the Baltic ports to have them ultimately exchanged against corn that, brought to England, appeased the hunger of starving paupers.

The characteristic feature of capitalism is the traders' unconditional dependence upon the market, that is, upon the best possible and cheapest satisfaction of the most urgent demand on the part of the consumers. For every kind of production human labor is required as a factor of production. But labor as such, however masterfully and conscientiously performed, is nothing but a waste of time, material, and human effort if it is not employed for the production of those goods and services that at the instant of their being ready for use or consumption will best satisfy in the cheapest possible way the most urgent demand of the public.

The market is the prototype of what are called democratic institutions. Supreme power is vested in the buyers, and vendors succeed only by satisfying in the best possible way the wants of the buyers. Private ownership of the factors of production forces the owners—enterprisers—to serve the consumers. Eminent economists have called the market a democracy in which every penny gives a right to vote.

III

Both the political or constitutional democracy and the economic or market democracy are administered according to the decisions of the majority. The consumers, by their buying or abstention from buying, are as supreme in the market as the citizens who, through their voting in plebiscites or in the election of officers are supreme in the conduct of the affairs of state. Representative government and the market economy are the products of the same evolutionary process; they condition one another, and it would seem today that they are disappearing together in the great reactionary counter-revolution of our age.

Yet, reference to this striking homogeneousness must not prevent us from realizing that, as an instrument of giving expression to the genuine wants and interests of the individuals, the economic democracy of the market is by far superior to the political democracy of representative government. As a rule it is easier to choose between the alternatives which are open to a purchaser than to make a decision in matters of state and "high" politics. The average housewife may be very clever in acquiring the things she needs to feed and to clothe her children. But she may be less fit in electing the officers called to handle matters of foreign policy and military preparedness.

Then there is another important difference. In the market not only the wants and wishes of the majority are taken into account but also those of minorities, provided they are not entirely insignificant in numbers. The book trade publishes for the general reader, but also for small groups of experts in various fields. The garment trades are not only supplying clothing for people of normal size, but also merchandise for the use of abnormal customers. But in the political sphere only the will of the majority counts, and the minority is forced to accept what they may detest for rather serious reasons.

In the market economy, the buyers determine with every penny spent the direction of the production processes and thereby the essential features of all business activities. The consumers assign to everybody his position and function in the economic organism. The owners of the material factors of production are virtually mandatories or trustees of the consumers, revocably appointed by a daily repeated election. If they fail in their attempts to serve the consumers in the best possible and cheapest way, they suffer losses and, if they do not reform in time, lose their property.

Feudal property was acquired either by conquest or by a conqueror's favor. Once acquired, it could be enjoyed forever by the owner and his heirs. But capitalistic property must be acquired again and again by utilizing it for serving the consumers in the best possible way. Every owner of material factors of production is forced to adjust the services he renders to the best possible satisfaction of the continually changing demand of the consumers. A man may start his business career as the heir of a large fortune. But this does not necessarily help him in his competition with newcomers. The adjustment of an existing railroad system to the new situation created by the emergence of motor-cars, trucks, and airplanes was a more difficult problem than many of the tasks that had to be solved by enterprises newly started.

The fact that made the capitalistic methods of the conduct of business emerge and flourish is precisely the excellence of the services it renders to the masses. Nothing characterizes the fabulous improvement in the standard of living of the many better than the quantitative role that the entertainment industries play in modern business.

Capitalism has radically transformed all human affairs. Population figures have multiplied. In the few countries where neither the policies of the governments nor obstinate preservation of traditional ways on the part of the citizens put insurmountable obstacles in the way of capitalistic entrepreneurship, the living conditions of the immense majority of people have improved spectacularly. Implements never known before or considered as extravagant luxuries are now customarily available to the average man. The general standard of education and of material and spiritual well-being is improving from year to year.

All this is not an achievement of governments or of any charitable measures. More often than not it is precisely governmental action that frustrates beneficial developments which the regular operation of capitalistic institutions tends to bring about.

Let us look upon one special case. In the precapitalistic ages, saving and thereby the betterment of one's economic condition was really possible, apart from professional money-lenders (bankers), only to people who owned a farm or a shop. They could invest savings in an improvement or expansion of their property. Other people, the propertyless proletarians, could save only by hiding a few coins in a corner they considered as safe. Capitalism made the accumulation of some capital through saving accessible to everybody. Life insurance institutions, savings banks, and bonds give the opportunity of saving and earning interest to the masses of people with modest incomes, and these people make ample use of it. On the loan markets of the advanced countries, the funds provided by the numerous classes of such people play an important role. They could be an important factor in making the operation of the capitalistic system familiar to those who are not themselves employed in the financial conduct of business affairs. And first of all—they could more and more improve the economic and social standing of the many.

But unfortunately the policies of practically all nations sabotage this evolution in the most disgraceful manner. The governments of the United States, Great Britain, France, and Germany, not to speak of most of the smaller nations, were or are still committed to the most radical inflationist policies. While continually talking about their solicitude for the common man, they have without shame, again and again through government-made inflation, robbed the people who have taken out insurance policies, who are working under pension plans, who own bonds or savings deposits.

IV

The authors who in Western Europe at the end of the eighteenth century and in the first decades of the nineteenth century developed plans for the establishment of socialism were not familiar with the social ideas and conditions in Central Europe. They did not pay any attention to the *Wohlfahrtsstaat*, the welfare-state of the German monarchical governments of the eighteenth century. Neither did they read the classical book of German socialism, Fichte's *Geschlossener Handelsstaat*, published in the year 1800. When much later—in the last decades of the nineteenth century—the nations of the West, first among them England, embarked upon the Fabian methods of a temperate progress toward socialism, they did not raise the question why continental governments whom they despised as backward and absolutist had long before already adopted the allegedly new and progressive principles of social reform.

But the German socialists of the second part of the nineteenth century could not avoid dealing with this problem. They had to face the policies of Bismarck, the man of whom the pro-socialist *Encyclopaedia of the Social Sciences* says that he was "with reason regarded as the foremost exponent of state socialism in his day."[5] Lassalle toyed with the idea to further the cause of socialism by cooperation with this most "reactionary" paladin of the Hohenzollern. But Lassalle's premature death put an end to such plans and, very soon, also to the activities of the socialist group of which he had been the chief. Under the leadership of the disciples of Marx, the German socialist party turned to radical opposition to the Kaiser's regime. They voted in the Reichstag against all bills suggested by the government. Of course, being a minority party, their votes could not prevent the Reichstag's approval of various pro-labor laws, among them those establishing the famous social security system. Only in one case could they prevent the creation of a government-supported socialization measure, viz., the establishment

---

5 See W. H. Dawson, "Births," in *Encyclopaedia of the Social Sciences*, vol. 2 (New York: Macmillan, 1930), p. 573.

of a governmental tobacco monopoly. But all the other nationalization and municipalization measures of the Bismarck age were adopted in spite of the passionate opposition of the socialist party. And the nationalization policy of the German Reich that, thanks to the victories of its armies, in those years enjoyed all over the world an unprecedented prestige was adopted by many nations of Eastern and Southern Europe.

In vain did the German socialist doctrinaires try to explain and to justify the manifest contradiction between their fanatical advocacy of socialism and their stubborn opposition to all nationalization measures put into effect.[6] But notwithstanding the support the nationalization and municipalization policy of the authorities got from self-styled conservative and Christian parties, it very soon lost its popularity with the rulers as well as with those ruled. The nationalized industries were rather poorly operated under the management of the administrators appointed by the authorities. The services they had to render to the customers became highly unsatisfactory, and the fees they charged were more and more increased. And, worst of all, the financial results of the management of public servants were deplorable. The deficits of these outfits were a heavy burden on the national treasuries and forced again and again an increase in taxation. At the beginning of the twentieth century, one could no longer deny the obvious fact that the public authorities had scandalously failed in their attempts to administer the various business organizations they had acquired in the conduct of their "state socialism."

Such were conditions when the outcome of the First World War made the socialist parties paramount in Central and Eastern Europe and also considerably strengthened their influence in Western Europe. There was in those years in Europe practically no serious opposition to most radical pro-socialist plans.

The German revolutionary government was formed in 1918 by members of the Marxian social-democratic party. It had no less power than the Russian government of Lenin, and, like the Russian leader, it considered socialism as the only reasonable and possible solution to all political and economic problems. But it was also fully familiar with the fact that the nationalization measures adopted by the Imperial Reich before the war had brought unsatisfactory financial results and rather

---

6 About the lame excuses of Frederick Engels and Karl Kautsky, see my book *Socialism*, J. Kahane, trans. (New Haven, Conn.: Yale University Press, 1951), pp. 240ff.

poor service and also that the socialist measures resorted to in the years of the war had been unsuccessful. Socialism was in their opinion the great panacea, but it seemed that nobody knew what it really meant and how to bring it about properly. Thus, the victorious socialist leaders did what all governments do when they do not know what to do. They appointed a committee of professors and other people considered to be experts. For more than fifty years the Marxians had fanatically advocated socialization as the focal point of their program, as the nostrum to heal all earthly evils and to lead mankind forward into the new Garden of Eden. Now they had seized power, and all of the people expected that they would redeem their promise. Now they had to socialize. But at once they had to confess that they did not know what to do, and they were asking professors what socialization meant and how it could be put into practice.

It was the greatest intellectual fiasco history has ever known, and it put in the eyes of all reasonable people an inglorious end to all the teachings of Marx and hosts of lesser-known utopians.

Neither was the fate of the socialist ideas and plans in the West of Europe better than in the country of Marx. The members of the Fabian Society were no less perplexed than their continental friends. Like these, they too were fully convinced that capitalism was stone dead forever and that henceforth socialism alone would rule all nations. But they too had to admit that they had no plan of action. The flamboyantly advertised scheme of Guild Socialism was, as all people had to admit very soon, simply nonsense. It quietly disappeared from the British political scene.

But, of course, the intellectual debacle of socialism and especially of Marxism in the West did not affect conditions in the East. Russia and other Eastern countries of Europe and China turned to all-round nationalization. For them, neither the critical refutation of the Marxian and other socialist doctrines nor the failure of all nationalization experiments meant anything. Marxism became the quasi religion of the backward nations which were anxious to get the machines and, first of all, the deadly weapons developed in the West, but which abhorred the philosophy that had brought about the West's social and scientific achievements.

The Eastern political doctrine asking for immediate full socialization of all spheres of life and the pitiless extermination of all opponents gets rather sympathetic support on the part of many parties and influential politicians in the Western countries. "Building bridges to the communist sector of the world" is a task rather prevalent with many governments of the West. It is fashionable with some snobbish people to praise the unlimited despotism of Russia and China. And, worst of all, out of the taxes collected from the revenues of private business some governments, first of all that of the United States, are paying enormous subsidies to governments that have to face tremendous deficits precisely because they have nationalized many enterprises, especially railroads, post, telegraph and telephone service, and many others.

In the fully industrialized parts of our globe, in the countries of Western and Central Europe and North America, the system of private enterprise not merely survives, but continually improves and expands the services it renders. The statesmen, the bureaucrats, and the politicians look askance upon business. Most of the journalists, the writers of fiction, and the university teachers are propagating various brands of socialism. The rising generation is imbued with socialism in the schools. Only very rarely does one hear a voice criticizing socialist ideas, plans, and actions.

But socialism is for the peoples of the industrial world no longer a living force. There is no longer any question of nationalizing further branches of business.[7]

None of the many governments sympathizing with the socialist philosophy dares today seriously to suggest further measures of nationalization. On the contrary. For example, the American government as well as every reasonable American would have reason to be glad if the new Administration[8] could get rid of the Post Office with its proverbial inefficiency and its fantastic deficit.

Socialism started in the age of Saint-Simon as an attempt to give articulation to the ripeness of Caucasian man's Western civilization. It tried to preserve this aspect when it later looked upon colonialism and imperialism as its main targets. Today it is the rallying cry of the East, of the Russians and the Chinese, who reject the West's ideology, but eagerly try to copy its technology.

---

7 The British Labor cabinet paid homage to its party ideology in dealing with the steel industry. But everybody knows that this is merely a facade to conceal a little the great failure of all that the various British left-wing parties were aiming at for many decades.
8 [This was the first administration of Richard Nixon; he was elected president in 1968. — Ed.]

CHAPTER 14

On Equality and Inequality

I

The doctrine of natural law that inspired the eighteenth-century decla-
rations of the rights of man did not imply the obviously fallacious proposition that all men are biologically equal. It proclaimed that all men
are born equal in rights and that this equality cannot be abrogated by
any man-made law, that it is inalienable or, more precisely, imprescrip-
tible. Only the deadly foes of individual liberty and self-determination,
the champions of totalitarianism, interpreted the principle of equality
before the law as derived from an alleged psychical and physiological
equality of all men. The French declaration of the rights of the man
and the citizen of November 3, 1789, had pronounced that all men are
born and remain equal in rights. But, on the eve of the inauguration of
the regime of terror, the new declaration that preceded the Constitution of June 24, 1793, proclaimed that all men are equal *par la nature.*
From then on this thesis, although manifestly contradicting biological
experience, remained one of the dogmas of "leftism." Thus we read
in the *Encyclopaedia of the Social Sciences* that "at birth human in-
fants, regardless of their heredity, are as equal as Fords."[1]

However, the fact that men are born unequal in regard to physical
and mental capacities cannot be argued away. Some surpass their fellow men in health and vigor, in brain and aptitudes, in energy and
resolution and are therefore better fitted for the pursuit of earthly affairs
than the rest of mankind—a fact that has also been admitted by Marx.
He spoke of "the inequality of individual endowment and therefore
productive capacity (*Leistungsfähigkeit*)" as "natural privileges" and of

[This article is reprinted from *Modern Age* (Spring 1961).—Ed.]
1 Horace Kallen, "Behaviorism," in *Encyclopaedia of the Social Sciences*, vol. 2 (New York: Macmillan, 1930), p. 498.

"the unequal individuals (and they would not be different individuals if they were not unequal)."[2] In terms of popular psychological teaching we can say that some have the ability to adjust themselves better than others to the conditions of the struggle for survival. We may therefore—without indulging in any judgment of value—distinguish from this point of view between superior men and inferior men.

History shows that from time immemorial superior men took advantage of their superiority by seizing power and subjugating the masses of inferior men. In the status society there is a hierarchy of castes. On the one hand are the lords who have appropriated to themselves all the land and on the other hand their servants, the liegemen, serfs, and slaves, landless and penniless underlings. The inferiors' duty is to drudge for their masters. The institutions of the society aim at the sole benefit of the ruling minority, the princes, and their retinue, the aristocrats.

Such was by and large the state of affairs in all parts of the world before, as both Marxians and conservatives tell us, "the acquisitiveness of the bourgeoisie," in a process that went on for centuries and is still going on in many parts of the world, undermined the political, social, and economic system of the "good old days." The market economy—capitalism—radically transformed the economic and political organization of mankind.

Permit me to recapitulate some well-known facts. While under precapitalistic conditions superior men were the masters on whom the masses of the inferior had to attend; under capitalism the more gifted and more able have no means to profit from their superiority other than to serve to the best of their abilities the wishes of the majority of the less gifted. In the market economic power is vested in the consumers. They ultimately determine, by their buying or abstention from buying, what should be produced, by whom and how, of what quality and in what quantity. The entrepreneurs, capitalists, and landowners who fail to satisfy in the best possible and cheapest way the most urgent of the not yet satisfied wishes of the consumers are forced to go out of business and forfeit their preferred position. In business offices and in laboratories the keenest minds are busy fructifying the most complex achievements of scientific research for the production of ever better implements and gadgets for people who have no inkling of the theories

2 Karl Marx, *Critique of the Social Democratic Program of Gotha* [Letter to Bracke, May 5, 1875] (New York: International Publishers, 1938).

that make the fabrication of such things possible. The bigger an enterprise is, the more is it forced to adjust its production to the changing whims and fancies of the masses, its masters. The fundamental principle of capitalism is mass production to supply the masses. It is the patronage of the masses that make enterprises grow big. The common man is supreme in the market economy. He is the customer who "is always right."

In the political sphere, representative government is the corollary of the supremacy of the consumers in the market. Officeholders depend on the voters, as entrepreneurs and investors depend on the consumers. The same historical process that substituted the capitalistic mode of production for precapitalistic methods substituted popular government—democracy—for royal absolutism and other forms of government by the few. And wherever the market economy is superseded by socialism, autocracy makes a comeback. It does not matter whether the socialist or communist despotism is camouflaged by the use of aliases like "dictatorship of the proletariat" or "people's democracy" or "*Führer* principle." It always amounts to a subjection of the many to the few.

It is hardly possible to misconstrue more thoroughly the state of affairs prevailing in capitalistic society than by calling the capitalists and entrepreneurs a "ruling" class intent upon "exploiting" the masses of decent men. We will not raise the question of how the men who under capitalism are in business would have tried to take advantage of their superior talents in any other thinkable organization of production. Under capitalism they are vying with one another in serving the masses of less gifted men. All their thoughts aim at perfecting the methods of supplying the consumers. Every year, every month, every week, something unheard of before appears on the market and is soon made accessible to the many.

What has multiplied the "productivity of labor" is not some degree of effort on the part of manual workers, but the accumulation of capital by the savers and its reasonable employment by the entrepreneurs. Technological inventions would have remained useless trivia if the capital required for their utilization had not been previously accumulated by thrift. Man could not survive as a human being without manual labor. However, what elevates him above the beasts is not manual labor and the performance of routine jobs, but speculation, foresight that provides for the needs of the—always uncertain—future. The characteristic mark of production is that it is behavior directed by the mind. This fact cannot be conjured away by a semantics for which the word "labor" signifies only manual labor.

II

To acquiesce in a philosophy stressing the inborn inequality of men runs counter to many people's feelings. More or less reluctantly, people admit that they do not equal the celebrities of art, literature, and science, at least in their specialties, and that they are no match for athletic champions. But they are not prepared to concede their own inferiority in other human matters and concerns. As they see it, those who outstripped them in the market, the successful entrepreneurs and businessmen, owe their ascendancy exclusively to villainy. They themselves are, thank God, too honest and conscientious to resort to those dishonest methods of conduct that, as they say, alone make a man prosper in a capitalistic environment.

Yet, there is a daily growing branch of literature that blatantly depicts the common man as an inferior type: the books on the behavior of consumers and the alleged evils of advertising.[3] Of course, neither the authors nor the public that acclaims their writings openly state or believe that that is the real meaning of the facts they report.

As these books tell us, the typical American is constitutionally unfit for the performance of the simplest tasks of a householder's daily life. He or she does not buy what is needed for the appropriate conduct of the family's affairs. In their inwrought stupidity they are easily induced by the tricks and wiles of business to buy useless or quite worthless things. For the main concern of business is to profit not by providing the customers with the goods they need, but by unloading on them merchandise they would never take if they could resist the psychological artifices of "Madison Avenue." The innate incurable weakness of the average man's will and intellect makes the shoppers behave like "babes."[4] They are easy prey to the knavery of the hucksters.

Neither the authors nor the readers of these passionate diatribes are aware that their doctrine implies that the majority of the nation are morons, unfit to take care of their own affairs and badly in need of a paternal guardian. They are preoccupied to such an extent with their envy

3 [For example, John K. Galbraith, *The Affluent Society* (Boston: Houghton Mifflin, 1958). — Ed.]
4 Vance Packard, "Babes in Consumerland," *The Hidden Persuaders* (New York: Cardinal Editions, 1957), pp. 90–97.

and hatred of successful businessmen that they fail to see how their description of consumers' behavior contradicts all that the "classical" socialist literature used to say about the eminence of the proletarians. These older socialists ascribed to the "people," to the "working and toiling masses," to the "manual workers" all the perfections of intellect and character. In their eyes, the people were not "babes" but the originators of what is great and good in the world, and the builders of a better future for mankind.

It is certainly true that the average common man is in many regards inferior to the average businessman. But this inferiority manifests itself first of all in his limited ability to think, to work, and thereby to contribute more to the joint productive effort of mankind. Most people who satisfactorily operate in routine jobs would be found wanting in any performance requiring a modicum of initiative and reflection. But they are not too dull to manage their family affairs properly. The husbands who are sent by their wives to the supermarket "for a loaf of bread and depart with their arms loaded with their favorite snack items"[5] are certainly not typical. Neither is the housewife who buys regardless of content, because she "likes the package."[6]

It is generally admitted that the average man displays poor taste. Consequently business, entirely dependent on the patronage of the masses of such men, is forced to bring to the market inferior literature and art. (One of the great problems of capitalistic civilization is how to make high-quality achievements possible in a social environment in which the "regular fellow" is supreme.) It is furthermore well known that many people indulge in habits that result in undesired effects. As the instigators of the great anti-capitalistic campaign see it, the bad taste and the unsafe consumption habits of people and the other evils of our age are simply generated by the public relations or sales activities of the various branches of "capital"—wars are made by the munitions industries, the "merchants of death"; dipsomania by alcohol capital, the fabulous "whiskey trust," and the breweries.

This philosophy is not only based on the doctrine depicting the common people as guileless suckers who can easily be taken in by the ruses of a race of crafty hucksters. It implies in addition the nonsensical theorem that the sale of articles which the consumer really needs and

5 Ibid., p. 95.
6 Ibid., p. 93.

would buy if not hypnotized by the wiles of the sellers is unprofitable for business and that on the other hand only the sale of articles which are of little or no use for the buyer or are even downright detrimental to him yields large profits. For if one were not to assume this, there would be no reason to conclude that in the competition of the market the sellers of bad articles outstrip those of better articles. The same sophisticated tricks by means of which slick traders are said to convince the buying public can also be used by those offering good and valuable merchandise on the market. But then good and poor articles compete under equal conditions, and there is no reason to make a pessimistic judgment on the chances of the better merchandise. While both articles—the good and the bad—would be equally aided by the alleged trickery of the sellers, only the better one enjoys the advantage of being better.

We need not consider all the problems raised by the ample literature on the alleged stupidity of the consumers and their need for protection by a paternal government. What is important here is the fact that, notwithstanding the popular dogma of the equality of all men, the thesis that the common man is unfit to handle the ordinary affairs of his daily life is supported by a great part of popular "leftist" literature.

III

The doctrine of the inborn physiological and mental equality of men logically explains differences between human beings as caused by postnatal influences. It emphasizes especially the role played by education. In the capitalistic society, it is said, higher education is a privilege accessible only to the children of the "bourgeoisie." What is needed is to grant every child access to every school and thus educate everyone.

Guided by this principle, the United States embarked upon the noble experiment of making every boy and girl an educated person. All young men and women were to spend the years from six to eighteen in school, and as many as possible of them were to enter college. Then the intellectual and social division between an educated minority and a majority of people whose education was insufficient was to disappear. Education would no longer be a privilege; it would be the heritage of every citizen.

Statistics show that this program has been put into practice. The number of high schools, of teachers and students multiplied. If the present trend goes on for a few years more, the goal of the reform will be fully attained; every American will graduate from high school.

But the success of this plan is merely apparent. It was made possible only by a policy that, while retaining the name "high school," has entirely destroyed its scholarly and scientific value. The old high school conferred its diplomas only on students who had at least acquired a definite minimum knowledge in some disciplines considered as basic. It eliminated in the lower grades those who lacked the abilities and the disposition to comply with these requirements. But in the new regime of the high school the opportunity to choose the subjects he wished to study was badly misused by stupid or lazy pupils. Not only are fundamental subjects such as elementary arithmetic, geometry, physics, history, and foreign languages avoided by the majority of high school students, but every year boys and girls who are deficient in reading and spelling English receive high school diplomas. It is a very characteristic fact that some universities found it necessary to provide special courses to improve the reading skill of their students. The often passionate debates concerning the high school curriculum that have now been going on for several years prove clearly that only a limited number of teenagers are intellectually and morally fit to profit from school attendance. For the rest of the high school population the years spent in classrooms are simply wasted. If one lowers the scholastic standard of high schools and colleges in order to make it possible for the majority of less gifted and less industrious youths to get diplomas, one merely hurts the minority of those who have the capacity to make use of the teaching.

The experience of the last decades in American education bears out the fact that there are inborn differences in man's intellectual capacities that cannot be eradicated by any effort of education.

IV

The desperate but hopeless attempts to salvage, in spite of indisputable proofs to the contrary, the thesis of the inborn equality of all men are motivated by a faulty and untenable doctrine concerning popular government and majority rule.

This doctrine tries to justify popular government by referring to the supposed natural equality of all men. Since all men are equal, every individual participates in the genius that enlightened and stimulated the greatest heroes of mankind's intellectual, artistic, and political history. Only adverse postnatal influences prevented the proletarians from equaling the brilliance and the exploits of the greatest men. Therefore, as Trotsky told us,[7] once this abominable system of capitalism will have given way to socialism, "the average human being will rise to the heights of an Aristotle, a Goethe, or a Marx." The voice of the people is the voice of God, it is always right. If dissent arises among men, one must, of course, assume that some of them are mistaken. It is difficult to avoid the inference that it is more likely that the minority errs than the majority. The majority is right, because it is the majority and as such is borne by the "wave of the future."

The supporters of this doctrine must consider any doubt of the intellectual and moral eminence of the masses as an attempt to substitute despotism for representative government.

However, the arguments advanced in favor of representative government by the liberals of the nineteenth century—the much-maligned Manchestermen and champions of laissez faire—have nothing in common with the doctrines of the natural inborn equality of men and the superhuman inspiration of majorities. They are based upon the fact, most lucidly exposed by David Hume, that those at the helm are always a small minority as against the vast majority of those subject to their orders. In this sense every system of government is minority rule and as such can last only as long as it is supported by the belief of those ruled that it is better for themselves to be loyal to the men in office than to try to supplant them by others ready to apply different methods of administration. If this opinion vanishes, the many will rise in rebellion and replace by force the unpopular officeholders and their systems by other men and another system. But the complicated industrial apparatus of modern society could not be preserved under a state of affairs in which the majority's only means of enforcing its will is revolution. The objective of representative government is to avoid the reappearance of such a violent disturbance of the peace and its detrimental effects upon morale, culture, and material well-being. Government by the people, i.e., by elected representatives, makes peaceful change possible. It warrants the agreement of public opinion and the principles according to which the affairs of state are conducted. Majority

---

7 Leon Trotsky, *Literature and Revolution*, R. Strunsky, trans. (London: George Allen and Unwin, 1925), p. 256.

rule is for those who believe in liberty not as a metaphysical principle, derived from an untenable distortion of biological facts, but as a means of securing the uninterrupted peaceful development of mankind's civilizing effort.

V

The doctrine of the inborn biological equality of all men begot in the nineteenth century a quasi-religious mysticism of the "people" that finally converted it into the dogma of the "common man's" superiority. All men are born equal. But the members of the upper classes have unfortunately been corrupted by the temptation of power and by indulgence in the luxuries they secured for themselves. The evils plaguing mankind are caused by the misdeeds of this foul minority. Once these mischief-makers are dispossessed, the inbred nobility of the common man will control human affairs. It will be a delight to live in a world in which the infinite goodness and the congenital genius of the people will be supreme. Never-dreamt-of happiness for everyone is in store for mankind.

For the Russian Social Revolutionaries this mystique was a substitute for the devotional practices of Russian Orthodoxy. The Marxians felt uneasy about the enthusiastic vagaries of their most dangerous rivals. But Marx's own description of the blissful conditions of the "higher phase of Communist Society"[8] was even more sanguine. After the extermination of the Social-Revolutionaries the Bolsheviks themselves adopted the cult of the common man as the main ideological disguise of their unlimited despotism of a small clique of party bosses.

The characteristic difference between socialism (communism, planning, state capitalism, or whatever other synonym one may prefer) and the market economy (capitalism, private enterprise system, economic freedom) is this: in the market economy the individuals *qua* consumers are supreme and determine by their buying or not-buying what should be produced, while in the socialist economy these matters are fixed by the government. Under capitalism the customer is the man for whose patronage the suppliers are striving and to whom after the sale they say "thank you" and "please come again." Under socialism the "comrade"

---

8 Marx, *Critique of the Social Democratic Program of Gotha.*

gets what "big brother" deigns to give him, and he is to be thankful for whatever he got. In the capitalistic West the average standard of living is incomparably higher than in the communistic East. But it is a fact that a daily increasing number of people in the capitalistic countries—among them also most of the so-called intellectuals—long for the alleged blessings of government control.

It is vain to explain to these men what the condition of the common man both in his capacity as a producer and in that of a consumer is under a socialist system. An intellectual inferiority of the masses would manifest itself most evidently in their aiming at the abolition of the system in which they themselves are supreme and are served by the elite of the most talented men and in their yearning for the return to a system in which the elite would tread them down.

Let us not fool ourselves. It is not the progress of socialism among the backward nations, those that never surpassed the stage of primitive barbarism and those whose civilizations were arrested many centuries ago, that shows the triumphant advance of the totalitarian creed. It is in our Western circuit that socialism makes the greatest strides. Every project to narrow down what is called the "private sector" of the economic organization is considered as highly beneficial, as progress, and is, if at all, only timidly and bashfully opposed for a short time. We are marching "forward" to the realization of socialism.

VI

The classical liberals of the eighteenth and nineteenth centuries based their optimistic appreciation of mankind's future upon the assumption that the minority of eminent and honest men would always be able to guide by persuasion the majority of inferior people along the way leading to peace and prosperity. They were confident that the elite would always be in a position to prevent the masses from following the pied pipers and demagogues and adopting policies that must end in disaster. We may leave it undecided whether the error of these optimists consisted in overrating the elite or the masses or both. At any rate it is a fact that the immense majority of our contemporaries is fanatically committed to policies that ultimately aim at abolishing the social order in which the most ingenious citizens are impelled to serve the masses in the best possible way. The masses—including those called the intellectuals—passionately advocate a system in which they no longer will be the customers who give the orders but wards of an omnipotent authority. It does not matter that this economic system is sold to the common man under the label "to each according to his needs" and its political and constitutional corollary, unlimited autocracy of self-appointed officeholders, under the label "people's democracy."

In the past, the fanatical propaganda of the socialists and their abettors, the interventionists of all shades of opinion, was still opposed by a few economists, statesmen, and businessmen. But even this often lame and inept defense of the market economy has almost petered out. The strongholds of American snobbism and "patricianship," fashionable, lavishly endowed universities and rich foundations, are today nurseries of "social" radicalism. Millionaires, not "proletarians," were the most efficient instigators of the New Deal and the "progressive" policies it engendered. It is well known that the Russian dictator was welcomed on his first visit to the United States with more cordiality by bankers and presidents of big corporations than by other Americans.

The tenor of the arguments of such "progressive" businessmen runs this way: "I owe the eminent position I occupy in my branch of business to my own efficiency and application. My innate talents, my ardor in acquiring the knowledge needed for the conduct of a big enterprise, my diligence raised me to the top. These personal merits would have secured a leading position for me under any economic system. As the head of an important branch of production I would also have enjoyed an enviable position in a socialist commonwealth. But my daily job under socialism would be much less exhausting and irritating. I would no longer have to live under the fear that a competitor can supersede me by offering something better or cheaper on the market. I would no longer be forced to comply with the whimsical and unreasonable wishes of the consumers. I would give them what I—the expert—think they ought to get. I would exchange the hectic and nerve-wracking job of a businessman for the dignified and smooth functioning of a public servant. The style of my life and work would resemble much more the seigniorial deportment of a grandee of the past than that of an ulcer-plagued executive of a modern corporation. Let philosophers bother about the true or alleged defects of socialism. I, from my personal point of view, cannot see any reason why I should oppose it. Administrators of nationalized enterprises in all parts of the world and visiting Russian officials fully agree with my point of view."

There is of course, no more sense in the self-deception of these capitalists and entrepreneurs than in the daydreams of the socialists and communists of all varieties.

VII

As ideological trends are today, one has to expect that in a few decades, perhaps even before the ominous year 1984, every country will have adopted the socialist system. The common man will be freed from the tedious job of directing the course of his own life. He will be told by the authorities what to do and what not to do, he will be fed, housed, clothed, educated, and entertained by them. But, first of all, they will release him from the necessity of using his own brains. Everybody will receive "according to his needs." But what the needs of an individual are will be determined by the authority. As was the case in earlier periods, the superior men will no longer serve the masses, but dominate and rule them.

Yet, this outcome is not inevitable. It is the goal to which the prevailing trends in our contemporary world are leading. But trends can change and hitherto they always have changed. The trend toward socialism too may be replaced by a different one. To accomplish such a change is the task of the rising generation.

CHAPTER 15

The Clash of Group Interests

I

To apply the term "group tensions" to denote contemporary antagonisms is certainly a euphemism. What we have to face are conflicts considered as irreconcilable and resulting in almost continual wars, civil wars, and revolutions. As far as there is peace, the reason is not, to be sure, love of peace based on philosophical principles, but the fact that the groups concerned have not yet finished their preparations for the fight and, for considerations of expediency, are waiting for a more propitious moment to strike the first blow.

In fighting one another, people are not in disagreement with the consensus of contemporary social doctrines. It is an almost generally accepted dogma that there exist irreconcilable conflicts of group interests. Opinions differ by and large only with regard to the question, which groups have to be considered as genuine groups and, consequently, which conflicts are the genuine ones? The nationalists call the nations (which means in Europe the linguistic groups), the racists call the races, and the Marxians call the "social classes" the genuine groups. But there is unanimity with regard to the doctrine that a genuine group cannot prosper except to the detriment of other genuine groups. The natural state of intergroup relations, according to this view, is conflict.

This social philosophy has made itself safe against any criticism by proclaiming the principle of polylogism. Marx, Dietzgen, and the radicals among the representatives of the "sociology of knowledge" teach that the logical structure of mind is different with different social classes. If a man deviates from the teachings of Marxism, the reason is either that he is a member of a nonproletarian class and therefore con-

[Reprinted from *Approaches to National Unity*, Lyman Bryson, ed. (New York: Harper and Row, 1945).—Ed.]

stitutionally incapable of grasping the proletarian philosophy; or, if he is a proletarian, he is simply a traitor. Objections raised to Marxism are of no avail because their authors are "sycophants of the bourgeoisie." In a similar way the German racists declare that the logic of the various races is essentially different. The principles of "non-Aryan" logic and the scientific theories developed by its application are invalid for the "Aryans."

Now, if this is correct, the case for peaceful human cooperation is hopeless. If the members of the various groups are not even in a position to agree with regard to mathematical and physical theorems and biological problems, they will certainly never find a pattern for a smoothly functioning social organization.

It is true that most of our contemporaries, in their avowal of polylogism do not go so far as the consistent Marxians, racists, etc. But a vicious doctrine is not rendered less objectionable by timidity and moderation in its expression. It is a fact that contemporary social and political science makes ample use of polylogism, although its champions refrain from expounding clearly and openly the philosophical foundations of polylogism's teachings. Thus, for instance, the Ricardian theory of foreign trade is simply disposed of by pointing out that it was the "ideological superstructure" of the class interests of the nineteenth-century British bourgeoisie. Whoever opposes the fashionable doctrines of government interference with business or of labor-unionism is—in Marxian terminology—branded as a defender of the unfair class interests of the "exploiters."

The very way in which social scientists, historians, editors, and politicians apply the terms "capital" and "labor" or deal with the problems of economic nationalism is the proof that they have entirely adopted the doctrine of the irreconcilable conflict of group interests. If it is true that such irreconcilable conflicts exist, neither international war nor civil war can be avoided.

Our wars and civil wars are not contrary to the social doctrines generally accepted today. They are precisely the logical outcome of these doctrines.

II

The first question we must answer is: What integrates those groups whose conflicts we are discussing?

Under a caste system the answer is obvious. Society is divided into

rigid castes. Caste membership assigns to each individual certain privileges *(privilegia favorabilia)* or certain disqualifications *(privilegia odi-
osa)*. As a rule a man inherits his caste quality from his parents, remains
in his caste for life, and bestows his status on his children. His personal
fate is inseparably linked with that of his caste. He cannot expect an
improvement of his conditions except through an improvement in the
conditions of his caste or estate. Thus there prevails a solidarity of interests among all caste members and a conflict of interests among the
various castes. Each privileged caste aims at the attainment of new
privileges and at the preservation of the old ones. Each underprivileged
caste aims at the abolition of its disqualifications. Within a caste society
there is an irreconcilable antagonism between the interests of the various castes.

Capitalism has substituted equality under the law for the caste system of older days. In a free-market society, says the liberal[1] economist,
there are neither privileged nor underprivileged. There are no castes
and therefore no caste conflicts. There prevails full harmony of the
rightly understood (we say today, of the long-run) interests of all individuals and of all groups. The liberal economist does not contest the
fact that a privilege granted to a definite group of people can further
the short-term interests of this group at the expense of the rest of the
nation. An import duty on wheat raises the price of wheat on the domestic market and thus increases the income of domestic farmers. (As
this is not an essay on economic problems, we do not need to point out
the special-market situation required for this effect of the tariff.) But it
is unlikely that the consumers, the great majority, will lastingly acquiesce in a state of affairs which harms them for the sole benefit of the
wheat growers. They will either abolish the tariff or try to secure similar
protection for themselves. If all groups enjoy privileges, only those are
really benefited who are privileged to a far greater degree than the rest.
With equal privilege for each group, what a man profits in his capacity
as producer and seller is, on the other hand, absorbed by the higher
prices he must pay in his capacity as consumer and buyer. But beyond
this, all are losers because the tariff diverts production from the places
offering the most favorable conditions for production to places offering
less favorable conditions and thus reduces the total amount of the na-

1 [Mises uses the term "liberal" in its nineteenth-century European sense, meaning laissez
faire. —Ed.]

tional income. The short-run interests of a group may be served by a privilege at the expense of other people. The rightly understood, i.e., the long-run interests, are certainly better served in the absence of any privilege.

The fact that people occupy the same position within the frame of a free-market society does not result in a solidarity of their short-run interests. On the contrary, precisely this sameness of their place in the system of the division of labor and social cooperation makes them competitors and rivals. The short-run conflict between competitors can be superseded by the solidarity of the rightly understood interests of all members of a capitalist society. But—in the absence of group privileges—it can never result in group solidarity and in an antagonism between the interests of the group and those of the rest of society. Under free trade the manufacturers of shoes are simply competitors. They can be welded together into a group with solidarity of interests only when privilege supervenes, e.g., a tariff on shoes (*privilegium favorabile*) or a law discriminating against them for the benefit of some other people (*privilegium odiosum*).

It was against this doctrine that Karl Marx expounded his doctrine of the irreconcilable conflict of class interests. There are no castes under capitalism and bourgeois democracy. But there are social classes, the exploiters and the exploited. The proletarians have one common interest, the abolition of the wages system and the establishment of the classless society of socialism. The bourgeois, on the other hand, are united in their endeavors to preserve capitalism.

Marx's doctrine of class war is entirely founded on his analysis of the operation of the capitalist system and his appraisal of the socialist mode of production. His economic analysis of capitalism has long since been exploded as utterly fallacious. The only reason which Marx advanced in order to demonstrate that socialism is a better system than capitalism was his pretension to have discovered the law of historical evolution; namely, that socialism is bound to come with "the inexorability of a law of nature." As he was fully convinced that the course of history is a continuous progress from lower and less desirable modes of social production toward higher and more desirable modes and that therefore each later stage of social organization must necessarily be a better stage than the preceding stages were, he could not have any doubts about the blessings of socialism. Having quite arbitrarily taken for granted that the "wave of the future" is driving mankind toward socialism, he believed that he had done everything that was needed to prove the superiority of socialism. Marx not only refrained from any analysis of a socialist economy, he outlawed such studies as utterly "utopian" and "unscientific."

Every page of the history of the past hundred years belies the Marxian dogma that the proletarians are necessarily internationally minded and know that there is an unshakable solidarity of the interests of the wage earners all over the world. Delegates of the "labor" parties of various countries have consorted with one another in the various International Working Men's Associations. But while they indulged in the idle talk about international comradeship and brotherhood, the pressure groups of labor of various countries were busy in fighting one another. The workers of the comparatively underpopulated countries protect, by the means of immigration barriers, their higher standard of wages against the tendency toward an equalization of wage rates, inherent in a system of free mobility of labor from country to country. They try to safeguard the short-run success of "pro-labor" policies by barring commodities produced abroad from access to the domestic market of their own countries. Thus they create those tensions which must result in war whenever those injured by such policies expect that they can brush away by violence the measures of foreign governments that are prejudicial to their own well-being.

Our age is full of serious conflicts of economic group interests. But these conflicts are not inherent in the operation of an unhampered capitalist economy. They are the necessary outcome of government policies interfering with the operation of the market. They are not conflicts of Marxian classes. They are brought about by the fact that mankind has gone back to group privileges and thereby to a new caste system.

In a capitalist society the proprietary class is formed of people who have well succeeded in serving the needs of the consumers and of the heirs of such people. However, past merit and success give them only a temporary and continually contested advantage over other people. They are not only continually competing with one another; they have daily to defend their eminent position against newcomers aiming at their elimination. The operation of the market steadily removes incapable capitalists and entrepreneurs and replaces them by parvenus. It again and again makes poor men rich and rich men poor. The characteristic features of the proprietary class are that the composition of its membership is continually changing, that entrance into it is open to everybody, that continuance in membership requires an uninterrupted sequence of successful business operations, and that the membership is divided against itself by competition. The successful businessman is not interested in a policy of sheltering the unable capitalists and entrepreneurs against the vicissitudes of the market. Only the incompetent capitalists and entrepreneurs (mostly later generations) have a selfish interest in such "stabilizing" measures. However, within a world of pure capitalism, committed to the principles of a consumers' policy, they have no chance to secure such privileges.

But ours is an age of producers' policy. Present-day "unorthodox" doctrines consider it as the foremost task of a good government to place obstacles in the way of the successful innovator for the sole benefit of less-efficient competitors and at the expense of the consumers. In the predominantly industrial countries the main feature of this policy is the protection of domestic farming against the competition of foreign agriculture working under more-favorable physical conditions. In the predominantly agricultural countries it is, on the contrary, the protection of domestic manufacturing against the competition of foreign industries producing at lower costs. It is a return to the restrictive economic policies abandoned by the liberal countries in the course of the eighteenth and nineteenth centuries. If people had not discarded these policies then, the marvelous economic progress of the capitalist era would never have been achieved. If the European countries had not opened their frontiers to the importation of American products— cotton, tobacco, wheat, etc.—and if the older generations of Americans had rigidly barred the importation of European manufactures, the United States would never have reached its present stage of economic prosperity.

It is this so-called producers' policy that integrates groups of people, who otherwise would consider each other simply as competitors, into pressure groups with common interests. When the railroads came into being, the coach drivers could not consider joint action against this new competition. The climate of opinion would have rendered such a struggle futile. But today the butter producers are successfully struggling against margarine, and the musicians against recorded music. Present-day international conflicts are of the same origin. The American farmers are intent upon barring access to Argentinian cereals, cattle, and meat. European countries are acting in the same way against the products of the Americas and of Australia.

The root causes of present-day group antagonisms must be seen in the fact that we are on the point of going back to a system of rigid castes. Australia and New Zealand are democratic countries. If we overlook the fact that their domestic policies are breeding domestic pressure groups fighting one another, we could say that they have built up homogeneous societies with equality under the law. But under their immigration laws, barring access not only to colored but no less to white immigrants, they have integrated their whole citizenry into a privileged caste. Their citizens are in a position to work under conditions safeguarding a higher productivity of the individual's work and thereby higher wages. The nonadmitted foreign workers and farmers are excluded from the enjoyment of such opportunities. If an American labor union bars colored Americans from access to its industry, it converts the racial difference into a caste quality.

We do not have to discuss the problem whether or not it is true that the preservation and the further development of occidental civilization require the maintenance of the geographical segregation of various racial groups. The task of this paper is to deal with the economic aspects of group conflicts. If it is true that racial considerations make it inexpedient to provide an outlet for the colored inhabitants of comparatively overpopulated areas, this would not contradict the statement that in an unhampered capitalist society there are no irreconcilable conflicts of group interests. It would only demonstrate that racial factors make it inexpedient to carry the principle of capitalism and market economy to its utmost consequences and that the conflict among various races is, for reasons commonly called noneconomic, irreconcilable. It would certainly not disprove the statement of the liberals that within a society of free enterprise and free mobility of men, commodities, and capital, there are no irreconcilable conflicts of the rightly understood interests of various individuals and groups of individuals.

III

The belief that there prevails an irreconcilable conflict of group interests is age-old. It was the essential proposition of Mercantilist doctrine. The Mercantilists were consistent enough to deduce from this principle that war is an inherent and eternal pattern of human relations. Mercantilism was a philosophy of war.

I want to quote two late manifestations of this doctrine. First a dictum of Voltaire. In the days of Voltaire, the spell of Mercantilism had already been broken. French Physiocracy and British Political Economy were on the point of supplanting it. But Voltaire was not yet familiar with the new doctrines, although one of his friends, David Hume, was their foremost champion. Thus he wrote in 1764 in his *Dictionnaire Philosophique*: "être bon patriote, c'est souhaiter que sa ville s'enrichisse par le commerce et soit puissante par les armes. Il est clair qu'un pays ne peut gagner sans qu'un autre perde, et qu'il ne peut vaincre sans faire des malheureux."[2] Here we have in beautiful French the formula of modern warfare, both economic and military. More than eighty years later we find another dictum. Its French is less perfect, but its phrasing is more brutal. Says Prince Louis Napoleon Bonaparte, the later Emperor Napoleon III: "La quantité des marchandises qu'un pays exporte est toujours en raison directe du nombre des boulets qu'il peut envoyer à ses ennemis, quand son honneur et sa dignité le commandent."[3]

Against the background of such opinion we must hold the achievements of the classical economists and of the liberal policies inspired by them. For the first time in human history a social philosophy emerged that demonstrated the harmonious concord of the rightly understood interests of all men and of all groups of men. For the first time, a philosophy of peaceful human cooperation came into being. It represented a radical overthrow of traditional moral standards. It was the establishment of a new ethical code.

All older schools of morality were heteronomous. They viewed the moral law as a restraint imposed upon man by the unfathomable decrees of Heaven or by the mysterious voice of conscience. Although a mighty group has the power to improve its own earthly well-being by inflicting damage upon weaker groups, it should abide by the moral law and forgo furthering its own selfish interests at the expense of the weak. The observance of the moral law amounts to sacrificing some advantage which the group or the individual could possibly secure.

In the light of the economic doctrine things are entirely different. There are, within an unhampered market society, no conflicts among the rightly understood selfish interests of various individuals and groups.

2 This quote from Voltaire is translated as: "to be a good patriot is to hope that one's town enriches itself through commerce and is powerful, in arms. It is clear that a country cannot gain unless another loses and it cannot prevail without making others miserable."

3 Louis Napoleon Bonaparte, *Extinction du Paupérisme* (Paris: La Guilotiére, 1848), p. 6, and is translated as: "The quantity of goods which a country exports is always directly related to the number of bullets which it can send against its enemies when its honor and dignity demand it."

In the short run, an individual or a group may profit from violating the interests of other groups or individuals. But in the long run, in indulging in such actions, they damage their own selfish interests no less than those of the people they have injured. The sacrifice that a man or a group makes in renouncing some short-run gains, lest they endanger the peaceful operation of the apparatus of social cooperation, is merely temporary. It amounts to an abandonment of a small immediate profit for the sake of incomparably greater advantages in the long run.

Such is the core of the moral teachings of nineteenth-century utilitarianism. Observe the moral law for your own sake, neither out of fear of hell nor for the sake of other groups, but for your own benefit. Renounce economic nationalism and conquest, not for the sake of foreigners and aliens, but for the benefit of your own nation and state.

It was the partial victory of this philosophy that resulted in the marvelous economic and political achievements of modern capitalism. It is its merit that today there are living many more people on the earth's surface than at the eve of the Industrial Revolution, and that in the countries most advanced on the way to capitalism, the masses enjoy a more comfortable life than the well-to-do of earlier ages.

The scientific basis of this utilitarian ethics was the teachings of economics. Utilitarian ethics stands and falls with economics.

It would, of course, be a faulty mode of reasoning to assume beforehand that such a science of economics is possible and necessary because we approve of its application to the problem of peace preservation. The very existence of a regularity of economic phenomena and the possibility of a scientific and systematic study of economic laws must not be postulated a priori. The first task of any preoccupation with the problems commonly called economic is to raise the epistemological question whether or not there is such a thing as economics.

What we must realize is this: if this scrutiny of the epistemological foundations of economics were to confirm the statements of the German Historical School and of the American Institutionalists that there is no such thing as an economic theory and that the principles upon which the economists have built their system are illusory, then violent conflicts among various races, nations, and classes are inevitable. Then the militarist doctrine of perpetual war and bloodshed must be substituted for the doctrine of peaceful social cooperation. The advocates of peace are fools. Their program stems from ignorance of the basic problems of human relations.

There is no social doctrine other than that of the "orthodox" and "re-actionary" economists that allow the conclusion that peace is desirable and possible. Of course, the Nazis promise us peace for the time after their final victory, when all other nations and races will have learned that their place in society is to serve as slaves of the Master Race. The Marxians promise us peace for the time after the final victory of the proletarians, precisely, in the words of Marx, after the working class will have passed "through long struggles, through a whole series of histori-cal processes, wholly transforming both circumstances and men."[4]

This is meager consolation indeed. At any rate, such statements do not invalidate the proposition that nationalists and Marxians consider their violent conflict of group interests as a necessary phenomenon of our time and that they attach a moral value either to international war or to class war.

IV

The most remarkable fact in the history of our age is the revolt against rationalism, economics, and utilitarian social philosophy; it is at the same time a revolt against freedom, democracy, and representative government. It is usual to distinguish within this movement a left wing and a right wing. The distinction is spurious. The proof is that it is impossible to classify in either of these groups the great leaders of the movement. Was Hegel a man of the Left or of the Right? Both the left-wing and the right-wing Hegelians were undoubtedly correct in refer-ring to Hegel as their master. Was Georges Sorel a Leftist or a Rightist? Both Lenin and Mussolini were his intellectual disciples. Bismarck is commonly regarded as a reactionary. But his social security scheme is the acme of present-day progressivism. If Ferdinand Lassalle had not been the son of Jewish parents, the Nazis would call him the first Ger-man labor leader and the founder of the German Socialist Party, one of their greatest men. From the point of view of true liberalism, all the supporters of the conflict doctrine form one homogenous party.

The main weapon applied by both the right- and the left-wing anti-liberals is calling their adversaries names. Rationalism is called super-ficial and unhistoric. Utilitarianism is branded as a mean system of

4 Karl Marx, *Der Bürgerkrieg in Frankreich*, Pfemfert, ed. (Berlin: Politische Aktions Bibliothek, 1919), p. 54.

stockjobber ethics. In the non–Anglo-Saxon countries it is, besides, qualified as a product of British "peddler mentality" and of American "dollar philosophy." Economics is scorned as "orthodox," "reactionary," "economic royalism," and "Wall Street ideology."

It is a sad fact that most of our contemporaries are not familiar with economics. All the great issues of present-day political controversies are economic. Even if we were to leave out of account the fundamental problem of capitalism and socialism, we must realize that the topics daily discussed on the political scene can be understood only by means of economic reasoning. But people, even the civic leaders, politicians, and editors, shun any serious occupation with economic studies. They are proud of their ignorance. They are afraid that a familiarity with economics might interfere with the naive self-confidence and complacency with which they repeat slogans picked up by the way.

It is highly probable that not more than one out of a thousand voters knows what economists say about the effects of minimum wage rates, whether fixed by government decree or by labor-union pressure and compulsion. Most people take it for granted that to enforce minimum wage rates above the level of wage rates which would have been established on an unhampered labor market is a policy beneficial to all those eager to earn wages. They do not suspect that such minimum wage rates must result in permanent unemployment of a considerable part of the potential labor force. They do not know that even Marx flatly denied that labor unions can raise the income of all workers and that the consistent Marxians in earlier days therefore opposed any attempts to decree minimum wage rates. Neither do they realize that Lord Keynes's plan for the attainment of full employment, so enthusiastically endorsed by all "progressives," is essentially based on a reduction of the height of *real* wage rates. Keynes recommends a policy of credit expansion, because he believes that "gradual and automatic lowering of real wages as a result of rising prices" would not be so strongly resisted by labor as any attempt to lower money wage rates.[5] It is not too bold a statement to affirm that with regard to this primordial problem the "progressive" experts do not differ from those popularly

5 John Maynard Keynes, *The General Theory of Employment, Interest and Money* (London: Macmillan, 1936), p. 264. For a critical examination of this idea, see H. Albert Hahn, *Deficit Spending and Private Enterprise* (Postwar Readjustments Bulletin, no. 8, U.S. Chamber of Commerce, 1944), pp. 28–29.

disparaged as "reactionary labor baiters." But then the doctrine that there prevails an irreconcilable conflict of interests between employers and employees is deprived of any scientific foundation. A lasting rise in wage rates for all those eager to earn wages can be attained only by the accumulation of additional capital and by the improvement in technical methods of production which this additional wealth makes feasible. The rightly understood interests of employers and employees coincide.

It is no less probable that only small groups realize the fact that the free traders object to the various measures of economic nationalism because they consider such measures as detrimental to the welfare of their own nation, not because they are anxious to sacrifice the interests of their fellow citizens to those of foreigners. It is beyond doubt that hardly any German, in the critical years preceding Hitler's rise to power, understood that those fighting aggressive nationalism and eager to prevent a new war were not traitors, ready to sell the vital interest of the German nation to foreign capitalism, but patriots who wanted to spare their fellow citizens the ordeal of a senseless slaughter.

The usual terminology classifying people as friends or foes of labor and as nationalists or internationalists is indicative of the fact that this ignorance of the elementary teachings of economics is an almost universal phenomenon. The conflict philosophy is firmly entrenched in the minds of our contemporaries.

One of the objections raised against the liberal philosophy recommending a free-market society runs this way: "Mankind can never go back to any system of the past. Capitalism is done for because it was the social organization of the nineteenth century, an epoch that has passed away."

However, what these would-be progressives are supporting is tantamount to a return to the social organization of the ages preceding the Industrial Revolution. The various measures of economic nationalism are a replica of the policies of Mercantilism. The jurisdictional conflicts between labor unions do not essentially differ from the struggles between medieval guilds and inns. Like the absolute princes of seventeenth- and eighteenth-century Europe, these moderns are aiming at a system under which the government undertakes the direction of all economic activities of its citizens. It is not consistent to exclude beforehand the return to the policies of Richard Cobden and John Bright if one does not find any fault in returning to the policies of Louis XIV and Jean-Baptiste Colbert.

V

It is a fact that the living philosophy of our age is a philosophy of irreconcilable conflict and dissociation. People value their party, class, linguistic group, or nation as supreme, believe that their own group cannot thrive but at the expense of other groups, and are not prepared to tolerate any measures which in their opinion would have to be considered as an abandonment of vital group interests. Thus a peaceful arrangement with other groups is out of the question. Take for instance the implacable intransigence of Leninism or of the French *nationalisme integral* or of the Nazis. It is the same with regard to domestic affairs. No pressure group is ready to renounce the least of its pretensions for considerations of national unity.

It is true that powerful forces are fortunately still counteracting these tendencies toward disintegration and conflict. In this country the traditional prestige of the Constitution is such a factor. It has nipped in the bud the endeavors of various local pressure groups to break up the economic unity of the nation by the establishment of interstate trade barriers. But in the long run even these noble traditions may prove insufficient if not backed by a social philosophy, positively proclaiming the primacy of the interests of the great society and their harmony with the rightly understood interests of each individual.

CHAPTER 16

A Hundred Years of Marxian Socialism

I

In this year, 1967, in which the University of Chicago celebrates its seventy-fifth anniversary, the present-day world's most powerful political movement, Marxism, commemorates the two most important dates of its history. A hundred years ago the literary foundation of Marxism was laid by the publication of the first volume of *Das Kapital*, the only volume published by Marx himself. And fifty years later, in 1917, the first Marxian government was established in the vast expanses up to that time subject to the rule of the Tsars of Russia. It seems appropriate to choose these jubilees for an appreciation of the role Marxism played and still plays in the evolution of the modern world.

Karl Marx was in his lifetime known only to small groups of uninfluential people. In the circles of revolutionary agitators in which he moved he had more enemies than friends. When he died in 1883, many newspapers did not find it necessary to report the fact.

All the economic and sociological doctrines of Marx and all his interpretations of history have been conclusively disproved. The great overwhelming success of Marxism, the adoption of its programs by Russia and the other Slavonic countries of the European East as well as by China, constitutes in itself a spectacular refutation of the fundamental tenets of essential Marxian theories. For according to these teachings one had to expect either that all countries will at the same time turn communist or that the industrially most advanced nations of Western Europe and North America will take the lead.

All this and much more has to be said to demonstrate the futility of all the allegedly scientific achievements of Marx. But when all this is

[This article appears to have been written in 1967; previously unpublished. —Ed.]

said, there remains the fact that the ideas of this penniless writer, whose name even was unknown to most of his contemporary statesmen and politicians, influenced in the last seventy or eighty years the course of world affairs more than any other philosophy. Whatever one may think about Marx, one must not belittle the role he plays in our world. He is one of the great political leaders, perhaps the most influential political leader the world has ever known.

The history of literature preserves the names and sometimes also the writings of powerless dreamers who took pleasure in contriving plans for an earthly paradise. The common characteristic of all these schemes was that the inmates of the proposed utopia were destined to be unconditionally subject to the orders first of its founder and later of his successors. What the utopias envisioned were in fact all-embracing prisons. Perhaps one can excuse some of their authors as psychopaths.

The critical spirit that the Enlightenment generated killed the prestige of all utopian projects and thereby also of the communist idea. The historical role of Karl Marx was that he taught an epistemology in the light of which the discredited idea could be resurrected and made seemingly safe against any attempt at refutation. This Marxian theory consists of three dogmas:

1. As long as there is no socialism, mankind is divided into social classes the vital interests of which are irremediably opposed to one another.

2. A man's thinking is necessarily always determined by his class affiliation. His thoughts mirror the special interests of his class, incurably antagonistic to the interests of the members of all other classes.[1]

3. The conflict of the class interests results in the pitiless class-struggle that unavoidably leads to the victory of the most numerous and most wronged class, the proletariat. Then the everlasting age of socialism dawns.

As this doctrine sees it, there cannot be any peaceful discussion concerning any serious problems between people belonging to different classes. They can never come to an agreement. For the result of their thinking will always be "ideological," i.e., determined by the special

---

1 There is a flaw in this point of the doctrine, a special privilege granted to its authors, the bourgeois Marx and Engels. They belong, says the *Communist Manifesto,* to a group "of bourgeois ideologists who have raised themselves to the level of comprehending theoretically the historical movements as a whole."

interests of their own class. The war between the classes is permanent. It will come to an end only by the radical "liquidation" of all "exploiting classes" and their "sycophants," the wretched peoples who betray their class comrades.

There had been, long before Marx, doctrines teaching the total war leading to the radical extinction or enslavement of the defeated. There was the ominous aphorism, repeated again and again, that no man can profit but by the loss of others. It was precisely the great achievements of the classical liberal doctrine to have demonstrated by an irrefutable chain of reasoning the solidarity of the rightly understood interests of all individuals and classes of individuals, whatever mark may have been applied to characterize class membership.

But all these endeavors to provide a rational basis for peaceful human cooperation within the frame of society appear vain in the light of the Marxian epistemology. There is, as long as the "classless" society has not been established by the radical liquidation of the exploiting classes, no such thing as a doctrine the truth of which can and must be acknowledged by all reasonable people. There are only class ideologies, i.e., doctrines adequate to the special interests of the thinker's class that are implacably opposed to the interests of all other classes and their members. There cannot be any question of dealing with the pros and cons of any ideology that originated from a member of an exploiting class. All that has to be done to destroy it is to reveal the class affiliation of its author.

The essence of all that Marx said is: The trend of historical evolution leads irresistibly to the establishment of an ideal, in every regard perfect state of affairs called socialism. Those denying the truth of this statement are badly prejudiced and must be pitilessly "liquidated." Their cause is doomed, as in virtue of the ineluctable laws of cosmic becoming the future belongs to socialism.

The political success of the Marxian propaganda revived the aspirations of other militant groups. There are deadly foes of socialism who claim for their race or for their linguistic group hegemony on the surface of our planet in the same way in which Marx claims it for the proletarian class.

In the liberal age of the nineteenth century the most consistent liberal group, the British Manchester School, expected that the general adoption of free trade and laissez faire will result in perpetual peace. In our age there is no longer any question of such an "abolition of war."

There are on the one hand people who abhor foreign wars and preach revolution and civil war, and there are on the other hand people who want peace within their own nation or race and pitiless total war against all foreigners.

The philosophy of the Enlightenment considered as its most precious achievement the principle of toleration, the liberty to uphold one's opinions in religious and philosophical matters without being harassed by the government. It was no less anxious to give to everybody the right to choose the way by which he planned to integrate himself into the system of social cooperation. The great ideal of the age of classical liberalism was liberty, the freedom to make the plans for one's own life. Today people are longing and fighting for the substitution of "planning" for the market economy. Planning, as they employ the term, means: plans made by others will prescribe to me what I am to do and how to do it. All my life I will live like the boy in the boarding school, like the soldier in the army, like the prisoner in his cell. I will see, hear, read, and learn what my superiors will consider as fit for me. I will be a cog in a vast machine, the operation of which is directed by the authorities. There is only one philosophy, one ideology, one quasi religion that people are free to profess and to propagate. Any deviation from the tenets of this dogmatism is a death-deserving crime.

II

Thus Marxism is the most radical and unconditional rejection of all the ideals of freedom and liberty. It does not acknowledge any dissenting opinion's right to existence. In its endeavors to extirpate all traces of any view it deems heretical, it is in no way inferior to any persecutors, inquisitors, and witch-hunters of the darkest ages. But it parades as the only legitimate continuation of all the past struggles for freedom.

That Marxism could, in spite of all its inherent deficiencies, attain the powerful position it holds in the present-day world is due to the fact that statesmen, politicians, and the immense majority of our intellectuals and businessmen are entirely ignorant of the most blatant defects of the Marxian reasoning. Let us look at the central thesis of Marxism, at the doctrine of the inevitability of the great social revolution that will transform capitalism into the everlasting bliss of socialism.

The coming of this revolution, says Marx, is unavoidable because the "immanent laws of capitalistic production" must make "the mass of misery, oppression, slavery, degradation and exploitation" of the working-class grow to such a degree that the proletarians are finally driven into rebellion, expropriate their oppressors, and establish the socialist system that will last forever. Thus the progressing impoverishment of the working masses, that is allegedly inherent in the capitalistic mode of production, leads to the great social catastrophe out of which the final radical revolution and thereby the age of everlasting bliss are born.

Now let us first compare Marx's unconditional forecast with the facts of these one hundred years that have passed. Nobody will deny that in all capitalistic countries the average standard of living of the earners of wages and salaries has improved to an unprecedented and unexpected degree. These people enjoy amenities of which the richest princes and lords of ages gone by could not even dream.

Marx and all the others who developed similar doctrines entirely failed to realize that the characteristic feature of capitalism is that it is mass production for the satisfaction of the needs of the masses. In the precapitalistic ages the processing trades worked only for supplying the well-to-do. The innovation that capitalism brought consisted in the establishment of shops producing for the many. Thus, e.g., the textile industries and the garment industries were not substitutes for activities of artisans who had previously done spinning, weaving, and tailoring for the common man. Such a class of businessmen selling to the "lower strata" of the population did not exist in precapitalistic ages. The activities the textile and the garment industries displaced were those of the female members of the family. In the early stages of capitalism factories turning out consumers' goods worked almost exclusively for the poorer strata of the population. And also today only a fraction of all the products of industry is consumed by those in the upper income brackets. The much greater part is consumed by the same people who are working in the factories, shops, and offices.

This alleged law of the inevitably progressing pauperization of the working class, which has been spectacularly disproved by history, was for Marx and is still for his followers one of the two fundamental laws of economics and of historical evolution. Its companion law was, long before Marx adopted it, to the economists known as the "iron law of wages," a term that Marx for purely personal reasons disliked although all his economic doctrines as expounded in the *Communist Manifesto* and in *Das Kapital* are based upon this iron law. And now there are two rather important things to say about this alleged iron law: first that it had been rejected as nonsensical and contrary to fact by all reasonable men already before Marx published his *Kapital* book, and, secondly that it is logically incompatible with the other fundamental law of Marxism, the law of the progressive pauperization of the wage-earning masses.

This alleged iron law of wages declares that wages can never rise above the minimum requisite to keep the laborer in bare existence as a laborer. Any increase in wages above this height will lead to an increase in population, and then the competition of increased numbers for employment will force wages down again to the minimum. We do not have to deal with the inherent fallacy of this pseudo-law. But if one adopts its reasoning in order to demonstrate that in the long run no rise in the average wage rate above the minimum is possible, one must also imply that no fall in the average rate can occur. The progressive impoverishment of the working masses which those famous observations at the end of the twenty-fourth chapter of *Das Kapital* describe cannot happen in the capitalistic system as depicted and analyzed by Marx in the preceding chapters of his book. The main thesis of Marx's great historical prognostication, the progressive impoverishment of the wage-earning masses, contradicts the main thesis of Marx's economic doctrine, the iron law of wages. Besides, as has been said already, it has been spectacularly refuted by the facts.

III

To appreciate correctly the meaning and the historical effects of the Marxian philosophy, we must confront it with the economic teachings prevalent in the middle of the nineteenth century. By and large, economists at that time agreed in the statement that the improvement of the material well-being of all strata of the population depends on the accumulation of capital. Not only the capitalists but also all other people gain by the increase of the per-head quota of capital available. There are no means by which the wages of all those eager to sell their labor can be raised other than by accelerating the increase of capital as compared with population.

Daily experience showed to all not hopelessly prejudiced men that all the attempts to deny this fundamental truth were vain. The essential fact about the capitalistic industries, the flourishing of which excited the envy of the anticapitalistic authors, is and was that the main consumers of their products are the same people who are toiling in their production. Only a few years after the publication of the first volume of *Das Kapital,* Jevons, Menger, and Walras developed the marginal utility approach to economic problems that clearly demonstrated the stake the laborers have in the increase of capital available. Today nobody dares to deny that what is most badly needed for any improvement of people's material well-being is a richer supply of capital.

The precapitalistic method of fighting poverty was charity. Those who had were asked or forced to give to those who had less. The capitalistic method is to produce more and cheaper; its application requires the accumulation of larger quantities of capital through saving. Charity cannot improve the average standard of living. Saving and capital accumulation do.

Socialism cannot alter these basic ontological facts. Also in a socialist or communist commonwealth any improvement of the average standard of living is conditioned by a previous accumulation of additional capital. The only successful "war against poverty" consists in removing impediments that retard saving and in abolishing conditions making for capital decumulation.

We human beings, subject to all the frailties and errors of human existence, cannot know how our earthly affairs may look when viewed by a superhuman intellect. But we can observe the fact that all noncapitalistic peoples implicitly acknowledge the superiority of our capitalistic methods in eagerly clamoring for their products.

When the Bolsheviks took over the government of Russia, they and all their friends in other countries were fully convinced that their noisily propagandized five-year plan would transform Russia into an earthly paradise. The world has now the experience of half a century of communist management in the countries that offer in Europe and in northwestern Asia the most propitious conditions for agricultural production and are also extremely rich in mineral and other natural resources. The results achieved by the socialist methods of management were simply catastrophic. There is no need to stress the fact, not denied by any sane observer, that the capitalistic methods of production are by far superior to those advocated by the communist or socialist parties.

The superiority of the capitalistic system of production is due to the fact that it remunerates everybody according to his contribution to the satisfaction of his fellow men. It thus stimulates everybody, within the system of the social division of labor, to exert himself to the utmost. The better a man serves others, the better for him. In the capitalistic market economy the consumers are supreme. In his capacity as a producer of commodities and services everybody is forced to serve the consumers.

The wage earner is remunerated according to the price the consumer is prepared to pay for his contribution to the qualities of the product. If the employer were to pay more to the worker, he would suffer losses in selling his wares. If he were to pay less, he would gain a surplus, and this fact would attract new competitors whose endeavors to snatch away the workers would raise wage rates back to the break-even point.

It does not matter how people judge this system of remuneration from a more or less biased point of view. One may call unfair the fact that an opera singer or a boxing champion earns many times more than a stevedore or a charwoman. But then we must put the blame upon nature for not having endowed more people with the qualities required for singing or boxing.

Production of goods ready for consumption requires the use of capital goods, that is, of tools and of half-finished material. Capital comes into existence by saving, i.e., the temporary abstention from consumption. The share that goes to the owners of the capital goods does not deprive either the workers or the consumers. It is the price the capitalists receive for the postponement of consumption.

There is no such thing as production in general. The main problem of production is the plan: what to produce, in what quantity and quality, how and where. Production is necessarily always production for the satisfaction of future needs. As future conditions are uncertain, production is always speculative. It may result either in a surplus or in a deficit in the means of the entrepreneur.

In the market economy everybody is free to choose the way in which he plans to serve his fellow men. There is—and this distinguishes the capitalistic system from the status society of the past and from the totalitarian despotism of the contemporary dictatorial regimes—no compulsion forcing the individual to adopt a definite way of life and assigning to him a definite place in the frame of society. The sovereign consumers in their never relaxing greed for more goods are always anxious to entrust the entrepreneurial functions to those best fitted for the conduct of business affairs. And the entrepreneurs are always in search for the best managerial and technological help. Under capitalism everybody has the chance to attain a position in which he can best serve the consumers, i.e., his fellow men. The supremacy of the consumers is not contested by any capitalistic institution. Every piece of capital goods must be invested in the lines in which it contributes to the satisfaction of the most urgent of the not yet fully satisfied wants of the public.

The unprecedented success of capitalism is due to the fact that in its sphere the long-run interests of the individual always coincide with those of other individuals. Thus the individual in serving his own concerns serves also, or, at least, does not prejudice, the concerns of other people. The incompetency of the socialist society manifests itself in the fact that under prudent management the individual's interests do not agree with those of other individuals.

In the market economy the height of the individual worker's compensation is determined by the value his work adds to the merchandise. The better a man works, the higher is his pay. He is personally interested in doing a good job.

But under socialism the individual has no personal incentive to exert his strength fully. If he works more fervently, all the toil and trouble of his overexertion inconvenience him and him alone; but at best he will enjoy an infinitesimal fraction only of the additional product that his overexertion has brought about. In the socialist system, in which all the fruits of the various individuals' labor are appropriated by the supreme office of production management and then distributed among the comrades without any regard for the worth of their individual contribution, there is no inducement for an individual to exert his strength. Everyday experience proves again and again the correctness of this statement. And nobody realizes its truth better than all those men who are directing the affairs of communist Russia.

The individual citizen in the capitalistic countries knows that he will fare the better, the more and the better he is able to contribute to the well-being of his fellow citizens. In working for the satisfaction of others, he always works for his own benefit. This is valid for all members of the capitalistic society, for the capitalists, and for the entrepreneurs no less than for the wage earners.

A characteristic mark of all anticapitalistic ideas is their failure to comprehend the role capitalistic saving and its result, the accumulation of capital, play in the human endeavors to survive. Animals and savages live from hand to mouth. What characterizes man is that he accumulates goods that make it possible for him to embark upon more time-consuming roundabout methods of providing for his needs. All the cultural and spiritual eminence of man is conditioned by the accumulation of capital. Saving in order to make these roundabout methods of production possible is the fundamental and only method to improve the physiological, intellectual, and moral status of mankind. All that distinguishes the material conditions of this country from those of the countries one calls poor, backward, underdeveloped, or barbarian is due to the higher per-head quota of capital accumulated and employed — invested — in production processes.

Nature has endowed many parts of the earth's surface much better than the territories originally inhabited by the white men who have developed the modern capitalistic methods of production. All the achievements of Western civilization were made possible by the establishment of moral and legal institutions that protected the individuals' savings and their investment for productive purposes against the rapacity of the rulers. While in the East private property was practically at the mercy of the officeholders, the West's legal systems considered it the basic principle of society's organization.

IV

The market economy and the capitalistic system have been described as a consumers' democracy in which every penny gives a right to vote.[2] Such metaphorical descriptions are always optional. But if we accept the metaphor in this case, we must not forget to point out some very momentous differences between the two systems of what is called democracy.

First: In the political democracy of representative government, one votes for men. The voter renounces virtually his prerogative in favor of the elected officeholder. In the market democracy the objective of the voting process is not a man, but a man's achievements, the products of his exertion. The voter does not express blind confidence in the future comportment of one of the candidates. He approves or disapproves of an already accomplished service.

Secondly: The average voter is as a rule not qualified to form a pertinent judgment about the problems of governmental policies. But the average housewife is by and large capable of distinguishing between what is good and wholesome for her family and what is not.

Political democracy and economic democracy condition one another. A democratic constitution is the political corollary either of a primitive community of the owners of family farms or of a market

2 [Cf. Frank A. Fetter, *The Principles of Economics*, 2nd ed. (New York: The Century Company, 1910), p. 394. — Ed.]

economy. A socialist system implies unlimited dictatorial powers of the chief. What created representative government in the countries of Western civilization was the gradual substitution of capitalism for the disintegrating feudal system. What inaugurated a new age of bloody dictatorship was the step by step progress of government interference with business.

The socialist system not only abolishes the democracy of the market. It is no less incompatible with political democracy. Most people are misled in this regard by the inappropriate terminology of present-day political language, the spurious distinction between left-wing parties and right-wing parties. In the European parliaments of the early nineteenth century the parties fighting absolutism and asking for more parliamentarianism were traditionally seated to the left of the chairman, and their opponents, the stooges of absolutism, at his right. Today in this country one calls the advocates of constitutional and economic freedom "rightists," and the supporters of socialist or communist dictatorship "leftists." A really Babylonic confusion of tongues!

Many more things are to be said about the achievements of the capitalistic system and the failure of all socialist and half-socialist experiments. And there is first of all need to refer to the economists' fundamental critique of socialism, viz., the fact that a socialist system would not be able to establish any kind of economic calculation and would therefore lack any method of distinguishing between what is more and what is less fit to satisfy human wants. A world-embracing socialist system would therefore not merit the name of an economic system. It would rather be a groping about in the dark, not being able to distinguish what is, from its own point of view, i.e., from the point of view of the socialist managers and the people for whom they have to provide, more or less desirable. Today this inability to calculate does not yet trouble the dictators of the communist nations. They can use and do use for this purpose the prices established on the markets of the capitalistic nations.

The greatness and the incomparable efficiency of the market economy are due to the fact that all economic actions can be calculated. This means: it is possible to find out what the costs of every action are, what we have to renounce in order to get the thing the costs of which we are trying to determine in terms of money. There are also many actions that cost more than merely things that have a price on the market. But these things are objects the value of which is directly determined by those enjoying it. If a municipality considers a project that—apart from monetary costs—requires the demolition of a historical landmark, it can fully take into account its emotional significance without assigning to it a definite monetary appreciation.

Economic calculation is the vital power that animates all manifestations of human action and cooperation in matters commonly called economic. It is the triumph of the human mind, the intellectual instrument that has enabled man to bring about all that elevates his life above that of the brutes.

As present to our mind, the history of economic activities and technological achievements records only radical changes and innovations, turning points of mankind's intellectual and chrematistic evolution. It refers, e.g., to the adoption of steam power and deals with the conditions of what is called the age of steam power. In resorting to such a simplification one easily forgets that the concept "steam power" encompasses a great variety of methods employed for the utilization of steam. The oldest and most primitive specimens of a steam engine underwent a long series of transformations and improvements that adjusted the device for various uses. In the technology of the capitalistic economy there is nothing permanent or stable, but a continuous tendency to adapt production methods daily anew to the best possible and cheapest satisfaction of the wants of the consumers. A thousand or several thousand changes—most slight ones only, some, of course, of momentous consequences—transformed the automobile as it was constructed in the last decade of the nineteenth century into what is called an automobile today. What makes this inherent disposition toward improvement mentally possible is the system of bookkeeping by double entry. It enables the entrepreneur to calculate the costs of every item of his products and thus to discover the most appropriate methods for the conduct of his operations. It is the mental device that provides the opportunity to compare degrees in the usefulness of various methods of production. It makes it possible to eliminate technological waste of definite amounts of labor or of material, i.e., their employment for a production that withholds specific labor or material from an employment in which it would satisfy consumers' demand in a more satisfactory way.

The economic history of the last two or three centuries provides ample illustration for the beneficial effect of this capitalistic method. The average standard of living of the masses of Western and Central Europe was, seen from our present-day point of view, shockingly bad. What brought about a radical change were not authoritarian decrees, but the ideas and the deeds of enterprising men whose energy and diligence were challenged by the profit motive. It was such men that in a process that fortunately is still going on transformed the almost completely autarkic economies of their nations into predominantly industrial systems and the isolation of various economic regions into the world market. The present standard of living of these countries—a very high one when compared with that of all other countries but that of the United States—is entirely due to the export of manufactured goods, most of which are produced out of imported raw materials. Economic calculation enabled all these improvements and adjusts the activities of business daily anew to the continually changing state of demand and supply of various commodities and services.

V

Marx was not the author of the socialist idea, and he did not contribute anything to the futile attempts to demonstrate the soundness and the practicability of the plans for the establishment of a socialist commonwealth. He passionately rejected all such efforts as unscientific. For his own socialism, the prognostication of the inevitability of socialism's coming, he claimed the epithet scientific. In his opinion this settled the issue for the contemporaries of Darwin and Maxwell.[3] How could any decent fellow dare to question what science taught! In vilifying everything that existed as hopelessly contaminated by the capitalistic surrounding, Marxism acquired the aureole of representing the unspoiled excellence of pure science and the golden age to come.

Marx was opposed to all claims of nationalism and chauvinism. But among the factors that contributed to the adoption of the Marxian teachings these nationalistic sentiments played a not negligible role. Modern capitalism developed first in England. The chauvinists of Western and Central Europe had the uneasy feeling that their own peoples were only imitators of methods that the British had invented and perfected. With the spread of the capitalistic methods over all parts of the earth, this kind of resentment grew more and more. The Slavonic peoples of Europe and the inhabitants of Asia and Africa are plagued by the fact that in all matters of literary, artistic, scientific, social, tech-

---

3 [James Clark Maxwell developed the theory of electromagnetic waves.—Ed.]

nological, and economic affairs they are following in the wake of the advanced nations of Europe and their descendants. In condemning capitalism as the worst of all evils that befell mankind, Marxism re-establishes their moral equilibrium. In the light of the Marxian philosophy, *not* to be responsible for the emergence of this most unfair and harmful system is no longer seen as the proof of moral and intellectual inferiority but, on the contrary, as the test of eminence.

Under the impact of the socialist idea governments and municipalities embarked upon the nationalization and municipalization of various enterprises. Paramount in these policies was the Imperial Government of Germany led by Prince Bismarck whom the *Encyclopaedia of the Social Sciences* calls "the foremost exponent of state socialism in his day."[4] But the trend toward socialism prevailed also in all other countries. Already in the 'eighties of the nineteenth century Sidney Webb, the leader of Fabian socialism, declared that the socialist philosophy is "but the conscious and explicit assertion of principles of social organization which have been already in great part unconsciously adopted." And he added that the economic history of the nineteenth century was "an almost continuous record of the progress of socialism."[5] A few years later an eminent British statesman, Sir William Harcourt, stated: "We are all socialists now."[6] In 1913 an American author, Elmer Robert, qualified the economic policies of the German Imperial Government as "monarchical socialism."[7]

It was precisely these socialist actions of various governments and municipalities that for the first time directed general attention to the main problems of socialism, the inherent inefficiency of the public management of enterprises. Poor service and rising deficits were the characteristic features of almost all nationalized or municipalized undertakings. All people agreed that a radical reform of their conduct of affairs was peremptory. But no practical suggestions turned up.

The Germans whom the crushing defeat in the First World War had deprived of their moral and political equilibrium were in 1918 even more anxious to adopt integral socialism than were the Russians. They considered this as the best method to wreak vengeance upon

4 *Encyclopaedia of the Social Sciences,* vol. 2 (New York: Macmillan, 1930), p. 573.
5 Sidney Webb, in *Fabian Essays in Socialism,* first published in 1889 (New York: Humboldt, 1891), p. 4.
6 Cf. G. M. Trevelyan, *Shortened History of England* (London: Longmans, 1942), p. 510.
7 Elmer Roberts, *Monarchical Socialism in Germany* (New York: C. Scribner's Sons, 1913).

the victorious capitalist nations, the United States, Great Britain, and France. But there was first a great obstacle to overcome; there was the unsolved problem of funding a method that would make a satisfactory management of the socialized enterprises possible. This task the German Revolution entrusted to a committee of socialist luminaries and university professors. It was really an absurd spectacle. The revolutionary part of the social democrats, victorious after a struggle of more than half a century, fully convinced that thanks to their action mankind has reached the most momentous turning point in its history, is forced to admit that it does not know how to put the cardinal, the only, point in its program that matters into effect and expects that a committee of experts and professors will tell them what to do! And, of course, this committee, whose best-known members were Doctor Hilferding and Professor Schumpeter, produced a collection of volumes dealing with various subjects, but did not solve the insoluble problem for the solution of which it had been established. It did not indicate a method for a reasonable and successful conduct of business operated by other principles than those of capitalistic profit-seeking.

It is important to keep in mind these facts if one wants to understand the course history took in the last fifty years. The masses of the civilized and industrialized nations of the West were easily talked, by fanatical agitators, into accepting anticapitalistic doctrines and voting for the parties that aim at subjecting all economic activities to the orders of the authorities. In the civilized countries this side of the Iron Curtain the masses of the voters and the members of the government fully sympathize with the socialist creed, and at the educational institutions and in the press hardly any critics of the socialist ideas are tolerated. But there is the undeniable fact of the irremediable inadequacy of the socialist methods of work, to say nothing of the absolute impossibility of any kind of economic calculation in a world-embracing socialist system. Public management of any undertakings and concerns unavoidably results in financial failure and poor service. The inefficiency of the bureaucratic conduct of affairs is proverbial. The very thought of an expansion of public management of industries makes even the most bigoted socialist politicians shudder.

Russia went communist in 1917, and many half-civilized nations followed in its wake because their intellectuals did not know anything that could not be learned from reading the writings of Marx and Engels. Thus, e.g., Lenin thought that he could convincingly reject all qualms

about the proper functioning of the socialist conduct of business affairs by pointing out that these socialist organizations will work like the
post office![8] In his eyes the "chief things necessary for the organizing
of the first phase of Communist society" were "accounting and control," and these he asserted have been "simplified by capitalism to the
utmost, till they have become the extraordinary simple operations of
watching, recording and issuing receipts, within the reach of anybody
who can read and write and knows the first four rules of arithmetic."[9]

Such blatant nonsense could be told to the ignorant self-styled intellectuals of Russia who prided themselves on being the vanguard of
Marxism and thereby of progress and civilization. It gave comfort to
the chauvinists of all backward nations who had an uneasy feeling in
comparing their own country's culture with that of the West. But it did
not appeal to the industrialized nations of the West. Americans could
not be fooled by the promise that the socialist system will succeed and
will make everybody happy because it will take for its model the post
office and will organize the whole of society as "one office and one factory with equal work and equal pay."[10]

Such are today conditions in the countries of Western civilization.
People are by and large enthusiastic admirers of Marxism and socialism
or communism. The officeholders whom they elect seldom miss any
occasion to demonstrate their anticapitalistic fanaticism by seriously
disturbing the functioning of the market economy. But once the opportunity is given to them to put fully into practice their plans for all-round
socialization of business, they shrink back. Nobody expects any longer
that the West German Social Democrats or the British Labor Party will
put into effect the fundamental principle of their socialist program. All
they do is to harass the businessmen and to take pleasure in sabotaging
their efforts to improve the methods of production.

What divides the nations today is not the ideological antagonism of
capitalism and socialism. Also in the noncommunist countries the governments and the immense majority of those called the intellectuals
are more or less committed to the socialist creed. What prevents these
self-styled liberals and progressivists from adopting the Lenin methods
of all-round socialization is the fact that they cannot help reluctantly
admitting the lamentable inadequacy of the socialist methods of eco-

8 V. I. Lenin, *State and Revolution* (New York: International Publishers, 1917), pp. 43f.
9 Ibid., pp. 83f.
10 Cf. ibid., pp. 83f.

nomic management. They apprehend that every farther step forward on the road toward the socialization of enterprises will seriously impair the quantity and the quality of the products of every industry. Everybody knows that this will hurt, first of all, the workers, as the main beneficiaries of the capitalistic methods of doing business are the masses of those employed in offices and workshops. Very few, of course, have the courage to refer publicly to this fact; but everybody is aware of it.

Pre-Marxian socialist authors had developed detailed plans for the organization and operation of a socialist commonwealth. It was easy for economists to demonstrate the impractability and absurdity of these designs. Marx carefully avoided dealing with this tricky problem and condemned as utopian phantasies all attempts of earlier socialists to treat it. Socialism is bound to come as the highest stage of mankind's evolution, he repeated again and again, and will arrange everything in the best possible way. But the crux is that every step toward the realization of the socialist ideals invariably resulted and will always result in economic failure and that the socialists are at a loss to discover any method of avoiding this outcome.

What stopped and stops the progress of the socialist policies is the fact that people have today the opportunity to compare the working of socialism with the working of capitalism. The socialists of Eastern Germany, the self-styled German Democratic Republic, spectacularly admitted the bankruptcy of the Marxian dreams when they built a wall to prevent their comrades from fleeing into the nonsocialist part of Germany.

CHAPTER 17

Observations on the Russian Reform Movement

The bosses of the Russian Communist Administration are disturbed by the fact that economic conditions in the countries which have not adopted the methods of the Communist International are by far more satisfactory than those in their own country. If they could succeed in keeping their "comrades" in complete ignorance of the achievements of Western capitalism, they would not mind the low efficiency of their own plants and farms. But as some scanty information about the "affluence" in the West penetrates to Russia, its masters are upset by the fear of the pro-capitalist reaction in their own house. This fear impels them on the one hand to foment sedition all over the "capitalist sector" of the earth, and on the other hand to ventilate various projects aiming at some minor reforms in their own methods of management.

Nobody is today more firmly convinced of the incomparable superiority of the capitalistic methods of production than the "production tsars" of the countries behind the Iron Curtain. The present-day strength of communism is entirely due to the mentality of the pseudo-intellectuals in the Western nations who still enjoy the products of free enterprise.

I

The market economy—capitalism—is a social system of consumers' supremacy. There is in its frame only one method of earning a living and of acquiring property, viz., one must try to serve one's fellow men, the consumers, in the best possible way. A daily and hourly repeated plebiscite determines again and again every individual's earning and place in society. By their buying and abstention from buying the con-

[Reprinted from *The Freeman* (May 1966).—Ed.]

sumers allocate ownership of all the material factors of production to those who have succeeded in satisfying the most urgent of their not yet satisfied wants in the best possible and cheapest way. Ownership of the material factors of production can be acquired and can be preserved only by serving the consumers better than other people do. It is a revocable public mandate as it were.

The supremacy of the consumers is no less complete with regard to labor, the human factor of production. Wage rates are determined by the price the consumer, in buying the product, is prepared to refund to the employer for the worker's contribution to the process of its production. Thus the consumers' valuation fixes the height of every worker's remuneration.[1] And let us not forget: the immense majority of the consumers are themselves earners of salaries and wages and in this capacity instrumental in the determination of their own compensation.

The unique efficiency of the capitalistic system is due to the incentive it gives to everybody to exert his forces to the utmost in serving his fellow citizens. Not a vague altruism, but rightly understood selfishness impels a man to put forth all his strength in the service of his fellow men. The system of economic calculation in terms of money, the commonly used medium of exchange, makes it possible to compute precisely all projects in advance and the result of every action performed in retrospect, and, what is no less important, to ascribe to every factor the size of its contribution to the outcome.

The characteristic feature of socialism is precisely the fact that it substitutes for this market system of consumers' supremacy a dictatorial system, the "plan." In the planned economy the individuals are not driven by the desire to improve their own conditions but either by dutifulness or by the fear of punishment. It is impossible for the individual workers to improve their own material situation by working better and harder. If they intensify their own exertion, they alone are burdened by the implied sacrifices, but only an infinitesimal fraction of the product of their additional exertion will benefit themselves. On the other hand they can enjoy in full the pleasures of carelessness and laziness in the performances of the tasks assigned to them while the resulting impairment of the total national product curtails their own share only infinitesimally.

---

1 This is to what the jargon of the Hollywood industry refers in using the term "box office account." But it is no less valid for all other fields of business.

The economists always pointed to this inherent deficiency of socialism. Today all people in the socialist countries know that this criticism
was fully justified. All their projects for an improvement of the quality
and an increase in the quantity of economic goods and services turn
around this problem. They all aim—unfortunately in vain—at discovering a scheme that could make the individual members of a socialist
system self-interested in the effect of their own contribution to the collective's effort.

That the socialists acknowledge this fact and are anxious to find a
solution amounts in itself already to a spectacular refutation of two of
the most zealously advanced arguments in favor of socialism. On the
one hand the socialists asserted that in the market economy the wage
earners are not interested in improving the output of their own work.
They expected that socialism would bring about an unprecedented improvement of the individual worker's contributions because everybody
will be incited by the knowledge that he does not labor for an exploiter
but works for his own best interest. On the other hand the socialists
vilified profit-seeking as the most pernicious and "socially" injurious
institution and indulged in reveries about the blessings of what they
called a substitution of "production for use" for "production for profit."

No less significant an admission of the viciousness of the socialist
ideology is provided by the small plots the exploitation of which for
the account of the rural workers (falsely labelled for "private profit")
alone prevented famines in the country that includes a good deal of the
world's most fertile arable soil. The urgency of the Soviet productivity
problem is due to the fact that in the processing industries no analogous expedient is at hand.

II

The much discussed reform projects of Professor Liberman[2] and
other Russian authors do not refer to the essential characteristics of the
Soviet system of central planning of all activities commonly called eco-

---

2 [Yevsei Liberman in the 1960s began writing in the Soviet Union that profits should be "the
index of the efficiency of an enterprise." In 1966 a plan was instituted granting autonomy to
forty-three different enterprises in various industries. The result was an increase in productivity
and worker income, leading to greater individual savings and more exportable goods, *Socialism:
The Grand Delusion*, Brian Crozier and Arthur Seldon, eds. (New York: Universe Books, 1986),
pp. 138–39. The plan was an embarrassing success for the advocates of state socialism.—Ed.]

nomic. Neither do they deal in any way with the problem of economic calculation. (For present-day Russian planners this problem does not yet have primary importance as, operating within a world of the price system, they are in a position to rely upon the prices determined on the markets of the West.)

What the reformers want to attain is improvement in the conduct of factories and workshops turning out consumers' goods by the adoption of new methods for the remuneration of directors, supervisors, or foremen. The salaries of such people should henceforth be meted out in such a way that they should have a pecuniary interest in producing articles that are considered as satisfactory by the consumers.

It is a serious blunder to employ in dealing with this issue any reference to the concept of "profit" or to declare that the suggested method of payment would mean something like "profit-sharing." There is within a socialist system no room for the establishment and computation of a magnitude that could be called profit or loss.

The task of production is to utilize the available human and material factors of production for the best possible satisfaction of future wants concerning which there cannot be any *certain* knowledge today.

Technology indicates for what purposes the various factors of production could be employed; it thus shows goals that could be attained provided this is considered as desirable. To choose from this bewildering multitude of possible ways of production those which most likely are fit to satisfy the most urgent of the future wants of the consumers is in the market economy the specific task of the entrepreneur. If all entrepreneurs were right in their appreciation of the future state of the market, the prices of the various complementary factors of production would already have today attained the height corresponding to this future state. As, under these conditions, no entrepreneurs would have acquired some or all of the complementary factors of production at prices lower or higher than those which later events proved to be the correct ones, no profits or losses could emerge.

One profits by having expended less than one—later—receives from the buyers of the product, and one loses if one can sell only at prices that do not cover the costs expended in production. What determines profit or loss is choosing the goal to be set for the entrepreneurial activities and choosing the methods for its attainment.

Thus it is investment that results either in profit or in loss. As in a socialist system only "society" invests, only society can profit or suffer losses. But in a socialist system the material factors of production are *res extra commercium*. That means: they can neither be bought nor sold, and thus no prices for them are determined. Therefore it is impossible to find out whether a definite production activity resulted in profit or loss.

The eminence of capitalism consists precisely in the fact that it tends to put the direction of production into the hands of those entrepreneurs who have best succeeded in providing for the demands of the consumers. In the planned economy such a built-in process of selection is lacking. There it does not matter whether the planning authorities have erred or not. The consumers have to take what the authorities offer them. Errors committed by the planning authority do not become known, because there is no method to discover them.

In the market economy the emergence of profit demonstrates that in the eyes of the consumers one entrepreneur served them better than others did. Profit and loss are thus the effect of comparing and gauging different suppliers' performance. In the socialist system there is nothing available to make possible a comparison between the commodities fabricated and the services rendered by the plan and its executors with something originating from another side. The behavior of the people for whom the plan and its executors are supposed to provide does not indicate whether or not a better method of providing for their needs would have been feasible. If in dealing with socialism one speaks of profits, one merely creates confusion. There are no profits outside the "profit and loss system."

If the authorities promise to the director of a shoe factory a bonus to be determined as a percentage of sales, they do not give him a share in "profits." Still less can it be called a return to the profit system. Profits can only be calculated if one deducts total costs from total receipts. Any such operation is unfeasible under the conditions of the case. The whole factory, fully equipped, was handed over by the authorities to the care of the director and with it all the material needed and the order, to produce, with the help of workers assigned to the outfit, a definite quantity of footwear for delivery to definite shops. There is no method available to find out the costs incurred by all the operations preceding the first interference of the director. The bonus granted to him cannot have any relation to the numerical difference between such total costs and the proceeds from the sale of the final product.

III

In fact the problem of reform as today passionately discussed in the communist countries does not deal with the profitability of the various plants and productive processes. It turns virtually around a different problem: Is it possible within a socialist system to remunerate a worker, especially also the supreme foreman of a plant, according to the value the consumers, the people, attach to his contribution to the accomplishment of the product or the service?

In the capitalistic or market economy the employer is bound to pay a hired worker the price the consumers are prepared to refund to him in buying the product. If he were to pay more, he would suffer losses, would forfeit his funds, and would be eliminated from the ranks of the entrepreneurs. If he tried to pay less, the competition of other employers would make it impossible for him to find helpers. Under socialism no such connection between the amounts expended in the production of a commodity and its appreciation by the consumers prevails. There cannot therefore *in general* be any question of remunerating workers according to their "productivity" as appreciated by the consumers. Only in exceptional cases is it possible to separate the contribution of one worker in such a way from those of all other contributors that its separate valuation by the consumers and therefore its remuneration according to this valuation become feasible. For instance: all seats in the opera house can be sold at the regular price of m. But if a tenor of world fame sings the main part, the house is sold out even if the price of admission is raised to $m + n$. It is obvious that such cases are extremely rare and must not be referred to in dealing with the problem of wage rate determination under socialism.

Of course, a socialist management can determine for many kinds of work "normal" tasks to be performed by the laborer and on the one hand reward those who accomplish more and on the other hand penalize those who fail to produce their quotas. But such a norm in no way depends on any market phenomena. It is the outcome of a more or less arbitrary decision of the authorities.

In the market economy the salaries paid to people who turn out commodities or render services that cannot be sold on the market and for which therefore no prices are available are indirectly determined by the structure of the market. The employer—in such cases as a rule the government—must pay to such people enough to prevent them from preferring a job in the orbit of the market. Such indirect determination of the height of wage rates too is unfeasible in a socialist system.

Of course, the government is always free to grant to any of the officials it employs a salary equal to the value the supreme chief or planner attaches to this man's services. But this does not have any reference to the social problem around which the discussion turns.

CHAPTER 18

Observations on the Cooperative Movement

∾ The Cooperative Idea

I   Cooperatives Not a Method of World Reconstruction

In spite of their steady expansion and the growth of their turnover, the cooperatives as they exist and operate today are merely dim shadows of what they were designed to be in the ambitious schemes of their first promoters. Robert Owen, William King, and Ferdinand Lassalle planned a cooperative organization of industrial production as a "New System of Society." They wanted to eliminate the entrepreneurs and the capitalists altogether. Henceforth, associations of the workers themselves should operate the plants, "their" plants, without any interference on the part of the "useless exploiters."

The object of the movement was the abolition of the wages system and the organization of industry in the form of producers' cooperatives. Each worker should own an equal share in the plant, workshop, or farm in which he was employed. He should share equally in the products or the earnings of this outfit. He should become his own employer, controlling its operations and retaining its proceeds.

Nobody will deny that all attempts to realize these far-fetched plans failed lamentably. If there are any producers' cooperatives today, their number is so negligible that hardly anybody pays attention to them. Even most of the books dealing with the cooperative movement avoid reference to the schemes for cooperative producers' associations.

The farmers are producers. But the farmers' cooperatives do not organize the farmers in their capacity as agricultural producers; they

[This article is part one in *Cooperatives in the Petroleum Industry*, a report prepared by the Petroleum Industry Research Foundation for the Empire State Petroleum Association and the Illinois Petroleum Marketers Association, 1947. — Ed.]

organize the farmers only as buyers of various equipment and articles required for their production and as sellers of the products. The individual farmer remains an independent entrepreneur and is, as far as his production activities are concerned, not integrated into a cooperative production outfit.

The purchasing cooperatives have entered the field of production in many branches of business. But these plants are not producers' cooperatives. They are not owned by the people employed in them. They are owned by the various cooperatives or associations of cooperatives. The employees are hired hands like the wage earners hired by any other enterprise. They have no say in the conduct of the business. The proceeds go to the owners, i.e., the cooperatives or associations of cooperatives, not to the employees. There is no question of abolition of the wages system.

All that remains of the ambitious projects of the glorified pioneers of cooperation are three types of cooperative organizations: consumers' cooperatives, farmers' purchasing cooperatives, and farmers' marketing cooperatives. It is a rhapsodic overstatement to speak, in referring to these cooperatives, of the cooperative way as a method of world reconstruction.[1]

II   Not the Cooperatives, but Private Profit-Seeking Business Is the Harbinger of Economic Improvement

The capitalistic market economy, the system of private profit-seeking enterprise, is essentially social cooperation under the division of labor. The various specialized enterprises and branches of industry cooperate with one another. The objective of each of them is collaboration for the production of all those goods and services which the consumers want to use. Within each enterprise, the various divisions and subdivisions cooperatively turn out products which are delivered to other enterprises which again use them for the production of more elaborate products. Finally, when all these cooperative processes come to an end, the finished product reaches the consumer. Seen from this point of view, the system of capitalism appears as a world-embracing cooperative organization in which each individual promotes his own well-being by serving his fellow men.

1 J. P. Warbasse, *The Cooperative Way, a Method of World Reconstruction* (New York: Barnes and Noble, 1946).

Now, the cooperatives have sequestrated to themselves the exclusive use of the epithet "cooperative." It is implied that they alone are cooperative and all other business enterprises non-cooperative. It is indeed a poor semantic makeshift.

In the face of this pretentious attitude on the part of the various cooperative associations, there is a need to stress the fact that they have contributed nothing to the substantial improvement of the material conditions of the people. For many decades, they have been thriving very well under the benevolent assistance granted to them by the authorities. But there is no record of any important innovation which owes its introduction to the cooperatives. While private business, overburdened by taxes from which the cooperatives are exempt, improves, year by year, the quality and increases the quantity of products and fills the markets with new articles unheard of before, the cooperatives are sterile. Not the cooperatives, but the much abused profit-seekers, are the harbingers of economic progress. If we look into the home of an average American worker or farmer and at his family's daily life, we may learn about the enormous changes which were brought about by the operation of private enterprise. The cooperatives hardly played any role in this miraculous transformation. The "rise of the consumer"[2] was not an accomplishment of the cooperative movement. It was an achievement of the "production for profit" engineered by "rugged individualists" and "economic royalists."

III   The Marketing Cooperatives of the Farmers and
      the Consumers' Cooperatives

Within the cooperative movement of all countries, it is possible to distinguish two main groups: the farmers' cooperatives and the consumers' cooperatives of the non-farming population.

The objectives of the farmers' cooperatives are the marketing of farm products on the one hand and the distribution of farm supplies and the consumers' goods which the farmers require on the other hand. Both objectives are in themselves perfectly legitimate and could, apart from the problem of tax and credit privileges, be approved by everybody.

However, it is impossible to look upon the farmers' cooperatives as an isolated phenomenon and not to notice that they are merely one device in a complex system of farm policies and political activities of

2 H. M. Kallen, *The Decline and Rise of the Consumer* (Chicago: Packard, 1945).

the farmers' organizations. As a pressure group, the organized farmers aim at enhancing the prices of agricultural products. In the plans for the realization of this goal an important role is assigned to the marketing cooperatives. They are a cog in a political machine constructed for the raising of the price of food, an objective radically opposed to that of the consumers' cooperatives of the non-rural population.

It is not the task of a study concerning the cooperatives to bring into full relief all the aspects of this great antagonism between the political organizations of the food producers and those of the masses of the food consumers. What must be said, however, is that the aims of the farmers' cooperatives are irreconcilably opposed to the aims which the consumers' cooperatives pretend to seek. The consumers' cooperatives say that they want to cheapen the prices of the necessities of life. The farmers' cooperatives aim avowedly at raising the prices of food and of other articles like cotton, tobacco, and wool. It is therefore strange indeed that between these two classes of cooperatives there is amicable collaboration and friendship and that they are united in cooperative alliances.

The consumers' cooperatives make light of this contradiction by pointing out that both branches of the cooperative movement agree in their eagerness to eliminate superfluous middlemen. Thus, it will be possible to raise the price the farmer receives for his product and at the same time to lower the price the consumer must expend for its purchase. The plea is lame. First, it is not true that the elimination of the private businessman, the "middleman," has reduced sales costs. It has, on the contrary, increased them. The proof is that the farmers' marketing cooperatives could not stand the competition of private business without the aid of tax exemptions and cheap credit. Second, the elimination of the middleman is only a minor issue in the comprehensive program of the pressure groups of farming. Their main goal is to raise the prices of foodstuffs and other agricultural products by various governmental measures.

The vast propaganda literature of the cooperatives deals much more with the consumers' cooperatives than with the two types of farmers' cooperatives. It passes over in silence the conflict between the interests of the urban consumers of agricultural products and the endeavors of the farmers' cooperatives to make the government resort to various restrictive measures with regard to these products. Most of the arguments advanced in favor of cooperativism refer exclusively to the cooperatives of urban consumers. This is especially paradoxical in the United States where the cooperatives of urban consumers play only an insignificant role when compared with the farmers' cooperatives.

IV   The Philosophy and Theology of Consumption

Capitalism needs neither propaganda nor apostles. Its achievements speak for themselves. Capitalism delivers the goods.

But the cooperatives cannot do without passionate propaganda. They call their promotional campaigning "cooperative education."

The end and sole purpose of production is consumption. All that profit-seeking business aims at is to serve the consumer in an unceasing effort to turn out more, better, and cheaper goods. The businessman is fully aware of the fact that there is no means of increasing consumption other than by increasing production. Since consuming causes delight and is in itself pleasant, there is no need to expatiate copiously on its pleasurableness. It is supererogatory to teach people how gratifying it is to consume more and better amenities. Even the untutored mind knows all about the sweetness of a higher standard of living.

But the toil and trouble required for production are painful. There are very few people who fail to take advantage of an opportunity to increase their own consumption. But there are many people who look with disdain upon work. The temptation of idleness is very great and a serious danger to society. This is why parents and educators since time immemorial have been intent upon teaching the rising generation the philosophy of travail. Young people must learn that the gratification of the good life must be paid for by exertion and hard work. They must realize that he who wants to consume must first produce. There cannot be any question of "a consumer economy."[3] The economy must always be an economy of production for the sake of consumption.

It is vain to speak of the "primacy of consumption."[4] Production must invariably precede consumption. It is futile to propagate an alleged philosophy of consumption as opposed to the philosophy of production.

In their excessive zeal, the champions of cooperativism have also entered the field of theology. They would have us believe "that the social teachings of the Christian and Jewish religions naturally lead to

3 Ibid., pp. 196–97.
4 Ibid., p. 422.

the formation of cooperatives."[5] They find "the beatitudes of Jesus" in "the practice and principles of the cooperatives."[6] It seems appropriate to leave the examination of this dogmatical issue to the doctors of the various churches and to the rabbis.

V   The True Objectives of the Cooperative Movement

The avowed objective of consumers' cooperatives and of the farmers' purchasing cooperatives is to provide their members with commodities and services at lower prices than those which they would have to expend in the absence of these associations. This is a perfectly legitimate task. We shall have to examine whether and how cooperatives really attain this end.

To save money in making a purchase is certainly a good thing. We can understand the satisfaction a man derives from such a reduction in his expenses. We may heartily congratulate him on his success. But it is quite a different thing when the champions of the cooperatives deal with these mammonistic economies in high-flown language. The members of cooperatives are people who want to buy at the lowest possible price. The employees of the cooperatives are people who believe that the most remunerative job they can find is a job with their employer, a cooperative. In defending the tax privileges and other prerogatives granted to the cooperatives, these cooperators and cooperative employees fight for their own material interests. They want to improve their own standard of living; they are eager to consume more. It is not seemly for them to resort to phrases which are appropriate only in describing the self-denying work of devout monks and nuns nursing people affected with leprosy.

A cooperative business enterprise aims at lowering the price of soap and gasoline; it is not "a concrete expression of the brotherhood of man."[7] In their purchases, cooperatives bargain with the purveyors; in hiring help, they bargain with employees. The mutual contractual relations between the cooperative association and its members are precisely determined by articles of incorporation, by-laws, and statutes carefully drafted by lawyers. To apply the term "brotherhood" to such purely

5 Cf. E. S. Bogardus, *Dictionary of Cooperation* (New York and Chicago: Cooperative League of the U.S.A., 1943 and 1945), p. 54.
6 Cf. Kallen, *The Decline and Rise of the Consumer*, p. 294.
7 Cf. Bogardus, *Dictionary of Cooperation*, p. 54.

mammonistic issues guided by the principle "do ut des" is an insult to the intelligence of the public. If this be brotherhood, then the operations of I. G. Farben, the world's biggest manufacturer of beneficial medicinal substances, were likewise manifestations of the brotherhood of man. The phraseology of the propaganda literature of the cooperative movement is disgusting. They speak of spiritual values,[8] of culture, of liberty, and freedom,[9] where the issue is to reduce the price of various things by a few cents.

In his *Utopia*, Plato refers to the ancient saying, "friends have all things in common."[10] If this is true, the cooperators are badly mistaken in calling their associations friendly societies. They have no "things in common." They have a punctilious system of accounting and auditing. The rights and the duties of the members of the cooperatives are neatly defined.[11]

〜 The Principles and Methods of Cooperatives

I The Origin of Cooperation

The world-embracing system of the social division of labor originated from occasional assistance mutually granted to one another by neighbors. John, more efficient in the processing of iron, manufactured a ploughshare for Paul, who was less efficient in this art. On the other hand, Paul, more efficient in leatherwork, fabricated a pair of shoes for John, who was less gifted in this kind of production. It was all friendship and neighborly fellow-feeling. Out of these modest beginnings developed the marvelous specialization of industry as it operates today.

It would be nonsense to refer to those remote sources of the division

---

8 Cf. Kallen, *The Decline and Rise of the Consumer*, p. 294.

9 Ibid., p. 435.

10 Plato, *The Laws*, bk 5, p. 739.

11 The most amazing product of cooperative propaganda is the already mentioned book by Professor Kallen. On pp. 436–59, Professor Kallen introduces a fictitious character, President Robert Adam Owen Smith, who, in the year 2044 addresses the "Cooperative Union of the World" and in this address narrates the history of the cooperative movement, viz., also for the years which separate our generation from the year 2044. This is what Mr. Smith says about the future history of the cooperative movement: "Big business . . . used all its cunning and all its power to wreck it, resorting to arms as well as to financial oppression. . . . These endeavors having failed, armed gangs were employed to destroy cooperative establishments and murder cooperators" (p. 443). No comment is needed.

of labor in dealing with present-day industrial conditions. Nobody is so unreasonable as to base any claims and pretensions upon the fact that the exchange of commodities and services was originally a display of pure brotherly sympathies. No modern steel corporation asks for any privileges or subsidies on account of the fact that once, in the ages of primitive mankind, a mythical John offered his services voluntarily to his no less mythical neighbor, Paul.

In the treatment of the affairs of the cooperatives, however, such a procedure is quite common.

We may admit, for the sake of argument, that cooperation originated from friendly relations between neighbors. The villager John went to town to buy five pounds of coffee. His neighbor Paul asked him to buy five pounds for him too. When John came back and handed the five pounds of coffee over to Paul, Paul reimbursed John for what John had expended for them. Perhaps the two also shared the transportation costs incurred by John. On the other hand, if the purchase of ten pounds of coffee was done at a wholesale price, John passed the difference on to his friend, Paul, and the latter also enjoyed the advantages inherent in wholesale buying.

This all was certainly comradeship and amicable sodality. But it is an impermissible display of naivete to refer to these mythical characters, John and Paul, in matters of the cooperatives as they operate today. These cooperatives are big businesses with millions of members who never meet one another. Their turnover amounts to billions of dollars. They are organized in a complicated hierarchy of simple cooperatives, super-cooperatives, and super-super associations. They have established gigantic vertical organizations. They do business with the government and are active in international trade. They own factories, oil wells, and transportation facilities; they engage in financial operations and enter all divisions of commercial and industrial activities. Their affairs are so complicated that their handling requires the employment of hosts of directors, managers, clerks, accountants, and lawyers. There are special schools for the training of the personnel of the cooperatives. Many universities have established chairs for the teaching of the cooperative methods of business management and accounting and of the laws of cooperatives.

It is ridiculous to conjure up the specters of mythical John and Paul in dealing with these mammoth enterprises.

In the writings of those fighting for the preservation of cooperative privileges, the cooperatives are described as agents of the memberships. However, no matter how lawyers define the term "agent" from the point of view of the valid laws of the nation, which, after all, are liable to alteration on the part of the legislature, from the economic point of view it is obvious that the cooperatives cannot be considered in any other sense as agents or mandatories of their membership than any other enterprise operating under the division of labor. If the cooperative is called the member's agent because it passes the gasoline it acquires on to the members, the term also fits the activities of any other enterprise. Then the steel corporation is the agent of all those whose well-being depends on the use of steel. If there were no steel works, every individual would have to produce the steel he needs for himself. The operation of steel works relieves the individuals from the necessity of taking care of an important branch of production for themselves. The steel corporations do not turn out products for their own use, but for that of all. Without a radical change in their standard of living and their daily activities, people could do without the services rendered by cooperatives; but they would fall back into the conditions of primitive barbarism and penury if the specialized industries were to go out of business.

When a cooperative buys some commodities, it looks after the interests of its members who ask for these commodities. But the same is no less the case when the businessmen and farmers are intent upon producing all those things which the average man needs for his own consumption.

Decency would require that the champions of the cooperatives cease to boast of their own idealism and disinterestedness. All those whose work contributes to the business of the cooperatives make their living from this job. To establish this truth is not to disparage these men. They are no less honest and useful citizens than any businessman, farmer, or wage earner. But they cannot be called idealists in any other sense than that which would apply to every other man engaged in a gainful occupation. Civil society is not based upon mere idealism and unselfishness. Its driving force is the rightly understood selfishness of every reasonable man. Selfishness, rightly understood, urges everybody to integrate himself into the system of the social division of labor. In rendering useful services to his fellow men, he furthers his own vital concerns.

The reference to idealism, unselfishness, and similar high-sounding notions is especially inappropriate with regard to farmers' cooperatives.

The farmers are businessmen and entrepreneurs of the type which the cooperative literature denounces as hard-boiled callous egoists. They do not till the soil for a heavenly reward, but for their own gain. They do not fill the markets with cereals to perform an act of charity for the consumers, but to make money and to buy the products of the processing trades. They use their political power and form pressure groups in order to attain special privileges enhancing their incomes. They are anxious to pay lower taxes than the rest of the people, to receive subsidies out of the public funds, to be protected by import duties, and to enjoy a thousand other privileges and prerogatives. There is certainly no idealism involved in the anti-margarine laws.

The endeavors of the farmers' cooperatives to save the farmers some money are perfectly sound and legitimate insofar as they do not ask for special privileges at the expense of all the people. Farmers are manufacturers, and it is all right for them to be concerned with keeping down costs of production. But it is quite another thing if they want to attain this aim by evading taxes and other burdensome obligations which must be borne by all other producing citizens.

II   Producers and Consumers

The characteristic feature of the free society of competitive capitalism is the unlimited sovereignty of the consumers. The capitalists, the owners of land and the entrepreneurs, are by the inescapable law of the market forced to employ their ingenuity and the material factors of production at their disposal in such a way as to fill the most urgent of the not yet satisfied wants of the consumers in the best possible and cheapest way. Businessmen are not irresponsible production tsars. They are unconditionally subject to the supremacy of the consumers. If they fail to obey the orders of the consuming public, they suffer losses. If they do not alter their conduct of affairs very soon in such a way as to adjust it to the demands of the public, they are forced to go out of business and forfeit their eminent position. The consumers, by their buying and abstention from buying, make poor people rich and rich people poor. They determine who should own the capital and the land and who should run the enterprises. They determine what should be produced, of what quality, and in what quantity. The market economy is a democracy of the consumers.

It is true that sinister elements are intent upon sapping the unhampered market economy and substituting a producers' supremacy for the consumers' supremacy. A general tendency prevails among present-day governments and political parties to shelter the less efficient producer against the competition of the more efficient producer. The very essence of government interference with business is to paralyze the operation of the unhampered market which invariably tends toward the attainment of that end which is today, not very appropriately, called "freedom from want." While flamboyantly advertising their alleged concern about the masses' material well-being, those in political office are firmly committed to restrictive practices which curtail the quantity of commodities available for consumption. They call their pernicious acts "social policy," "Sozialpolitik," "New Deal," "progressivism" and smear all opponents as "reactionaries" and "economic Bourbons."

The most enthusiastic supporters of restrictions are the organized pressure groups of the farmers and of the wage earners. Deluded by fallacious pseudo-economic doctrines, these pressure groups believe that they can improve their own material well-being by all kinds of restriction and featherbedding, by subsidies, and other privileges.

Now, it is true that a privilege granted to a special group of producers improves in *the short run* the material conditions of those favored by this privilege at the expense of the rest of the population. Within a society based on the social division of labor, each specialized group is only a minority. If a privilege is granted to such a minority group, the result is certainly an improvement of its members' conditions. But it is quite hopeless for such a minority to remain lastingly in the exclusive possession of a privileged position. However gullible the rest of the people may be, they will finally discover that they are suckers who must foot the bill for the privileges granted to a comparatively small group. They will not tolerate the preservation of such a state of affairs. They will either abolish the privileges granted to other people or they will secure for themselves similar privileges.

Unfortunately, what prevails in our day is the second alternative. Faced with the problem of privilege, those not privileged do not ask for the abolition of all privileges. They ask for privileges for themselves too. They are too dull to comprehend that this system, when carried to its ultimate logical consequences, is the acme of nonsense. What a man may gain *qua* producer by a privilege granted to his branch of production, he loses *qua* consumer in buying the products of the other equally privileged branches. What remains is merely a deterioration in the material well-being of all people on account of the general drop in the productivity of labor.

It seems to be a very good thing for the milk farmers to outlaw margarine and for the musicians to outlaw recorded music. But if in every other branch of production, progress is likewise stopped, nobody gains and all people are hurt. The milk farmers' and the musicians' incomes are raised, but the prices of all the goods they want to buy are raised concomitantly. What remains is that all people miss all those advantages they could derive from technological progress.

This nonsensical and self-defeating policy of privilege parades today under the misleading label of "producers' policy." The worst sin of capitalism, contend the champions of the producers' privileges, is that it assigns primacy to the "idle" consumer and not to the "industrious" producer. They fail to realize that producers and consumers are the same people. It is only the thinking of economic analysis that distinguishes between man as a producer and man as a consumer. In life and reality these two aspects of each individual are inextricably linked together. You cannot favor man in his producer quality without hurting him in his consumer quality. The primacy of consumption as manifested in the unhampered operation of the capitalistic market economy is the consummation of the fact that consumption is the sole end and purpose of production.

If the cooperative movement were to attack the errors of this alleged "pro-producer" policy, it would render a very valuable service to the promotion of welfare. However, in spite of the lip service they pay to what they call the primacy of the consumer, the consumers' cooperatives are far from raising any objections to the restrictive practices of our day. They are, on the contrary, among the most zealous supporters of these disastrous methods. Many of their members are precisely those people who most obtrusively ask for such producers' policies: farmers and labor union members.

All this bombastic talk about the alleged blessings of cooperation is vain, as the cooperatives acquiesce in the existence of vast producers' privileges. The farmer may save pennies as a member of a cooperative, but he loses dollars on account of featherbedding and hostility to technological improvement as displayed by labor unions. The wage earner may at best save pennies when buying in a cooperative store, but the pro-farmer privileges cost him dollars.

There is only one really efficient way to further the interests of the consuming masses, namely, the way of free private enterprise. Not to hinder the more efficient producer to outdo the less efficient rival is a much better method to have the farmer and the urban consumer supplied more amply and at lower costs than anything else. In diverting the public's attention from the main economic evil, viz., the policy of restriction and producers' privileges, and in concentrating upon the trifling issue of saving pennies where dollars are at stake, the cooperative movement does more harm than good.

The cooperators have certainly no claim to glorify themselves as the champions of the consumers. Their achievements are meager indeed when compared with those of the businessmen who succeed in turning out more, better, and cheaper products.

III   The Place of the Cooperatives Within the Frame of the Competitive System

Economic liberalism, today disparaged as Manchesterism, maintains that the government should not place any obstacles in the way of people who want to serve their fellow citizens. As the liberals interpret the principle of consumers' sovereignty, the consumers alone should decide whether a business unit is good or bad. This is what the much abused slogan "laissez faire" means: let the consumers choose for themselves and not a *Führer* for them.

The market economy gives everybody a chance. What a man needs to become a captain of industry is merely good ideas and the ability to make these ideas work. No inherited wealth and no capital are required in order to succeed. The capitalists, driven by their own selfish interests and eager to find the most profitable investment for their funds, are always in search of ingenious men to whom they can entrust their funds.

The harbingers of totalitarian government omnipotence would have us believe that under present conditions, in the era of what they call "mature" capitalism, this is no longer true. Today, they say, conditions are rigid. There is no longer any opportunity for a penniless newcomer to challenge the vested interests of the old firms and big corporations. The poor are doomed to remain poor forever, and the rich are getting richer from day to day.

This fable distorts the actual state of affairs no less than all the other Marxian and Keynesian fables. It is, of course, correct that today all branches of government cooperate in the effort to prevent technological progress and the emergence of new enterprises and new millionaires. But in spite of all these handicaps there is still room left for the success of self-made men. The greater part of the present-day leaders of business are not sons and still fewer grandsons of the millionaires of days gone by. As far as a family succeeds in preserving its place on the top of the social ladder for several generations, it owes its eminence to the ability and zeal of its younger generations. There is nothing in the operation of the unhampered market economy that could, in the long run, afford to vested interests a safe protection against the competition of improved methods of production, new products, better quality, and cheaper prices. It is precisely because such protection is absent in the unhampered market that those who by indulgence in routine, lack of inventiveness, incompetence, laziness, and negligence endanger their own prosperity are asking for protection on the part of the government.

The principle of not interfering with market conditions and giving a chance to everybody applies no less to new methods of business organization. The corporative form of business enterprise owes its present role not to any assistance offered on the part of the laws and the administrative officers. On the contrary. From its early beginnings it had to meet the hostility of those in power. This hostility developed in the last decades into undisguised persecution. The authorities discriminate in many respects, first of all in the field of taxation, against the corporations. The corporations are singled out for much more burdensome taxation than non-corporate business. But the enormous efficiency of the corporate form of business has victoriously withstood the onslaughts of the power to destroy.

The cooperatives entered the scene of business with passionate diatribes against the merchants and especially against the retailers. It would have been comprehensible if the retailers had asked the authorities to suppress these new competitors who seemed to expect less from serving their members than from smearing the established firms. A demand of retail business for outlawing the cooperatives and suppressing their activities altogether would not have been more perverse than are the endeavors of the farmers to outlaw margarine and to cut down the importation of meat and cereals. But apart from the angry utterances of a few hotspurs, no such demands were ever raised. The fairness of the much calumniated merchants and their full endorsement of the principle of free competition manifested themselves in the attitude these men showed in dealing with the cooperatives. They did not ask the police to silence these insidious slanderers and defamers. All they asked was that they not be coddled with privileges and prerogatives. Fully committed to the fundamental maxim of free enterprise and free competition, all that private businessmen are aiming at is equality in the treatment of all forms of business enterprise. They ask for neither privileges for themselves nor hostile discrimination against any group of rivals. All they ask is that the government stay neutral. Neither privileges nor discrimination. The freedom of the public to choose between the multiplicity of competing sellers and to prefer the shop that best serves them should not be curtailed by virtual subsidies granted to less efficient enterprises. For the sake of consumers' sovereignty and for the benefit of the whole people, there should be equality in the treatment of all kinds and varieties of business enterprise.

IV   The Character of the Cooperatives' Profits

There are three different elements included in the conception of profit as popularly employed in mundane language and in statistics: interest on invested capital, compensation for the entrepreneur's own labor expended in the conduct of the business, and, finally, profit proper. In the case of corporations and cooperatives, the second of these elements is absent, as the owners of the enterprise are legally distinguished from those performing any labor in the conduct of business even if these latter own stock in the corporation or are members of the cooperative.

Profit proper is the surplus an enterprise earns from selling at prices exceeding the total amount of costs expended. There is no need to enter into an examination of the conditions required for the emergence of profits proper, their economic significance, and the role they play in the operation of all economic affairs. Such an analysis is the task of treatises dealing with economic theory.

The cooperatives contend that the objective of their conduct of business is not profit making and that the surplus they are passing on to their customers in proportion to the purchases each of them made is not a dividend, but a "patronage refund"; that it is not profit, but savings resulting from the conduct of the business. Upon this doctrine the cooperatives base their vast claims to a privileged position and especially to tax exemption.

It is possible to imagine a method of conducting a cooperative's business in such a way that no such surplus emerges at all. The cooperative could sell every article at a price which merely includes the costs the cooperative itself incurred in acquiring it plus full compensation for the costs incurred in the manipulation of this article. Actually no cooperative has adopted this procedure. The cooperatives sell above costs. At the end of a definite period, there remains, provided the conduct of operations was successful, a net profit, i.e., a surplus of sales proceeds over costs.

Mrs. Beatrice Potter Webb (Lady Passfield), that adamant apologist of the worst excesses of Bolshevism, tried to explain why the cooperatives do not realize "the Owenite ideal of eliminating profit in the transaction of business," why they do not sell "their commodities at cost price plus the expenses of management." As Mrs. Webb saw it, the blame must be put upon the imperfection of monetary institutions. The sale of small quantities at cost price, she contended, "involves the use of fractions not represented in current coin."[12] Yet the fact that the divisibility of coins is not unlimited has never prevented business from nicely adjusting prices to each height required by the structure of the market. In the retailing of fruit and other necessities of daily life, such prices as "five pieces for seven cents" and "three pieces for eleven cents" are quite common. There is no reason why the cooperatives should not adopt the same procedure. Actually they do adopt it, as it is indispensable. But when they adopt it, their aim is not the elimination of profit, but rather the necessity of competing with their rivals.

Mr. Jacob Baker explains these procedures of the cooperatives in a different way. In his opinion, it would take too much bookkeeping to calculate the wholesale cost and proportional share of operating expenses on each dozen of eggs and each pound of butter.[13] However, a businessman who would not figure out neatly what his own costs are and would grope about in the dark is a clumsy bungler and headed for bankruptcy. Competition enjoins upon every seller—whether profit-seeking merchant or allegedly altruistic cooperative store or oil station—the necessity of not asking more than the market price. But every seller must know whether each of his transactions involves a profit or a loss. If he were to ignore this and to sell below his own costs, he would

12 Cf. B. Potter Webb, *The Cooperative Movement in Great Britain*, 10th ed. (London: G. Allen, 1920), p. 65.
13 Cf. J. Baker, *Inquiry on Cooperative Enterprise* (Washington, D.C.: U.S. Government Printing Office, 1937), p. 7.

very soon forfeit his position in the framework of the social division of labor. If economic calculation shows a businessman that he cannot carry a definite article without losing money, he must as a rule discontinue this branch of activity. In exceptional cases, he may go on deliberately carrying this article for special considerations such as not making his customers stop patronizing his shop or similar matters. But even then, he must be fully aware of the import of his conduct. In the operation of commerce, there is no room left for ignorance and carelessness. Computing costs as correctly as possible is the backbone of trade.

Actually, the immense majority of well-run cooperatives have fully adopted the well-tried accounting methods as developed by many generations of businessmen. They even boast of their achievements in the field of bookkeeping and financial statements.[14]

The method of selling above costs must certainly not be excused by referring to the alleged fact that cooperatives do not know what their own costs are.

The true reasons for these methods are very different from those advanced by these apologetic doctrines.

A surplus of sales proceeds over costs appears only if the transaction was successful. Even the most ingenious businessman cannot always avoid losses. He may sometimes misjudge the trend of prices and expend more in the acquisition of an article than later actual developments would have justified. Business is always speculative, as it is based upon the anticipation of the future from which business profits and losses stem. In a world without change, in which the tomorrow does not differ from the today, there would be neither profit nor loss. Our actual world is fortunately not stagnant. There is continuous change in conditions and—at least still in this country—a continuous trend toward improvement. Under such a state of affairs, prices are in ceaseless fluctuation. He who buys in order to sell can only reap a profit if he has bought at a price which is lower than the price at which he sells minus total sales costs.

Cooperative enterprise is no exception. It too is subject to the law of the market. If a cooperative buys 10,000 pounds of an article at $2,000 and its operating sales costs are five cents per pound if there is

14 Cf. *Learning the Language of Study and Action* (Cooperative League of the U.S.A.: Pamphlet no. 43).

to be no loss. But if in the time lag between the purchase and the sale, the retail price drops to eighteen cents, it is forced to sell at a loss of seven cents per pound and a total loss of $700. Of course, a cooperative that would engage exclusively in such unwise deals would very soon go to the dogs. With a prosperous cooperative, over a definite period of time, the total amount of profits must at least equal the total amount of losses. But in every business enterprise, whether cooperative or other, the various individual deals contribute in different ways to the final result of business transacted over a definite period of time. Some of these individual deals are more profitable, others either less profitable or producing losses of various amounts.

It is these hard facts that make it peremptory for the cooperatives not to sell each article precisely at the proportional shares of their own total costs (wholesale price expended plus operating or sales costs). If they were to try this, they could not sell at all that part of their stock which was bought at prices which appear unreasonable when seen from the angle of the present structure of retail prices.

Cognizance of the state of affairs explodes entirely the cooperative doctrine concerning patronage refunds or patronage dividends. These refunds have nothing at all to do with the purchases of the individual members. They are not adjusted to the margin above costs at which the concrete purchases were billed to the individual members. They are distribution of the total profit earned by the cooperative over a definite period of time. They have no relation whatever to the individual's purchases. A member who bought only articles in the sale of which the cooperative suffered losses is no less entitled to a refund in proportion to the total amount of his purchases than any other member.

If the cooperative were merely an agent of the members, the members would have the obligation of absorbing their share of the cooperative's purchases and to make good all the costs incurred by the cooperative no matter whether or not this is advantageous for them. They would have the obligation of buying even if this would mean for them buying above the price they would have to expend in buying elsewhere. This is the inference to be drawn from the much talked about fable of John and Paul. If John asks Paul to buy a necktie for him in New York, he must take the necktie and reimburse Paul for what he has expended in the purchase. It is immaterial whether or not John discovers that he could have bought an equivalent necktie in his own place of residence at a much lower price. He has given to Paul the discretionary power to act as his agent in the purchase of a necktie and must bear the consequences.

It is therefore obvious that the doctrine of the cooperators according to which a private store *sells* articles *to* its customers while a cooperative store *buys* them *for* its members[15] is moonshine. The cooperative sells no less than a private store, and it must induce its own members to patronize the cooperative store by the same methods to which private retailers resort, namely, by asking lower prices than its competition. The cooperative's purchases are not more closely tied up with its sales than are the purchases and sales of every private retailing business. Membership in a cooperative does not enjoin upon any member the obligation to buy any commodities in the cooperative store or oil station, still less the obligation to reimburse the cooperative, in the purchase of any commodity he may buy, for all it has expended in acquiring this concrete article plus operating expenses. The individual cooperator has the right to buy in the cooperative store in the same way in which every man—cooperator and non-cooperator alike—has the right to buy in every private shop. The phrase "the cooperative buys for its members" is not a more correct description of the actual state of affairs than the phrase, "the private retailer buys for his customers."

The essential fact is that the surplus of total sales proceeds over total costs which the cooperative distributes among its customers does not stem from the various concrete purchases of the individual members, but from the successful conduct of the cooperative's aggregate business over a definite period of time. Such a surplus appears only if the managers of the cooperative were skillful enough to buy at such low prices that the later sale can be made in a remunerative way.

The economic character of a cooperative does not differ from that of a private store. Success and failure result with a cooperative from the same sources from which they result with a private retail shop. Success nets profits, failure losses.

V   The Disposition of the Cooperatives' Profits

If a cooperative's conduct of business was successful over a definite period of time and consequently the balance sheet shows a net surplus, i.e., a profit, this profit is handled in the same way in which every

15 Cf. Baker, *Inquiry on Cooperative Enterprise*, p. 6.

private business handles its profits. The profit is either distributed or ploughed back into the business as an addition to its working capital, or it is partly distributed and partly ploughed back.

It is immaterial what legal forms are resorted to in this accumulation of undistributed profits and how this increment to the working capital is called in the book entries. What alone counts is that the whole amount of profit earned or a part of it is withheld from distribution and added to the capital stock. By not distributing profits, the cooperatives accumulate additional capital in the same way as all other types of business enterprises. Capital accumulation is always the result of not consuming the total amount of profits earned.

The evolution of cooperatives from simple independent stores into big businesses has brought about a very complicated variety of membership rights. There are active voting members who own regular membership shares corresponding to the common stock of corporations. There are shares of non-active members who have no right to vote and therefore do not share in the control of the cooperative. There are fully-paid shares and part-paid shares. Thus it is possible to choose sometimes for the accumulation of additional capital methods which seemingly appear as a payment of a dividend. If the dividend is paid in shares, the result is actually an increase in the capital ploughed back into the cooperative. It does not affect the value of the members' equity whether the profit is simply retained by the cooperative or whether it is retained by giving an additional share to each member. In both cases, the individual member's portion of the total amount of the cooperative's total net assets is the same.

Cooperatives employ their capital funds only partially in the conduct of their own affairs. They have founded large-size wholesale enterprises and production outfits. They have organized these enterprises in a hierarchy of super-cooperatives, super-super cooperatives and super-super-super cooperatives. Each of these associations earns its own profits and either retains them as undistributed profits or distributes them among its members, the cooperative associations of a lower rank.

VI   Is the Cooperative Movement Economically Sound?

The vast propaganda literature of the cooperatives boasts in extreme language of the achievements of the cooperative movement. From modest beginnings, the cooperatives developed into big business with an ample supply of capital. They have millions of members, many thousands of organizations, over a hundred mills, factories, oil wells, refineries, and pipelines. Their yearly turnover is enormous. This thriving condition is not limited to this country. It is a world phenomenon. The International Cooperative Alliance had at the outbreak of the Second World War affiliates with a membership of more than 70 million in thirty-eight different countries. What a marvelous success!

At closer examination, however, one discovers some flaws in this fascinating picture. First of all, there is the fact that cooperation is much stronger abroad than it is in the United States. Before the war, the consumers' cooperatives of Finland handled about 30 percent of the country's retail trade; in Sweden the figure was 12 percent; in Great Britain, France, and Denmark, 10 percent. But in the United States, it was only a fraction of one percent.[16]

This is an amazing fact. Precisely in that country in which the common man's standard of living is highest, the role played by the cooperatives in the field of retailing is very modest when compared both with conditions abroad and with the total turnover of domestic retailing. The United States is foremost in the world with regard to the material well-being of the masses, but rather backward with regard to the development of consumers' cooperatives. Hence, it is obvious that the prosperity of the average citizens does not depend on the flowering of cooperatives but on other factors.

The second idea which comes to the mind of an impartial observer is that the cooperatives were denied the opportunity to test their efficiency under equal competitive conditions as against other types of enterprise. In all countries of the world, they were pampered in a lavish way by privileges, especially by tax exemptions and cheap credit. They did not stand the competition of the private or corporate retailer and the private or corporate manufacturer by their own means and by their own accomplishments. The virtual subsidies they received at the expense of the public revenue were considerable enough to make them flourish even in spite of lamentable inefficiency and wasteful and inept management. The experience of the long history of the cooperative movement cannot prove anything in favor of cooperative methods. It merely proves that tax privileges in this age of confiscatory taxation are

16 Cf. M. S. Stewart, *Cooperatives in the United States—a Balance Sheet* (Public Affairs Pamphlets no. 32, 1944), p. 6.

very valuable and make those privileged prosper. The ardor with which the spokesmen of the cooperatives are fighting for the preservation of these privileges and their reiterated assertions that the abolition of these privileges would doom the cooperative movement suggest that they themselves have very little confidence in the power of the cooperatives to hold their own against the competition of private business.

The very fact that the private retailer is able to stand the rivalry of a cooperative store bears witness to the economic superiority of profit-seeking free enterprise. The cooperative enjoys ample tax privileges; it is backed by an organization whose capital by far exceeds that of the average retailer, and it enjoys many other privileges. Private business is in every institutional and political respect handicapped in its competitive effort. It owes its flowering exclusively to its superior efficiency and to the fact that it serves the customer best.

The pro-cooperative propaganda overflows with arguments purporting to show why profit-seeking retail trade must necessarily be wasteful and costly and why the cooperatives are more economical and can sell at cheaper prices. If these statements were right, the cooperatives would long since—even without the ample subsidies they enjoy in the shape of tax privileges—have superseded private retailing. But the fact remains that the cooperatives are not able to outdo the private distributor either in regard to the height of prices (i.e., the net charge to the buyer) or in regard to the other services they render to their patrons. The fact that the overwhelming majority of the American housewives patronize the private retailers and that by and large only less than one cent of each dollar spent by the consumers goes into the cooperative stores amounts to a striking expression of the nation's acknowledgment of the private storekeeper's superiority. There is no need to unmask the fallacies implied in all these sophisticated demonstrations of the alleged shortcomings of private business. The housewife, passing by the cooperative store and walking into the private distributor's shop, explodes them more convincingly than any theorist could.

The cooperative doctrine's fundamental error is the misconstruction of the role played by the distributors and retailers. As the champions of the cooperative doctrine see it, retailing is sterile because it does not add anything to the physical and chemical properties of the merchandise. The merchant is merely a superfluous middleman whose interposition enhances the price without improving the quality of the product or rendering any valuable services. One could easily dispose of this drone and of his undeserved gain.

If the cooperatives had not enjoyed their ample tax privileges, they would have very soon learned from experience that this seemingly plausible argument is utterly wrong. The retailer is not just a dispensable intermediary. Retailing is a necessary function within the operation of the market economy. It is one of the devices daily adjusting production anew to the changing demands of the consumers. Although as a rule, the retailer does not alter the physical and chemical properties of the merchandise, he adds to its value by keeping it ready for use precisely at those places and at that time in which it is most urgently asked for. The services that the retailer renders to the public are not overpaid, as competition—always very acute in the field of distribution—keeps their prices within the most narrow margin possible. In dealing with the consumers' cooperatives one cannot often enough stress the point that the cooperatives, in spite of their tax prerogatives, are not in a position to supplant the private merchant. It is this fact that demolishes all the verbose disquisitions of the cooperative literature.

VII   The Political Element in the Cooperative Movement

From its very beginnings, the cooperative movement was primarily a political movement. It was, in the plans of its initiators, not so much an instrument for improving the conditions of its members as a weapon to be used for the destruction of the "bourgeoisie" and the "bourgeois or capitalistic mode of production." Because they appreciated the cooperatives from this point of view, the socialist parties always sympathized with the cooperative movement. Apart from the farmers' cooperatives, a great many of the members of consumers' cooperatives are socialists. In the imagination of these socialist cooperators, the socialist paradise of the future will be organized as an association of the associations of consumers' cooperatives. The foundation of a new cooperative store and the expansion and improvement of already operating cooperatives are steps forward on the road that leads to mankind's social salvation.

Now, all this is utterly confused and contradictory talk. Within the frame of a socialist system of production there cannot be any question of cooperatives. Socialism is the very antithesis of any freedom and discretion granted to the consumers. It abolishes the market, market exchange, and all the rights of the buyers. Under socialism, the individual must be content with what the authority deigns to give him. Socialism is the supremacy of the production tsar.

It is, of course, possible for a socialist commonwealth to retain the name "cooperative" and to call its distribution shops "cooperatives." The communists in Soviet Russia, as well as the Nazis in Hitler Germany, resorted to this trick. But nobody can be fooled by such a terminological makeshift.

One of the characteristic features of the capitalist system (which the Marxians dub the system of "wage-slavery," where "labor is a commodity") is that the wage earner is free to spend his earnings as he likes. The consumer's buying and abstention from buying ultimately determine what should be produced and in what quantity and quality. This supremacy of the consumer is warranted by the competitive order of industrial production which all producers, however different their products may be, compete with one another for the greatest possible share in the buyer's dollar. If there is only one producing agency, viz., the government, this competition ceases; then the housewife must take in the shop what the agent of the government is prepared to give her. Under capitalism, the shopkeeper, whether he is a private merchant or the employee of a cooperative, is anxious to serve the patrons; once the deal is finished, he thanks the customer for having patronized his shop and asks him to patronize it in the future too. Under socialism, the shopkeeper is eager to please the government, his superiors; he dispenses the merchandise as a favor and admonishes the recipient to be grateful to the sublime donor, the great dictator.

Those people who associate with the word socialism the image of clean cooperative stores, amply stocked with merchandise, in which courteous salesmen attend on the customers are badly mistaken. The cooperative stores are clean, amply stocked with goods, and staffed with obliging clerks because they must compete with private profit-seeking retailing. The stores of a socialist system will be very different.

VIII   Monopolistic and Totalitarian Tendencies in the Cooperative Movement

The managers of the cooperatives are fully aware of the fact that the cooperatives would not be able to stand the competition of private business if they had to vie with them under equal conditions. It is this insight which on the one hand makes them passionately defend their precious privileges and on the other hand, pushes them toward monopolistic and totalitarian ventures.

The writings and the speeches of the cooperative propaganda never tried to conceal cooperatives' monopolistic ambitions. They disparage competition as such and exuberantly praise the blessings of what they call unity. In each country, the local cooperatives tend to unite to form a national organization. The national societies of the world are federated in the International Cooperative Alliance. It is the avowed ideal of the champions of cooperativism to abolish every kind of competition by eliminating not only private free enterprise but also state-owned and -operated outfits. They dream of a world-embracing "Cooperative Union of the World" into which virtually supreme power will be vested in the coming "Consumers' Cooperative Era."[17] This "Union," supreme and unrivalled in both production and distribution, is to enjoy a monopolistic position in every field of economic activities. It will have precisely the same exclusive totalitarian power the Nazis assigned to their *Reichswirtschaftsministerium* and the Bolsheviks to their *Gosplan*.

In this imperfect world, however, the cooperatives are forced to moderate their pretensions. They are anxious to combine and to conspire for the elimination of competition and for the restraint of trade. Their activities provide the classical example both of horizontal and vertical combination. They tend to ramify into all fields, even in such as are only loosely associated with their main activities. In these efforts, they are greatly encouraged by the direct and indirect support various departments of the federal and the state governments accord to them. But the inherent inferiority of the cooperative way of business offsets all these privileges and favors. The progress which the consumers' cooperatives have made on the way toward their final goal, the monopolistic control of the retail markets, is comparatively slow because it is not easy to fool the housewife. The fact that in the United States the consumers' cooperatives are but small and insignificant when compared with those of many European countries is the proof of the American consumers' greater shrewdness and greater capacity to distinguish between better and poorer merchandise.

IX Are the Cooperatives Democratic?

The more manifest the weakness of the economic arguments advanced in favor of cooperativism becomes, the more its protagonists lay stress upon its alleged democratic character. As they see it, cooperativism is

17 Cf. Kallen, *The Decline and Rise of the Consumer*, p. 436.

democratic while profit-seeking business is reactionary; the establishment of political democracy demands the establishment of economic democracy, viz., supremacy of the cooperatives.

The truth is that the market economy is the full and only possible realization of the principle of economic democracy. The market process is a daily repeated voting in which every penny gives a right to vote. The buyers, by preferring those commodities which in regard to price and quality are best-fitted to satisfy their needs, make the conduct of each enterprise profitable or unprofitable, make small-size business big, and penniless beginners rich. On the market, nothing ultimately counts but the buyer's dollars. It is true, these ballot papers are not equally distributed among the public. The rich put more of them into the ballot-box than their less prosperous fellow citizens. But to be rich is in itself the outcome of a vote taken, as in the market economy not only the acquisition but no less the preservation of wealth requires continuous success in best supplying the consumers. The capitalist who does not invest his funds in those lines in which they serve the satisfaction of the most urgent wants of the public is penalized by losses and loses his wealth entirely if he does not alter his conduct in time.

Political democracy as embodied in representative government is the corollary of the economic democracy of the market. From the point of view of a consistent application of Marxian dialectic materialism, one must describe parliamentarism, government by the people, and all the freedoms granted by the bills of rights as the "ideological and political superstructure of the capitalistic system of private enterprise." At any rate, the Marxians were consistent enough to deprecate and to disparage democracy as "pluto-democracy" and parliamentarism as a "bourgeois bogus." Never were there more adamant foes of any kind of democratic institutions than the Bolsheviks. Only when the menace of the Nazis made them beseech the aid of the capitalistic nations of the West, did they begin to arrogate to themselves the appellation democratic. Only then did the communists and their allies in Western Europe and America discover that the cooperatives are democratic institutions, even the very paragon of economic democracy.

In resorting to this semantic innovation, the pro-cooperative agitators adopted a terminology which owes its origin to Mrs. Beatrice Potter Webb (Lady Passfield). It was Mrs. Webb who camouflaged the labor union movement as "industrial democracy" and described the coop-

erative movement as one aspect of industrial democracy.[18] There is no
need to enter into an examination of these claims. What Mr. and Mrs.
Sidney Webb call democracy and freedom is the very opposite of both.
In their eyes, the Soviet dictatorship is true democracy, and the ruthless extermination of all those who do not fully agree with the rulers is
genuine freedom.

The cooperative as a type of business organization is neither democratic nor anti-democratic. It is one of the legal patterns for group ownership. In a free society, cooperatives are allowed to function in the
same way in which other types of the business corporation are allowed.
If the cooperatives were not to enjoy any government favors, one would
be right in declaring that they owe the role they play and the rise of
their turnover to the voluntary support of their patrons as manifested
in the democratic process of the market. But this is precisely not the
case. The cooperatives are amply subsidized by government favoritism.
What makes their membership rolls swell is neither their own achievements nor the services they render to the patrons but the cumulation
of government favors. In joining the cooperative, the consumer does
not approve of the cooperative idea; what he aims at is to share in the
benefits which the government bestows upon the cooperators.

The cooperative propaganda lays great stress upon the fact that the
cooperatives are voluntary associations. Such statements entirely distort the true state of affairs.

First, the government interferes in a momentous way with the final
decision of an individual on the point of choosing between joining
or not joining a cooperative. The cooperative is privileged to the disadvantage of all taxpayers who are not enlisted members. If from two
competing bus lines, the red line and the blue line, the tickets of the
former are subject to a tax while those of the latter are exempt, it would
be misleading to say that a passenger who prefers the blue line made
his choice voluntarily. He acted under duress, as, due to the government's interference, the choice of the red line is penalized.

Second, it is a sad fact that in many communities the cooperators
resort to social pressure and to more or less open threats in order to
increase enrollment. It is true that these abuses are less frequent in the
United States than in the European countries. But this is not a proof

18 In 1891. Cf. Webb, *The Cooperative Movement in Great Britain*, p. xxiii.

that the American cooperators are more democratically minded and have due respect for the rights and freedoms of their fellow citizens. It merely shows that the United States is still a country in which laws and legality are enforced.

The cooperatives are neither more nor less democratic than any other business organization to which the democratic market economy offers the opportunity to show what they are able to achieve. However, the cooperatives do not dare to risk the trial of such an examination and are looking for the shelter of favoritism.

∾ The Privileges, Prerogatives, and Immunities
of the Cooperatives

I The Governments' Bias in Favor of the Cooperatives

No human being can free himself from partiality and particular bias in favor of or against persons, institutions, or things. A government is always composed of mortal men and is therefore never aloof from the strife of peoples, parties, and ideologies. Only state idolatry describes the rulers as unaffected arbiters and directors of earthly affairs. Realistic observers know how different the real officeholders and administrators are.

What is wrong with contemporary governments is not merely that they are excessive in their predilections and prepossessions, but still more that they are guided by blind prejudices. The result is that their best intentions are frustrated and that they invariably spread havoc.

The whole fabric of modern economic developments is built upon the functioning of two main types of business organization: individual and proprietorship and partnership on the one hand and the corporation on the other hand. All the unprecedented achievements of modern industrialism that have procured a continually improving standard of living for an ever-increasing population were effected by these two types of business organization. It was exclusively profit-seeking business that transformed the world of horses, sailing ships, and windmills into the world of steam power, electricity, and mass production for the needs of the masses. It was profit-seeking private business that accumulated the capital, i.e., the tools and machines, which alone have the power to raise the productivity of labor and thereby wage rates. Even the most bigoted partisans of cooperativism cannot dare to claim any of these merits for the cooperatives. The best that could be said to the praise of the cooperatives is that—of course, taking advantage of the lavish privileges accorded to them—they more or less aptly copied some of the well-tried technical methods of profit-seeking business. It would be impossible to write the history of our age without assigning the first place to the efforts of private business that daily supplies the household of the average with new, better, and cheaper products. But the historian would omit nothing noteworthy if he did not mention the fact that some of these products are distributed or marketed through cooperatives and that some of the more simple processes of manufacturing are also executed in plants owned by cooperative associations. There is no American whose daily life would not be less comfortable if private business had been prevented from accomplishing all that it has brought about in the last hundred years. But the great majority of the nation would not be in any respect worse off if there had never been cooperatives.

Nonetheless the governments behave as if private business were an objectionable thing and as if the salvation of mankind were to depend on the cooperatives. They openly and avowedly discriminate against private business in subjecting its surpluses to a burdensome taxation from which a surplus made by a cooperative is exempt. They discriminate especially against the corporations in taxing corporate incomes both on the corporation and on the shareholders who receive dividends. Confiscatory rates of personal-income taxation curtail the amount of venture capital available for the conduct of private business while the cooperatives are allowed to accumulate capital either without being taxed at all or without being taxed to the extent private business is taxed.

In all countries of the world, the cooperatives enjoy ample privileges.

In the United States, both state and federal laws provide that the ordinary activities of the cooperative associations are not to be deemed violations of anti-trust laws. The Department of Agriculture makes available to farmers' cooperatives free legal, statistical, and technical advisory service. Government agencies supply the cooperatives with loans at low rates of interest.

The most valuable privileges are those granted in the field of taxation. Some of these exemptions do not count very much, e.g., the exemption from the annual franchise taxes. But the exemptions in the matter of income taxation are of primordial importance.

From its very beginnings, the federal income tax legislation exempted cooperatives. These exemptions were widened and enlarged in the later Acts. On the other hand, they became the more helpful and profitable as the tax rates increased to confiscatory levels. With the present tax rates, they are tantamount to lavish subsidies at the expense of all taxpayers and the whole nation.

II The Essential Problems Concerning the Tax Privilege

In defending and justifying their tax privileges, the cooperatives purposely dwell upon trifling technicalities and legalistic syllogisms in order to divert the public's attention from the essential issue.

As has been pointed out already, from the beginning of the federal income tax legislation it was the intention to exempt the cooperatives. The political constellation in the nation and in Congress was such that no law could be passed without the votes of certain senators and representatives from whom these tax exemptions were of paramount importance. Hence, all the definitions and provisions of the tax laws were so formulated as to leave the cooperatives unmolested. When the practical experience of the laws' application and the rulings of the courts demonstrated that these privileges were not so broad as the cooperatives wanted them to be and when, with the tax burden continually becoming heavier, the cooperatives' appetite for exemptions increased, these formulations were again and again redrafted. Although some congressmen tried to make the fundamental constitutional principle of equality under the law prevail, the cooperatives' prerogatives were virtually always enlarged by such redrafting.

Under this state of affairs, it is easy to understand why the cooperators are eager to make the discussion turn around the problem whether or not the cooperatives make profits in the technical sense that the income tax laws attribute to this term. This present legal definition of income was influenced by the intention of making the cooperatives exempt. It is no wonder that it can be interpreted by the cooperatives in their own favor.

Of course, these interpretations are contradictory and indefensible. No dialectical artifices can bring about a tenable definition of income that would include the surplus earned by a corporation and exclude that earned by a cooperative. But the exemption of the cooperatives does not depend on the definition of income as written into the law. The cooperatives are specifically exempt both by the federal and by the state laws.

A discussion concerning what the law should be must radically differ from the interpretation of the existing law. While the latter problem is strictly limited to the letter and the spirit of the law, the former knows only one yardstick, viz., public welfare and economic expediency.

Taxes are levied in order to raise the funds needed for the conduct of government affairs. To contribute one's share to these funds is a civic duty. It is not a penalty. The government does not penalize its citizens for owning a home, smoking cigarettes, or travelling on the railroad. It taxes them according to the standards provided by these conditions.

The same holds true for the income tax. It is not a penalty for having earned profits. Its idea is that people whose income is higher have a greater faculty or ability to pay than those with smaller incomes. (There is no need to investigate whether this ability principle of taxation is sound and whether it is not already at the point of showing its own absurdity.) But the cooperators, entangled in their prepossession that private profits earned by businessmen are an evil that must be eradicated, consider the income tax as a fine imposed upon the "profiteers." In their opinion the income tax is the legal vehicle to brush away profit-seeking business and to give to the cooperatives that role that the most ambitious cooperators are aiming at, namely, the exclusive monopoly in supplying the consumers with all commodities and services they are asking for and the control of the plants turning out these commodities.

At the bottom of the cooperatives' argument lies the idea that selling a commodity at a price exceeding costs incurred is unfair and should be penalized by confiscation of at least a part of the surplus. But if this were true, it would apply no less to the surpluses earned by the cooperatives than to those earned by corporations.

Let us review in detail the arguments advanced by the cooperatives in favor of their tax privileges.

1. The transaction between a cooperative and its members is not a sale and a purchase. The process, says an eminent spokesman of the cooperatives, Mr. James Peter Warbasse, President Emeritus of the Cooperative League of the U.S.A., is "simple. A group of people pool a certain amount of money with which they buy goods to put on the

shelves of their retail store. They own the goods and so cannot sell them to themselves. When a member wants some of the goods, he goes to the store and takes away, for example, a can of peas. The peas are already his—he has already paid for them."[19] Now, this description is from the beginning to the end inappropriate and misleading.

The group of people of whom Mr. Warbasse is speaking do not merely pool a certain amount of money. They establish an association organized under the provisions of a specific statute of their state. They act in this way purposely and with full consideration of the law because they desire that this association should be recognized by the laws and the courts as a legal entity which can sue and be sued only in the corporate name and that the individual associates should not be liable for the debts of the association. Consequently it is not true that the members "own the goods and cannot sell them to themselves." The goods are owned by the association and not by the individual members. If a member wants to acquire them in a legally correct way—and not through theft or embezzlement—he must buy them from the association. He must not "take them away from the shelves." In this respect, there is not the slightest difference between a corporation and a cooperative. The member of a cooperative has no better title to take away a can of peas from the shelves of the cooperative store than has the shareholder of a department store with regard to the cans on the shelves of the department store.

This is not merely a legal technicality. It is the life blood of the cooperative that it is regarded by the laws as a person whose assets and liabilities are distinct from the assets and liabilities of its members. The whole system of cooperative business would immediately collapse if this principle were to be abandoned.

2. Even if one were to accept the vicious argument that the cooperatives in selling to members do not really *sell*, it would not fit all those frequent instances in which cooperatives sell to non-members. It is paradoxical that associations engaged in all kinds of wholesale and retail transactions, in export trade and in government contracts, resort to such a lame excuse.

3. The employment of the total gross surplus of sales proceeds over all costs expended is to be classified into three groups:

    a. One portion is laid aside in a depreciation fund to replace the equipment worn out.

19 Cf. Warbasse, *The Cooperative Way, a Method of World Reconstruction*, p. 115.

b. One portion is ploughed back into the business as an enlarge-ment of the capital invested either in the existing outfit itself or in its affiliates.

c. One portion is withdrawn from the business and goes to those entitled: the owner of the private firm, the shareholders of the corporation, and the members of the cooperative.

The portions *b* and *c* together are also from the legal point of view net income. The advocates of the cooperatives in contending that the patronage refunds are not profits refer only to the portion *c*. However, the portion *b* is no less important; it is even more important as the main social and historical function of profit making is the accumula-tion of additional capital. The enormous role that the ploughing back of profits and the investment of profits in new enterprises plays in the evolution of cooperative business is well known. Almost all equity capi-tal operating in the super-cooperatives and especially in their produc-tion and transportation enterprises was provided by such profits.

4. An examination of the principles and methods according to which the cooperatives conduct their business operations and of the rules they employ in bookkeeping and accounting clearly reveals that they are—like all other types of business enterprise—guided by the urge to make a surplus or profit and to avoid losses. Their reluctance to allow the use of the term "profit" with regard to their affairs is pure verbalism without any substantial foundation.

Let us look at an official document of the Cooperative League of the U.S.A., published under the title *Learning the Language of Study and Action*.[20] Here the authors freely admit that "we," i.e., the cooperatives, "are in business *to make money*." Hence, they say, many cooperators ask the same question the private businessman does, namely, the ques-tion: "Have we made a profit or loss?" The private businessman calls the statement which gives us the answer a "profit and loss statement." But the authors of the booklet do not like this appellation. Cooperative accountants and cooperative members, they say, should avoid the use of the term "profit and loss statement," preferring either "income and expense statement" or "operating statement."[21]

This is a purely semantic manipulation. The authors do not even venture to demonstrate that these ominous "earnings," which they want to withdraw from taxation, are not income or profit. All they do is to

---

20 Cooperative League of the U.S.A.: Pamphlet no. 43.
21 Ibid., p. 18.

give them another name. If it were enough to avoid income taxes by changing the name of the "profit and loss statement" to "operating statement," all private firms and corporations could do so.

The same verbalism manifests itself in the Cooperative League's suggestion to substitute the term "savings return" for "rebate," "patronage dividend," or "purchase refund."[22]

5. The cooperatives deny that they enjoy tax exemption and are thus privileged as against profit business. Their tax exemption, they say, is not a privilege, as the private businessman could easily enjoy the same freedom. Let him give back to his customers the difference between the cost price and the selling price, as the cooperatives do, and the problem is solved.[23] It is obvious that this reasoning does not apply to the tax exemption granted to that part of a cooperative's profits which is not distributed but reinvested. Neither does it apply to that part which stems from selling to non-members and from previous investment in affiliates. Setting aside these minor points, it must be observed that the concept of cost price is different with regard to cooperatives and with regard to the private owner of a store or a filling station. With the cooperative, it includes the salaries and other payments made to the officers and managers of the cooperative business. With the private grocer, it does not include a remuneration for the grocer's own labor performed. If the private grocer or owner of a filling station were to "give back" to the customers the difference between the cost price and the selling price, he would not have any income at all; he would work for a heavenly reward while only the staff of the cooperatives receives its pay.

III   How Capital and Labor Are Wasted by the Cooperatives

The eminence of the competitive market economy consists primarily in the fact that it ceaselessly tends to convey the means of production into the hands of those people who employ them in the most economical way for the best possible satisfaction of the needs of the consumers. It tends to eliminate the less efficient producers and to give control of production management to the most efficient. To comprehend the meaning of this function of the market, it is necessary to realize that everybody's material well-being is harmed if material factors of production or human labor are anywhere employed in such a way as

22 Cf. W. E. Regli, *A Primer of Bookkeeping for Cooperatives,* 2nd ed. (1937), p. 5.
23 Warbasse, *The Cooperative Way, a Method of World Reconstruction,* p. 158.

not to yield the highest output they could yield when more properly managed. As against more economical methods of operation, less-economical methods result in a restriction of total output. They make the nation as a whole and all its members poorer.

In the absence of government interference with business, an enterprise which requires a higher amount of capital and labor than is necessary under the given conditions cannot survive. As its costs of operation are higher, it is finally forced by more efficient competitors to go out of business. Only the most efficient outfits remain.

But as soon as the government interferes by subsidies, cheap credit, or tax exemptions, the state of affairs can be altered entirely. If the inefficient grocer A is exempt from a tax which his more efficient competitor B is forced to pay, the power of A to stand the competition of B is strengthened. A's operating costs proper (i.e., operating costs exclusive of taxes) are still higher than those of B. But against this difference in the operating costs proper must be held the advantage which A derives from tax exemption. Although A's conduct of affairs is wasteful, although it absorbs an amount of capital and labor which, without curtailment of the services received by the public, could be made available for the satisfaction of other wants which cannot be satisfied precisely on account of A's wastefulness, his shop can continue in business. The government shelters A against the consequences of his own inefficiency.

A's tax exemption is therefore not merely a matter that would concern exclusively him and B and would not affect the interests of all other people. What the government achieves by taxing B alone instead of distributing this tax equally between A and B is not merely a disarrangement of the mutual competitive position between A and B. The main social and economic effect is the preservation of a high-cost unit at the expense of a low-cost unit, the preservation of a quite useless and obviously pernicious squandering of scarce factors of production.

This inefficient A, whom the government pampers in order to make it possible for him to compete with B, is the cooperative in its capacity as a beneficiary of tax exemption and other government favors. It is of no avail how the friends of cooperativism try to justify these tax privileges in resorting to metaphysical arguments. The simple truth is: the government interferes in order to make it possible for the cooperatives to stand the competition of private business which they admittedly could not stand when unaided.

The fathers of the cooperative idea and the founders of the first co-

operatives were committed to the erroneous belief that the cooperatives could serve the public at lower costs than private business. However, a century of cooperative experience has exploded this assumption
as utterly delusive. The cooperatives did not stand the test. Where
they thrive and as far as they thrive, they owe their existence to various
government privileges, especially to tax exemptions and cheap government credit.

These privileges become the more valuable for the cooperatives
and the more detrimental for the nation's whole industrial effort and
economic well-being, the more the cooperatives engage in production
activities.

In the unhampered market economy there prevails a tendency to
invest capital available for the execution of new projects only in those
enterprises which offer the best expectations that they will avoid waste
and inefficiency. However, favoritism shown to the cooperatives coun-
teracts these tendencies. As the government on the one hand taxes
private business heavily and taxes the corporations twice and on the
other hand leaves the cooperatives free, it gives to inefficient cooperative factories the delusive appearance of efficiency and the opportunity
to amass a surplus. The champions of cooperativism are boasting that
today in the United States owners of factories approach cooperatives
and offer to sell their plants and that the banks come to the cooperatives and tell them where there is a factory that can be bought cheaply
and offer to lend the money to buy it.[24] Such offers are, however, not
as the cooperative champions assume, the proof of the superiority of
the cooperative mode of production. They merely show that factories
which on account of the fact that they are producing at too high a
cost are doomed on the free market, can quietly survive as soon as the
ample privileges of the cooperatives are granted to them.

While the tax system both of the federal government and of the states
considerably checks the accumulation of capital on the part of corporations, private firms, and individuals, it encourages capital accumulation on the part of the cooperatives. The cooperatives are fully aware
of the tremendous potentiality of this state of affairs. They have coined
the slogan "*Factories Are Free.*"[25] Their most eminent spokesman, in re-
porting a definite transaction of a consumers' cooperative, says: "It was

---

24 Ibid., pp. 45–46.
25 Ibid., p. 46.

good business for the members of the cooperative, for without sacrifice on their part they made themselves the owners of a manufacturing
business."[26] Now, there are no such things as can be acquired without
sacrifice. It is true that the members of the cooperative acquired the
manufacturing business in question "without sacrifice on *their* part."
But this was only the case because the government forced other people
to make a sacrifice for the benefit of the members of the cooperative. It
forced these other people to pay higher taxes in order to free the cooperative from the burden of taxes. The cooperative acquired the factory
by a subsidy which it received in the shape of tax exemption.

The cooperatives in dealing with their expansion pass over their
privileges in silence. They ascribe their success exclusively to the fact
that they "do not have to make any profit."[27] It is not necessary to enter
anew into an examination of all the problems implied in this profit
issue. Let us look at the matter from a purely pragmatic point of view.

The essential point in the reasoning of the fathers and pioneers of
cooperativism was this: the retailers and distributors, these quite useless middlemen, enhance the price of the commodities because they
are anxious to make profits. The cooperators will eliminate profit and
thereby be in a position to sell the goods to their members at lower
prices than those charged by private profit-seeking business. As everybody is eager to buy in the cheapest market, the evolution of the cooperatives will very soon supersede the private retailer.

History has entirely refuted this doctrine. The cooperatives are not
in a position to stand the competition of private profit-seeking business.
They would have long since completely disappeared if they were not to
enjoy ample privileges on the part of the government.

The very fact that in spite of these privileges they have not made
greater inroads into the field of retailing is a proof of their inherent
inefficiency.

By splitting hairs and indulging in subtle syllogisms concerning the
concepts of profits, savings, earnings, surplus, costs, and so on, the cooperators evade the discussion of the main issue. In a free country,
such as the United States, the immense majority of the buying public
prefers to patronize private business and not the cooperatives. The
cooperatives always insist upon the fact that they give back to their

26 Ibid., pp. 46–47.
27 Ibid., p. 46.

customers the difference between the cost price and the selling price in the shape of the patronage dividend while private business, as they say, retains this difference as profit. But the intelligent customer in choosing between private business and cooperative business takes into account all the terms of the contract, the quality of the merchandise as well as its price and the value of all the further services rendered by the seller; in considering a purchase with a cooperative, he also takes duly into account the patronage dividend to be expected. It is a fact that in the United States, this comparison between the private store and the cooperative store in the immense majority of cases decides in favor of private business. The conduct of the American people in buying bears witness to the fact that one buys cheaper or better or both cheaper and better in the private store notwithstanding the patronage rebate. Hence it is proved that the private businessman's profit is not due to overcharging the customer. It is earned by an enterprise that in the majority of cases serves the consumer better and cheaper than the "altruistic" cooperative. The cooperatives have no reason whatever to boast of the patronage dividends. The private retailer is giving the customer more, in the shape either of better merchandise or of a lower price or of other services.

IV   Cooperative Operation of Manufacturing and Other Production Enterprises

The spectacular expansion of manufacturing and other production and transportation activities of the cooperatives and of the various associations of cooperatives was, as has been already mentioned above, a consequence of the fact that the tax privileges of the cooperatives became the more valuable the more the taxes for the groups of business not tax exempt were made increasingly burdensome.

The differences between a production plant owned and operated by a cooperative or an association of cooperatives and such a plant owned and operated by a corporation or a private profit-seeking firm are two-fold:

1. The former's management is less efficient than the latter's.
2. The former enjoys privileges in the field of taxation and credit procurement which are denied to the latter.

Those who would be prepared to question the first of these statements are at a loss to explain why the competition of these privileged enterprises does not completely crush their non-privileged competitors. An eminent expert, Mr. A. G. Black, former governor of the Farm Credit Administration, declared prior to the Second World War that "when taxes are absorbing a large part of the earnings of private business, the cooperative form of business really provides an enormous advantage."[28] This enormous advantage is entirely swallowed by the cooperative bureaucracy to offset the inefficiency of their conduct of affairs. No part of it is passed on to the consumers, as the consumers, due regard being had to the quality of the products or services rendered, are not supplied by the cooperatives at lower net prices (that means: prices minus patronage dividends) than those of the private firms which are not tax-free. Neither do the workers employed in the cooperatives' plants receive higher pay than other workers.

The nation's treasury, in granting these tax privileges to the production activities of the cooperatives, renounces revenues which it would pocket if these plants were owned by corporations or if no privileges were granted to the cooperatives. Public expenditure must be curtailed correspondingly. Some benefits which a budgetary allowance could make must be forgone. Who profits from all this? The answer is: nobody. The equivalent of the drop in revenue is squandered by ineptitude, negligence, and clumsiness.

If this were not true, the cooperatives could either, selling at the same prices as other firms, reap enormous profits or, at lower prices, ruin all their rivals. In either case, they would have long since already reached what they consider as the ultimate goal of their movement, namely, a state of affairs under which the cooperatives produce in their own factories everything that their members require. The mere fact that their success was much more modest proves that there is in cooperativism itself a factor that checks its progress in spite of the enormous support they receive from the government. We cannot help calling this factor economic inferiority.

V   How Favoritism Harms the Cooperatives

Favoritism harms those favored no less than those at whose expense the favors are granted. It corrupts and enfeebles the protégé.

Placing their trust in political tutelage, the cooperatives have often neglected to appoint as officers, managers, and staff members men ef-

---

28 As quoted in *Tax-Free Manufacturing Cooperative Associations* (prepared by the National Tax Equality Association, 1945), p. 2.

ficient in the conduct of business and have given preference to people versed in political affairs, propaganda, and lobbying and popular with politicians and bureaucrats. In the continental countries of Europe, whose cooperative activities the American cooperators praise lavishly and set up as a pattern for their own activities, the cooperatives are in complete dependence on the various political parties. Each of the most important parties—especially the Social Democrats, the Catholic Socialists, the non-Catholic Christian parties, the various nationalist parties—has established its own system of cooperatives which closely collaborates with the political leadership.

Private business is eager to succeed by improving the quality of its products and services and by lowering their prices. It resorts to advertising in order to make the public familiar with the commodities it offers for sale. A profit-seeking merchant's advertisement sets into relief the advertiser's own achievements and the advantages which the prospective customers could derive from them. It never smears the competitors. The propaganda of the cooperatives is at a loss to find enough praiseworthy in the cooperatives' own accomplishments. Its leitmotif is the vilification of private enterprise and the insinuation that its profits are earned by cheating the customers.

When the private merchant is dissatisfied with the yield of his store, he tries to improve his conduct of affairs. When a cooperative works unsatisfactorily, the first thought of the responsible officers and managers is not the recourse to an appropriate reform of the operations. It is easier for them to ask for more tax exemption and for more and cheaper public credit.

The authors of the innumerable books, pamphlets, and periodicals published by the cooperative propaganda are so much preoccupied with the political aspects of cooperativism that they never raise the question which cannot be answered without entirely exploding the essential dogmas of the cooperative movement. They never ask: Were the fathers of cooperativism right in assuming that the elimination of profit will make it possible to supply the consumer more cheaply than he is supplied by profit-seeking business? If the answer to this question were to be given in the positive, it would be impossible to explain how private business—even apart from all the privileges granted to the cooperatives—could compete with the cooperatives. The spectacular failure of the consumers' cooperatives in the urban agglomerations of the United States is the only problem to be dealt with by a serious and honest book on cooperativism. How could this failure happen in spite of all taxes charged to private business and of all the ample privileges accorded to the cooperatives?

The champions of cooperativism think that they have sufficiently excused themselves from answering this question by heaping invective and insulting terms on all those who disagree with them. The foul language the pro-cooperative literature employs in its polemics is utterly disgusting. But the very fact that they resort to such abusive words proves that they are fully aware of their inability to refute the objections raised by the economists.

Neither is it of any use to throw dust in people's eyes by expatiating upon the success of cooperativism in other parts of the world. The fact that Iceland is in proportion to its population the "most highly cooperatized country in the world"[29] does not outweigh the fact that the United States, the country with the highest standard of living, is—as far as consumers' cooperatives are concerned—the least cooperatized one. The expansion of cooperativism in those countries of Eastern Europe which never experienced liberal institutions will certainly not count very much in the eyes of the citizens of free countries.

The cooperative literature lacks entirely the spirit of self-criticism and realistic appreciation of facts. It is full of conceit, vainglory, and self-adulation. It repeats again and again old fallacies, a hundred times refuted, and never gives a serious thought to any new idea. It thus faithfully mirrors the intellectual sterility of a movement which owes its development exclusively to the benevolent partisanship of the politicians.

Conclusion

The cooperative movement is entirely based on the very popular but utterly fallacious idea that profit is an unfair toll which the businessman levies on his patrons and on the contention that, by rights, the businessman should not ask more than what the merchandise cost him. The cooperatives were designed as devices for the general abolition of the vicious practice of selling above costs.

Experience of a hundred years of cooperative association has clearly proved that cooperatives are not able to take their chances on a free market. They cannot maintain themselves by their own efforts. At least

29 Cf. Warbasse, *The Cooperative Way, a Method of World Reconstruction*, p. 126.

it cannot be denied that there is no record of cooperatives which did stand the competition of private business without government favoritism. In all countries of the world, the cooperative movement owes its development and its present expansion, whatever they may be, to tax exemptions, cheap government credit, and other privileges. In passionately asserting that the abolition of these privileges would amount to a suppression of the cooperatives, the spokesmen of the cooperatives confess that they themselves consider these privileges as indispensable for the survival of cooperativism.

Business is not an end in itself. It exists and operates for the benefit of the public. The only justification of the conduct of a business lies in the patronage voluntarily given to it by a sufficient number of people. If people do not patronize a shop of their own accord, it is certainly not the task of government to favor it at the expense of the public revenue and thereby to bring to it as members people who are eager to share in the enjoyment of these favors. A business outfit that owes its survival to political pressure and not to the voluntary support of the buying public is parasitic. Its preservation results in the squandering of labor and material factors of production, it curtails the total amount of goods available for consumption, and it is pernicious from the point of view of public welfare.

The cooperative type of business organization can justify its existence only by renouncing the privileges which it enjoys today. Only as far as the cooperatives are able to hold their own without the support of tax exemptions, cheap government credit, and other favors can cooperativism be considered as a legitimate method of doing business in a free society.

CHAPTER 19

Some Observations on Current Economic Methods and Policies

I

If no radical changes in the prevailing political trends and tendencies occur very soon, the system of full government control of human activities will within a few years triumph in all countries this side of the Iron Curtain.

The doctrine today accepted by all those statesmen and politicians who do not openly embrace all the teachings of communism and totalitarianism maintains that it is the duty of the government to interfere with the operation of the market whenever the outcome of this operation appears to the government as "socially" undesirable. This means: the individuals in their production activities and in their buying and selling on the market are free as far as they precisely do what the government wants them to do; but they are not permitted to deviate from the course approved by the authorities. This doctrine of government omnipotence is, of course, today not yet completely enforced. The governments have not yet attained the formal power to control prices and wage rates. But the resistance offered to the enactment of such powers is weakening more and more. The government of the United States, in its endeavors to go on in its reckless inflationary policy, continually threatens the nation with the specter of all-round control of prices and wages. And only a few voices of protest are raised.

People who declare that they are in favor of the preservation of the market economy are called "extremists," and their arguments are not deemed worthy of a refutation. Even members of minority groups join in this enthusiasm for government omnipotence, although this system would deprive them of the only opportunity they have for overcoming

[This article was written in 1951; previously unpublished. —Ed.]

the animosity of the majority by excelling in the service of the public, the consumers. Almost all educational institutions, for the most part carefully avoiding the ticklish terms communism and socialism, are propagandizing for—all-round—planning and for "production for use."

Gone are the days when people, and first of all the youth, held liberty in esteem. Our contemporaries long for the "plan," the strict regimentation of everybody's life, work, and leisure by decrees of the paternal dictator.

II

The only goal of production is to provide for the satisfaction of wants, that is, consumption. The eminence of the market economy is to be seen in the fact that all production activities are ultimately directed by the consumers. Man is sovereign in his capacity as a consumer. In his capacity as a producer, he is bound to comply with the wishes of the consumers.

By their buying and by their abstention from buying, the consumers determine all that happens in the sphere of what is commonly called economic affairs. Their behavior ultimately determines everybody's place and function in the social apparatus of production. They allot ownership of the material factors of production to those who have succeeded in directing them into employments in which they best satisfy the most urgent of the needs of the consumers. Property in material factors of production, wealth, can be acquired and preserved in the capitalistic or market economy only by serving the consumers better or more cheaply than others do. Such property is a public mandate, as it were, entrusted to the proprietor under the condition that he use it in the best possible way for the benefit of the consumers. The capitalist must never relax in endeavors to serve the public better and more cheaply. If he feels that he cannot achieve this without help from other people, he must choose adequate partners or lend his funds to such men. Thus there is built into the system of the market economy a mechanism, as it were, that inexorably forces the owners of all material factors of production to invest them in those lines in which they best serve the consumers.

In a similar way, the consumers determine the height of the earnings of those working for salaries and wages. The employer is under the necessity of paying to each helper the full price the consumers are prepared to refund to him for what this worker has contributed to the qualities of the product. He cannot pay more, for then the employment of the worker would involve a loss; neither can he pay less, for then his competitors would lure away the job seekers from his plant. It is not the valuation of the employer, but that of the consumers that is instrumental in granting high wages to popular actors and athletes and low wages to street sweepers and charwomen.

That this system benefits all nations and all individuals within every nation has been spectacularly demonstrated by the unprecedented increase in population figures it has brought about. Wherever governments and pressure groups resorting to violent action have not fully succeeded in their endeavors to sabotage the operation of the market, industry has provided the masses with amenities of which the wealthiest princes and nabobs of the past did not even dream.

If one compares economic conditions in the most prosperous parts of the earth with those in the so-called underdeveloped countries, one cannot help realizing the correctness of the fundamental principle of nineteenth-century economic liberalism. Against the vagaries and revolutionary delusions of the socialist and communist agitators, the economists opposed the thesis: there is but one method available to improve the conditions of the whole population, viz., to accelerate the accumulation of capital as against the increase in population. The only method of rendering all people more prosperous is to raise the productivity of human labor, i.e., productivity per man-hour, and this can be done only by placing into the hands of the worker more and better tools and machines. What is lacking in the countries usually described as underdeveloped is saving and capital accumulation. There is no substitute for the investment of capital. If any further proof of this fundamental principle were needed, it is to be seen in the eagerness of all backward nations to get foreign capital for their industries.

III

In dealing with the pros and cons of socialist management, one unfortunately neglects to pay sufficient attention to those effects which are commonly considered as non-economic. One fails to pay attention to the human aspect of the problem.

The distinctive feature of man consists in his initiative. An animal's life takes precisely the course peculiar to all members of the species it belongs to. A deviation from this line can be brought about only by external force, the interference of a human will. But man is in a position to choose between various ways of conduct open to him. His fate depends to some extent on the mode in which he reacts to the conditions of his environment and integrates himself into the social system of peaceful cooperation. He is, within definite limits drawn by nature, the founder of his fortune. Not to be restricted in the pursuit of his own plans by anything else than the same freedom accorded to his fellow men is what is commonly called freedom. Freedom does not mean unbridled license to indulge in any acts of ferocity, and it does not conflict with the operation of a "state," i.e., a social apparatus, for the violent repression of the recourse to brute force on the part of unruly individuals or gangs. On the contrary, it can work only where the peaceful cooperation of individuals is protected in such a way against oppression and usurpation.

Constitutional government by elected officeholders—representative government—is an institution to give the citizens in the administration of public affairs a supremacy as far as possible analogous to the sovereignty they enjoy in their capacity as consumers in the market economy. Supplanting the rule of the aristocratic lords of the feudal ages and all systems of slavery and serfdom, it developed in the countries of Western civilization simultaneously with the gradual disintegration of the economic self-sufficiency of families, villages, counties, and nations and the evolution of the world-embracing system of the international division of labor. It is the political corollary of the economic democracy of the market economy, and it gives way to a dictatorial regime whenever and wherever the voluntary cooperation of men under the system of free markets is abolished by the establishment of any kind of socialist management.

The planned economy is the most rigid system of enslavement history has ever known. Its advocates implicitly admit it in calling it a method of social engineering, that is: a system that deals with human beings—with all of them but the supreme dictator—in the way in which the engineers deal with the dead material out of which they build houses, bridges, and machines. To the individual no other choice is left but between unconditional surrender or hopeless rebellion. Nobody is free to deviate from the role the plan assigns to him. From the cradle to the coffin all actions of a man as well as his behavior in the time styled leisure hours are exactly prescribed by the authorities.

Such are conditions in the regime after which the immense majority of our intellectuals and the masses of common men are passionately hankering. The children and grandchildren of the generations that were full of enthusiasm for liberty are enraptured by the image of a utopia in which they themselves will be nothing but pawns in the hands of other people. To those familiar with the long history of the struggles for freedom, it gives a peculiar impression to see today the old and the young, the professors and the ignorant, the artists and the boors longing for the unlimited rule of "big brother."

This infatuation of the intelligentsia as well as of the illiterate masses is so firm that no adverse experience can weaken it. The more information about the real state of affairs in the communist countries reaches the Western nations, the more fanatical become the daily swelling ranks of those longing for the "dictatorship of the proletariat."

IV

The radical change that has buried in oblivion the ideal of liberty and extols to the skies unconditional submission to the "plan" is reflected in the alteration of the meaning of almost all terms designating political parties and ideologies.

In the nineteenth century the term *liberal* (derived from liberty) denoted those aiming at representative government, at government by laws and not by men, and at restricting the power of the government to the preservation of peaceful interhuman relations against any possible attacks on the part of domestic gangsters or of external foes. Today in the United States to be *liberal* means: to advocate full government control of all human activities in domestic policy and, in foreign policy, to sympathize with all revolutions aiming at the establishment of a communist dictatorship. No term is left to signify those who favor the preservation of the market economy and of private property in the material factors of production. Such "reactionaries" are not considered worthy of having a party name.

In some parliamentary chambers of nineteenth-century Europe, the members of the party advocating government by the people and full civil liberties were seated to the left of the chairman. Hence the designation *left* came into use to signify them and the designation *right* to signify their opponents, the advocates of despotic government. In present-day American usage the meaning of these terms has been inverted. The champions of the "dictatorship of the proletariat," of the Russian and Chinese methods of unlimited tyranny of those in power, are nowadays called *leftists*, and the advocates of constitutional government and civil liberties *rightists*. In this terminology not only Lenin, who on January 6, 1918, dispersed the Constituent Assembly by military force, is to be called a *leftist*, but no less his predecessors in the impolite treatment of parliaments: Oliver Cromwell and the two Napoleons. But Karl Marx, who vehemently rejected this Bonapartist method of suppressing the opposition in one of his best-known pamphlets,[1] would have a fair claim to be qualified as a member of the "extreme right."

The truth is that any kind of socialist or communist regime is incompatible with the preservation of civil liberties and representative or constitutional government. Representative government and civil liberties are the constitutional or political corollary of capitalism, as unlimited despotism is the corollary of socialism. No semantic prattle can alter this fact. The socialist movement is not a continuation of the liberal movement of the nineteenth century, but the most radical reaction against it. The total state of the Lenin and Hitler pattern is the embodiment of the ideals of all the great tyrants of all ages.

V

Unintentionally the words a man chooses in his speaking and writing reveal something about his ideas that he would not be prepared to express directly.

The noun *revolution* originally signified a revolving motion and then a transformation. But since the American and the French Revolutions it means first of all violence, civil war, war against the powers that be. When Arnold Toynbee used for his rather biased account of the evolution of modern industrialism in England (first published in 1884) the title *Industrial Revolution*, he unintentionally disclosed his interpretation of history as a succession of violent conflicts, of killing and destroying.

The same disposition explains the use of the expression "the conquest of a market" to describe the fact that Ruritanian merchants succeeded in selling their wares in Laputania.

1 *The Eighteenth Brunmaire of Louis Bonaparte* [1852], Daniel de Leon, trans., 3rd ed. (Chicago: H. Kerr, 1913).

Many more examples could be quoted. But it is sufficient to mention one: the United States's "war against poverty." The only method of reducing poverty and of supplying people more amply with consumers' goods is to produce more, better, and cheaper. This is what profit-seeking business aims at and achieves, provided sufficient capital has been accumulated by saving. All that a government can do in this process is to protect the operation of the market economy against violent or fraudulent aggression. What lessens poverty is not taking something away from Paul and giving it to Peter, but making commodities more easily accessible by producing more, better, and cheaper. There is nothing in this sequence of events for the appellation of which the term "war" would seem to be adequate. A governmental system that spends every year billions of dollars of the taxpayers' money to make essential foodstuffs, cotton, and many other articles more expensive should certainly have the decency not to boast of an alleged war against poverty.

VI

What distinguishes the mentality of our contemporaries most radically from that of their grandparents is the way they look upon their relation to the government. To the nineteenth-century liberals, state and government appeared as institutions to give to the people the opportunity to live and to work in peace. Everything else, the development of material welfare as well as the cultivation of man's moral, intellectual, and artistic faculties, was the concern of the individuals.

The citizens had to comply with the laws of the country, and they had to pay taxes to defray the costs incurred by the government apparatus. In their household accounts the state was an item of expenditure. Today the individual sees in the state the great provider. Together with his fellows organized as a pressure group, he expects material assistance from the authorities. He is convinced that the state's funds are inexhaustible, as it can fleece the rich endlessly.

The state which the citizens supported in paying taxes could be democratic. The state from which the citizens are getting subsidies cannot remain democratic. People competing with one another for bounties submit humbly to the candidate for dictatorship bidding the most.

What the masses in their thirst for lucre do not see is that they themselves will have to pay the costs of the "presents" the government gives them. Inflation, the main source of the Santa Claus state's funds, makes their savings wither away. While investors in real estate and common stock profit from the progressive weakening of the monetary unit's purchasing power during an inflation, the investments of the less-wealthy strata, predominately consisting in savings deposits, bonds, and insurance policies, melt away. The popularity inflationary measures enjoy among the masses of wage earners, who are victimized by them more than the rest of the nation, shows clearly their inability to see what their genuine interests really are.

❧ Ideas

CHAPTER 20

The Role of Doctrines in Human History

I   Thought and Conduct

Earlier historians dealt almost exclusively with the deeds and exploits of kings and warriors. They paid little or no attention to the slowly working changes in social and economic conditions. They did not bother about the modifications of doctrines, creeds, and mentalities. Even such an unparalleled event as the expansion of Christianism was hardly mentioned by the historians of the first two centuries.

About a hundred and score years ago a new approach to history was entered upon. Cultural history studies the development of social, political, and economic institutions, the changes in technique and in methods of production, the alterations in the way of life, and the transformation of customs and habits. These studies must needs lead to the discovery of the dominant role played by the ideas guiding human behavior. Everything that men do is the result of the theories, doctrines, creeds, and mentalities governing their minds. Nothing is real and material in human history but mind. The essential problems of historical research are the modifications of the systems of thought which occupy man's spirit. Habits and institutions are the product of mind.

As an animal, man has to adjust himself to the natural conditions of the earth or the part of the earth where he lives. But this adjustment is a work of the brain. The geographical interpretation of history failed to recognize this deciding point. The environment works only through the medium of human mind. On the same soil where the white settlers have developed modern American civilization, the Indian aborigines did not succeed even in inventing wheels and carriages. The natural

[This article was probably written in either 1949 or 1950; previously unpublished until this volume. — Ed.]

conditions which render skiing a very useful means for travelling were present both in Scandinavia and in the Alps. But the Scandinavians invented the skis, whereas the inhabitants of the Alps did not. For hundreds, nay thousands, of years these peasants were closeted during the long winter months in their mountain homes and looked longingly upon the inaccessible villages down in the valleys and upon the unapproachable homesteads of their fellow farmers. But this desire did not activate their inventive spirit. When some forty or fifty years ago townsfolk imported skiing as an outdoor sport into the mountains, the natives sneered at what seemed to them to be a funny toy. Only very late they learned how useful these "toys" could be for them.

Not more conducive than this theory of the natural environment is the theory of the general environment as developed by various nineteenth-century sociologists. Every man is influenced by the social and cultural conditions of the milieu in which he has to live and to work. But these institutions and conditions are themselves already the product of the doctrines dominating the conduct of preceding generations. They themselves have to be explained; the appeal to them is not a substitute for an explanation. Taine was right when in dealing with the history of art he referred to the milieu in which artists and poets achieved their works. But general history has to go further; it has not to acquiesce in considering the conditions of environment as data which cannot be traced further back.

We do not intend to deny that human mind is influenced by the conditions under which man lives. In saying that we have to consider human thoughts as the ultimate source of human conduct, we do not wish to contend that mind is something indivisible or something final beyond which nothing else exists or that it is not subject to the limitations of the material universe. We do not have to deal with metaphysical problems. We simply have to take account of the fact that the present state of knowledge does not enable us to realize how the inner man reacts upon external things. Different men and the same men at different times respond in a different way to the same stimuli. Why did some people bend their knees before the idols, whereas others preferred to die rather than to commit an act of idolatry? Why did Henry IV change his faith in order to obtain the rule of France, whereas his scion Henry of Chambord refused to abandon the white flag with the *fleur-de-lis* for the tricolor, although he knew that he lost thereby the crown of France? There is no other answer possible to such questions than the reference to the ideas controlling human conduct.

The different readings of the very popular Marxian materialistic interpretation of history are fundamentally wrong. Both the state of technology and the productive forces are products rather of the working of mind than factors determining the state of mind. One merely moves in a circle when one tries to explain thought by something which itself is a result of human ideas. The obvious truth that man has to adjust himself to the natural conditions of the world in which he lives does not at all justify the naive and crude materialist metaphysics of Marx. This adjustment is effected by thought. Why did not the Negroes of Africa discover means to fight the germs which menace their lives and health, and why did European scholars discover efficient methods to fight these diseases? No materialism can answer such questions satisfactorily.

II   The Social Role of Doctrines

Science cannot provide us with a full explanation of everything. Every branch of knowledge has to stop at some given facts which it has—at least for the present time, maybe forever—to consider as ultimate and beyond which it cannot go. These ultimate facts are simply given to our experience; they cannot be traced back to other facts or forces; they are inexplicable. We call them by names like *electricity* and *life*, but we have to confess that we do not know what *electricity* and *life* are, whereas we know what *water* and *thunder* are.

Individuality is such an ultimate given for history. Every historical investigation reaches earlier or later a point where it cannot explain facts otherwise than by pointing to individuality.

We are fully aware of the fact that every individual is at any given moment the product of his past. At birth he brings into the world as innate qualities the precipitate of the history of all his ancestors, their fate, and their vicissitudes of life. We call it his biological inheritance or his racial characteristics. In his lifetime the individual is steadily influenced by his environment, both by the natural surrounding and by the social milieu. But we cannot explain how all these factors act on his thought. There is always something left which we cannot analyze further. We cannot explain why Descartes became a great philosopher, and Al Capone a gangster. Our last word is: individuality. *Individuum est ineffabile.*

In dealing with doctrines, their origin, their development, their logical implications, and their working in society, we do not wish to contend that they are ultimate facts. Doctrines have not a life of their own; they are products of human thought. They are a part only of the universe, and we may assume that nothing in their history justifies considering them as exempt from the laws of causality. But we have to realize that we know nothing, simply nothing, about the way in which man creates or produces ideas and mentalities. In this sense only are we entitled to call doctrines ultimate facts.

We may assume that there are doctrines whose applications favor man in his struggle for life and that other doctrines are detrimental. There are doctrines building up social cooperation and there are destructive ideas resulting in a disintegration of society. But nothing gives us the right to believe that destructive doctrines must needs lose their prestige because their consequences are pernicious. Reason has a biological function to fulfill; it is man's foremost tool in his adjustment to the natural conditions of life. But it would be a mistake to believe that a living being must always succeed in the struggle for life. There were species of plants and of animals which vanished because they failed in their endeavors to adjust themselves. There were races and nations which died out; there were societies and civilizations which disintegrated. Nature does not prevent man from thinking prejudicial ideas and from constructing hurtful doctrines. The fact that a doctrine has been worked out and that it succeeded in obtaining many supporters is not a proof that it is not destructive. A doctrine may be modern, fashionable, and generally accepted and nevertheless be detrimental to human society, civilization, and survival.

We have to study the history of doctrines because they alone give us the clue to the understanding of social, economic, and political changes.

III Experience and Social Doctrines

In the field of the natural sciences, especially in physics, we have the opportunity of applying the experimental method. The scientist isolates in the laboratory the various conditions of change and observes their action. Every statement can be verified or refuted by the result of experiments.

In the field of the sciences of human conduct, we cannot recur to the experimental method and cannot make experiments. Every experience is the experience of a complexity of phenomena. We never enjoy the advantage of observing the working of one factor only, other things being equal. Experience therefore can never verify or refute our statements and theories concerning social problems.

It is an undeniable fact that no nation has reached a somewhat higher stage of civilization without private ownership of the means of production. But nobody is prepared to maintain the statement that experience has proved that private property is a necessary and indispensable requisite of civilization. Social and economic experience does not teach us anything. The facts have to be commented by our theories; they are open to different explanations and conclusions. Every discussion concerning the meaning of historical facts falls back very soon to an examination of a priori theories and scrutinizes them without any reference to experience. These theories have logical precedence; they are anterior to historical experience, and we grasp the meaning of this experience only with the aid of them.

These theories and doctrines, whether sound or unsound, whether suitable or detrimental for survival, do not only guide human conduct, they are at the same time the mental tool through the aid of which we perceive their working in history. We cannot observe social facts but in the light in which our theories and doctrines show them. The same complex of events offers different aspects according to the point of view from which the observer sees it.

Some very fashionable opinions have badly misjudged these objectives. Positivism, empiricism, and historicism believed that social facts could be established in the same way in which physics establishes physical facts. (We do not have to scrutinize the bearing of the latest discoveries which let us foresee that also the physicists will have to acknowledge that the result of an observation differs according to the different ways in which the observer approaches it. It seems to be too early to draw conclusions from the contributions of Werner Heisenberg, Louis de Broglie, and other contemporary scientists.) They consider facts as something independent from the ideas of the observer, and social experience as something logically and temporarily antecedent to theories. They do not realize that the act by which we set off, out of the stream of events, some happenings and consider them as definite facts is necessarily guided by our theoretical insight or, as some people may prefer to say, by our doctrinal prejudices. Why do we consider the balance of payments of the United States as a fact, and why do we not pay any attention to the balance of payments of the state of Maryland or of the city of Boston or of the borough of Manhattan? Why do we, in dealing with the problems of Germany's currency, consider the state of Germany's balance of payments? Because the investigation of the economist who proceeds in this way is guided by a very definite (and, as I have to remark, erroneous) theory of money.

The statisticians are mistaken when believing that what they study are pure facts only. The statistician tries to discover the correlations existing between different series of figures, when his theoretical reasoning makes him assume that there exists a causal relation between them. In the absence of such theoretical assumptions, he does not pay any attention at all to obvious correlations, whereas he is quick in proving that a correlation exists when his preconceived theory postulates such a correlation. Jevons believed that he had succeeded in demonstrating a correlation between the economic crises and the sun spots. On the other hand no statistician ever paid any attention to the discovery of a correlation between the number of storks and the changes of natality.

In life and reality all things are linked with all other things. History is a continuous flow of events which are entangled into a uniform structure. The delimitation of our mental forces prevents us from grasping them as a whole by one act of perception. We have to analyze them step by step, starting from the isolation of small things and slowly proceeding to the study of more complicated problems. The act by which we separate some changes out of the whole context of the flux of life and consider them as facts is not a function of reality. It is the result of the working of our mind. In the field of the social sciences, there are no such things as pure facts. What we conceive as a fact is always the result of the way we look into the world. A superhumanly perfect intellect would see the same things in a different way. We of the twentieth century look at the same things in another way than Plato, Saint Thomas, or Descartes did. Our facts are different from their facts, and the facts of men who will live a hundred years after us will be different again.

A social fact is a piece of reality perceived by human intellect. What constitutes a fact is not only reality but no less the observer's mind.

An isolated figure or an isolated series of figures does not mean anything. Nor does any other isolated fact—such as: Brutus killed Caesar—mean anything. Assembling statements about isolated facts does not deepen our insight and is no substitute for theories and philosophies. But every attempt to combine different facts—whether by establishing correlations or by other methods—is the outcome of our theories and doctrines. In the context of different doctrines identical events get a different meaning. The same experience and the same facts are viewed in a quite different way by people who do not agree about the theories. The experience of Russian Bolshevism is not the same for Liberals (in the old sense of the term) and for Socialists, for free thinkers and for Catholics, for Nazis and for Slav Nationalists, for economists and for the patrons of the screen. The same is true for the American New Deal, for the breakdown of France, for the Treaty of Versailles, and for all other historical facts. Of course, every party is firmly convinced that its own interpretation only is sound and adequate to the facts and that all other opinions are radically wrong and biased by false theories. But the conflict of doctrines cannot be solved by silencing all those who have different ideas. A party which succeeds in making its own opinion the only legal one and achieves to outlaw all other opinions does not alter the characteristic feature of its creed. A doctrine remains a doctrine even when generally accepted and undisputed. It may be erroneous even when no contemporary challenges it.

In order to broaden our knowledge in the field of human conduct we have to study on the one hand the problems of praxeological and economic theory and on the other hand history. But the study of history has to center around the study of the development of ideas and doctrines. The first step to every attempt to investigate social, political, and economic changes has to be the study of the changes of the ideas which guided men to bring about these changes.

IV   Doctrines and Political Problems

The problems the politicians have to deal with are not set by nature and natural conditions; they are set by the state of doctrinal convictions.

For the sixteenth and seventeenth centuries there existed a religious problem for which no satisfactory solution seemed to be possible. In those days people could not grasp the idea that men of different denominations could peacefully live together in the same country. Torrents of blood were shed, flowering countries were devastated, civilizations were destroyed by wars for the establishment of religious uniformity. Today we do not see any problem at all in this issue. In Great Britain, in the United States, and in many other countries, Catholics and Protestants of various denominations cooperate and collaborate without any qualms. The problem has been solved; it disappeared with the change of the doctrines concerning the task of civil government.

On the other hand we have a new problem to deal with, the problem of the coexistence of various linguistic groups in the same territory. It was not a problem a hundred years ago and it is not a menacing problem in America. But it is a terrible menace in Central and Eastern Europe. Americans still find it difficult to recognize that it is a problem at all, because they are not familiar with the doctrines which made it a problem.

It would be inadequate to say that these great political issues which cause conflicts, wars, and revolutions are *apparent* problems only and make light of them. They are not less real and genuine than any other problem of human conduct. They are the outcome of the whole structure of ideas and reasonings which guide present-day politics. They actually exist in the social environment which is determined by these doctrines. They cannot be solved by a simple recipe. They may fade one day with the evanescence of the whole structure of ideas which have created them.

We have to separate the technological problems from the political ones. The adjustment of man to natural conditions of life is the outcome of his study of nature. The natural sciences may be styled by theologians and metaphysicians as an inadequate means to solve the riddles of the world and to answer the fundamental questions of being. But nobody can deny that they have succeeded in improving the external conditions of human life. That there are living today on the earth's surface many more people than some hundreds or thousands of years ago and that every citizen of a civilized country enjoys much more comfort than the preceding generations did is a proof of the usefulness of science. Every successful surgical operation contradicts the skepticism of sophisticated grumblers.

But scientific research and its application in the struggle for human life can be effected only in a society, i.e., in a world, where men cooperate by division of labor. Social cooperation is a product of reason and mind. It can be considered as a gift of God or as a natural phenomenon only as far as we have to realize that the power to think is a natural equipment of man. Man has, by making proper use of his faculties, created both technology and society. The progress of the natural sciences and of the social sciences and the development of technical skill and of social cooperation are inextricably linked together. Both are outcomes of mind.

We have not to dwell upon the matter that there are problems which the natural sciences cannot solve. As far as the experimental method of the laboratory can work, the natural sciences can attain statements which may be regarded as undisputed facts. Natural science marches forward by trial and error. That the experiments arranged in the laboratory effect the expected results and that the machines run in the way we want them to run provides us with a verification of the body of our physical insight which is beyond any doubt.

But in the field of the social sciences, we do not enjoy the advantage of the experimental method. We have to repeat this fact again and again, because its enormous bearing can hardly be overrated and because it is totally neglected by present-day epistemology and economics. The theories which build up or disintegrate social cooperation can only be proved or refuted by pure reasoning. They cannot be exposed to the simple examination of the experiment.

This explains fully why the conflict of social doctrines seems to be in such a hopeless state. When Lavoisier replaced the theory of the phlogiston with a more satisfactory theory, he met first with a stubborn opposition by the supporters of the older view. But this resistance disappeared very soon and forever; the experiments in the laboratory and the application of the new theory in technological practice put an end to it. No similar test could be brought forward in favor of the great economic achievements of Hume, Ricardo, and Menger. They have to undergo the scrutiny of abstract reasoning.

Then there is a second important difference. Within the framework of a capitalist society where there is private property of the means of production, a new idea can be put into practice in a limited field with small resources. Thus men like Fulton and Bell could succeed in realizing plans to which the majority of their contemporaries laughed. But social changes have to be brought about by measures which need the support of the majority. A free trader cannot realize free trade by the support of a few friends; peace cannot be established by an isolated small group of peace-loving people. To make social doctrines work, the support of public opinion is needed. Those scores of millions who ride on the railroads and listen to broadcasts without any idea of how railways have to be constructed and operated and how the radio works have to grasp the incomparably more difficult problems of social cooperation if society is to operate satisfactorily. Thus the great bulk of the low-browed, the masses who do not like to think and to reflect, the inert people who are slow in grasping new complicated ideas have to decide. Their doctrinal convictions, how crude and naive they may be, fix the course of events. The state of society is not the outcome of those theories which have the support of the small group of advanced spirits, but the result of the doctrines which the masses of laymen consider as sound ones.

It is generally believed that the conflict of social doctrines is due to the clash of group interests. If this theory were right, the cause of human cooperation would be hopeless. If unanimity cannot be reached, because the rightly conceived interests of individuals are running counter to each other or because the interests of society are in antagonism to the interests of individuals, then no lasting peace and no friendly cooperation between men can ever be attained. Then the present state of civilization which postulates peace cannot be maintained and mankind is doomed. Then the Nazis were right who considered war as the only normal, natural, and desirable shape of human intercourse. Then the Bolsheviks were right who did not argue with their adversaries but exterminated them. Then Western civilization was nothing but a shameless lie and its achievements, as Werner Sombart asserted, the work of the devil.

What we have to realize is that the social problems are the result of the state of social doctrines. What has to be considered is whether a state of social organization can be conceived which could be considered satisfactory from the—rightly conceived—interests of every individual. If the answer to this question has to be in the negative, then we have to see in the conflicts of our day the prelude to the unavoidable disintegration of society. If on the other hand the answer will be affirmative, we have to investigate what state of mind has led to conflicts in a world where another result is at least conceivable.

In any case, the conflicts are a result of the doctrines. Even those who believe that the conflicts are the unavoidable outcome of a real and necessary antagonism of interests do not deny that these real antagonisms have to be perceived by reason in order to guide the actions of men. Man can only act for his own interest if he knows what his interests are and what has to be done in order to promote them. Both the Marxians and the Nationalists agree that a state of mind could prevail, and prevailed, where classes, nations, and individuals are mistaken about their true interests and stick to doctrines which are detrimental to their own welfare. Notwithstanding their repeated assertions that being, by some mystical process, creates the proper ideas, they praise their great men for having discovered them, they acknowledge that some people conceive ideas unsuitable to their being, and they believe that propaganda is necessary to imbue people with the doctrines adequate to their being. Thus they, too, admit that the doctrines and not the bare state of things engender the conflicts.

There is another widely spread fallacy according to which men are by innate features or by environment disposed for a particular *Weltanschauung*, or philosophy. Men of different philosophies disagree about everything; their opinions can never harmonize, and no conformity can ever be reached. This too, if it were true, would render society and social cooperation impossible. But it is not true. All men, notwithstanding the party lines which divide them, want the same things in this world. They want to protect their own life and the lives of their kin against damage, and they want to increase their material well-being. They fight each other not because they wish to attain different aims, but on the contrary, because—striving for the same ends—they assume that the satisfaction which the other fellow may get hinders their own improvement. There were once ascetics who honestly and fully renounced every worldly ambition and were content to live the life of the fish in the water. We have not to dwell upon their case, because these rare saints certainly are not responsible for the struggles for more food and more luxuries. When people disagree about social doctrines, they do not disagree about *Weltanschauung*, they disagree about the methods to get more wealth and more joy. All political parties acting on the stage of history promise to their followers a better life on earth. They justify the sacrifices they exact from their partisans as necessary means for the acquisition of more wealth. They declare these sacrifices as temporary only, as investments which will bear multiple profits. The conflict of doctrines is a discussion about means, not about ultimate ends.

Political conflicts are the result of doctrines which maintain that the only way to happiness is to inflict harm on other people or to menace them with violence. Peace, on the other hand, can be achieved only by the conviction that peaceful cooperation gives better satisfaction than fighting each other. The Nazis embarked upon the way of conquest because their doctrines taught them that a victorious war is indispensable for their happiness. The people of the fifty American states live peacefully together because their doctrine teaches them that a peaceful cooperation suits better their objectives than warring does. When once, some hundred years ago, a different doctrine got hold upon the minds of Americans, bloody civil war resulted.

Thus the main subject of historical research has to be the study of social, economic, and political doctrines. What people do when making laws and constitutions, when organizing political parties and armies, when signing or breaking treaties, when living peacefully or kindling wars or revolutions is the application of these doctrines. We are born into a world shaped by doctrines, and we are living in an environment which continually changes by the operation of changing doctrines. Every man's fate is determined by the working of these doctrines. We sow, but the result of our toil and trouble depends not only on the acts of God; not less important for our harvesting is the conduct of other people, and this conduct is guided by doctrines.

V   The Expedience of Doctrines

It is not the task of a scientific inquiry to judge the various doctrines from the point of view of preconceived convictions or of personal preferences. We have not the right to measure other people's ideas by the standard of our morals. We have to eliminate from our reasoning the consideration of ultimate ends and values. It is not the duty of science to tell people what they should try to attain as their chief good.

There is only one standard which we have to apply when dealing with doctrines. We have to ask whether their practical application will succeed in attaining those ends which people wish to attain. We have to examine the fitness of doctrines from the point of view of those who apply them in order to reach some certain goals. We have to inquire whether they are suitable for the purpose which they have to serve.

We do not believe that there are men who take the old principle *fiat justitia pereat mundus* in its literal meaning. What they really want to say is *fiat justitia ne pereat mundus*. They do not wish to destroy society by justice, but on the contrary, they want to protect it against destruction. But if there were people who consider it as the ultimate end of their endeavors to destroy civilization in order to reduce mankind to the status of Neanderthal man, then we could not help applying to their doctrines the standard of their ultimate end. We could add: we and the large majority of our fellow men do not share this madness; we do not long for destruction but for advancement of civilization, and we are prepared to defend civilization against the assaults of its adversaries.

There is still a second point of view from which to judge a doctrine. We can ask whether it is logically coherent or self-contradictory. But this estimate is secondary only and has to be subordinated to the above-mentioned standard of expediency. A contradictory doctrine is wrong only because its application will not achieve the ends sought.

It would be a mistake to call this method of judging doctrines pragmatist. We are not concerned with the question of truth. We have to consider doctrines, i.e., recipes for action, and for these no other standard can be applied than that of whether these recipes work or do not work.

It would not be more correct to style our point of view a utilitarian one. Utilitarianism has rejected all standards of a heteronomous moral law, which has to be accepted and obeyed regardless of the consequences arising therefrom. For the utilitarian point of view, a deed is a crime because its results are detrimental to society and not because some people believe that they hear in their soul a mystical voice which calls it a crime. We do not talk about problems of ethics.

The only point which we have to emphasize is that people who do not apply the appropriate means will not attain the ends they wish to attain.

VI   Esoteric Doctrines and Popular Beliefs

Any attempt to study human conduct and historical changes has to make ample allowance for the fact of intellectual inequality of men. Between the philosophers and scholars who contrive new ideas and build up elaborate systems of thought and the narrow-minded dullards whose poor intellect cannot grasp but the simplest things, there are many gradual transitions. We do not know what causes these differences in intellectual abilities; we have simply to acknowledge their existence. It is not permitted to dispose of them by explaining them as brought about by differences in environment, personal experience, and education. There can be no doubt that at the root of them lies innate heterogeneity of individuals.

Only a small elite has the ability to absorb more-refined chains of thought. Most people are simply helpless when faced with the more-subtle problems of implication or valid inference. They cannot grasp but the primary propositions of reckoning; the avenue to mathematics is blocked to them. It is useless to try to make them familiar with thorny problems and with the theories thought out for their solution. They simplify and mend in a clumsy way what they hear or read. They garble and misrepresent propositions and conclusions. They transform every theory and doctrine in order to adapt it to their level of intelligence.

Catholicism had a different meaning for Cardinal Newman and for the hosts of the credulous. The Darwinian theory of evolution is something else than its popular version that man is a scion of apes. Freudian psychoanalysis is not identical with pan-sexualism, its version for the millions. The same dualism can be stated with all social, economic, and political doctrines. All doctrines are taught and accepted at least in two different, nay, conflicting varieties. An unbridgeable gulf separates the esoteric teaching from the exoteric one.

As the study of doctrines is not a goal for itself, it has to pay no less attention to the popular doctrines than to the doctrines of the philosophical authors and their books. Of course, the popular doctrines are derived from the logically elaborated and refined theories of the scholars and scientists. They are secondary, not primary. But as the application of social doctrines necessitates their endorsement by public opinion, and as public opinion mostly turns toward the popular version of a doctrine, the study of the latter is no less important than that of the perfect conception. For history a popular slogan may sometimes vouchsafe more information than the ideas formulated by scholars. There are popular and generally accepted beliefs which are so contradictory and manifestly indefensible that no serious thinker ever dared to represent them systematically. But if such a belief provokes action, it is for historical research no less important than any other doctrine applied in practice. History has not to limit its endeavors either to sound doctrines or to doctrines neatly expounded in scholarly writings; it has to study all doctrines which determine human action.

CHAPTER 21

The Idea of Liberty Is Western

I

The history of civilization is the record of a ceaseless struggle for liberty.

Social cooperation under the division of labor is the ultimate and sole source of man's success in his struggle for survival and his endeavors to improve as much as possible the material conditions of his well-being. But as human nature is, society cannot exist if there is no provision for preventing unruly people from actions incompatible with community life. In order to preserve peaceful cooperation, one must be ready to resort to violent suppression of those disturbing the peace. Society cannot do without a social apparatus of coercion and compulsion, i.e., without state and government. Then a further problem emerges: to restrain the men who are in charge of the governmental functions lest they abuse their power and convert all other people into virtual slaves. The aim of all struggles for liberty is to keep in bounds the armed defenders of peace, the governors and their constables. Freedom always means: freedom from arbitrary action on the part of the police power.

The idea of liberty is and has always been peculiar to the West. What separates East and West is first of all the fact that the peoples of the East never conceived the idea of liberty. The imperishable glory of the ancient Greeks was that they were the first to grasp the meaning and significance of institutions warranting liberty. Recent historical research has traced back to Oriental sources the origin of some of the scientific achievements previously credited to the Hellenes. But nobody has ever contested that the idea of liberty was created in the cities of ancient Greece. The writings of Greek philosophers and historians transmitted it to the Romans and later to modern Europe and America. It became

[Reprinted here from *American Affairs* (October 1950). — Ed.]

the essential concern of all Western plans for the establishment of the good society. It begot the laissez-faire philosophy to which mankind owes all the unprecedented achievements of the age of capitalism.

The meaning of all modern political and judicial institutions is to safeguard the individuals' freedom against encroachments on the part of the government. Representative government and the rule of law, the independence of courts and tribunals from interference on the part of administrative agencies, habeas corpus, judicial examination and redress of acts of the administration, freedom of speech and the press, separation of state and church, and many other institutions aimed at one end only: to restrain the discretion of the officeholders and to render the individuals free from their arbitrariness.

The age of capitalism has abolished all vestiges of slavery and serfdom. It has put an end to cruel punishments and has reduced the penalty for crimes to the minimum indispensable for discouraging offenders. It has done away with torture and other objectionable methods of dealing with suspects and lawbreakers. It has repealed all privileges and promulgated equality of all men under the law. It has transformed the subjects of tyranny into free citizens.

The material improvements were the fruit of these reforms and innovations in the conduct of government affairs. As all privileges disappeared and everybody was granted the right to challenge the vested interests of all other people, a free hand was given to those who had the ingenuity to develop all the new industries which today render the material conditions of people more satisfactory. Population figures multiplied, and yet the increased population could enjoy a better life than that of their ancestors.

Also in the countries of Western civilization there have always been advocates of tyranny—the absolute arbitrary rule of an autocrat or an aristocracy on the one hand and the subjection of all other people on the other hand. But in the Age of Enlightenment the voices of these opponents became thinner and thinner. The cause of liberty prevailed. In the first part of the nineteenth century the victorious advance of the principle of freedom seemed to be irresistible. The most eminent philosophers and historians got the conviction that historical evolution tends toward the establishment of institutions warranting freedom and that no intrigues and machinations on the part of the champions could stop the trend toward liberalism.

II

In dealing with the preponderance of the liberal social philosophy there is a disposition to overlook the power of an important factor that worked in favor of the idea of liberty, viz., the eminent role assigned to the literature of ancient Greece in the education of the elite. There were among the Greek authors also champions of government omnipotence, such as Plato. But the essential tenor of Greek ideology was the pursuit of liberty. Judged by the standards of modern liberal and democratic institutions, the Greek city-states must be called oligarchies. The liberty which the Greek statesmen, philosophers, and historians glorified as the most precious good of man was a privilege reserved to a minority. In denying it to metics and slaves, they virtually advocated the despotic rule of a hereditary caste of oligarchs. Yet it would be a grave error to dismiss their hymns to liberty as mendacious. They were no less sincere in their praise and quest of freedom than were, two thousand years later, the slaveholders George Washington and Thomas Jefferson. It was the political literature of the ancient Greeks that begot the ideas of the Monarchomachs, the philosophy of the Whigs, the doctrines of Althusius, Grotius, and John Locke, and the ideology of the fathers of modern constitutions and bills of rights. It was the classical studies, the essential feature of a liberal education, that kept awake the spirit of freedom in the England of the Stuarts and George III, in the France of the Bourbons, and in Italy, subject to the despotism of a galaxy of princes.

No less a man than Bismarck, among the nineteenth-century statesmen the foremost foe of liberty, bears witness to the fact that even in the Prussia of Frederick William III, the *Gymnasium* was a stronghold of republicanism.[1] The passionate endeavors to eliminate the classical studies from the curriculum of the liberal education and thus virtually to destroy its very character were one of the major manifestations of the revival of the servile ideology.

It is a fact that a hundred years ago only a few people anticipated the overpowering momentum which the anti-liberal ideas were destined to acquire in a very short time. The ideal of liberty seemed to be so firmly rooted that everybody thought that no reactionary movement

---

1 Cf. Otto von Bismarck, *Gedanken und Erinnerungen*, vol. 1 (New York: Cotta, 1898), p. 1.

could ever succeed in eradicating it. It is true, it would have been a hopeless venture to attack freedom openly and to advocate unfeignedly a return to subjection and bondage. But anti-liberalism got hold of people's minds camouflaged as super-liberalism, as the fulfillment and consummation of the very ideas of freedom and liberty. It came disguised as socialism, communism, and planning.

No intelligent man could fail to recognize that what the socialists, communists, and planners were aiming at was the most radical abolition of the individual's freedom and the establishment of government omnipotence. Yet the immense majority of the socialist intellectuals were convinced that in fighting for socialism they were fighting for freedom. They called themselves left-wingers and democrats, and nowadays they are even claiming for themselves the epithet liberals.

These intellectuals and the masses who followed their lead were in their subconsciousness fully aware of the fact that their failure to attain the far-flung goals which their ambition impelled them to aim at was due to deficiencies of their own. They were either not bright enough or not industrious enough. But they were eager not to avow their inferiority both to themselves and to their fellow men and to search for a scapegoat. They consoled themselves and tried to convince other people that the cause of their failure was not their own inferiority but the injustice of society's economic organization. Under capitalism, they declared, self-realization is only possible for the few. "Liberty in a *laissez-faire* society is attainable only by those who have the wealth or opportunity to purchase it."[2] Hence, they concluded, the state must interfere in order to realize "social justice." What they really meant is, in order to give to the frustrated mediocrity "according to his needs."

III

As long as the problems of socialism were merely a matter of debates, people who lack clear judgment and understanding could fall prey to the illusion that freedom could be preserved even under a socialist regime. Such self-deceit can no longer be nurtured, since the Soviet experience has shown to everybody what conditions are in a socialist commonwealth. Today the apologists of socialism are forced to dis-

2 Cf. H. Laski, "Liberty," in *Encyclopaedia of the Social Sciences*, vol. 9 (New York: Macmillan, 1930), p. 448.

tort facts and to misrepresent the manifest meaning of words when they want to make people believe in the compatibility of socialism and freedom.

The late Professor Laski—a self-styled noncommunist or even anti-communist—told us that "no doubt in Soviet Russia a Communist has a full sense of liberty; no doubt also he has a keen sense that liberty is denied him in Fascist Italy."[3] The truth is that a Russian is free to obey all the orders issued by the great dictator. But as soon as he deviates a hundredth of an inch from the correct way of thinking as laid down by the authorities, he is mercilessly liquidated. All those politicians, officeholders, authors, musicians, and scientists who were "purged" were—to be sure—not anti-communists. They were, on the contrary, fanatical communists, party members in good standing, whom the supreme authorities, in due recognition of their loyalty to the Soviet creed, had promoted to high positions. The only offense they had committed was that they were not quick enough in adjusting their ideas, policies, books, or compositions to the latest changes in the ideas and tastes of Stalin. It is difficult to believe that these people had "a full sense of liberty" if one does not attach to the word *liberty* a sense which is precisely the contrary of the sense which all people always used to attach to it.

Fascist Italy was certainly a country in which there was no liberty. It had adopted the notorious Soviet pattern of the "one-party principle" and accordingly suppressed all dissenting views. Yet there was still a conspicuous difference between the Bolshevik and the Fascist application of this principle. For instance, there lived in Fascist Italy a former member of the parliamentary group of communist deputies, who remained loyal unto death to his communist tenets, Professor Antonio Graziadei. He regularly received the pension which he was entitled to claim as professor emeritus, and he was free to write and to publish, with the most eminent Italian publishing firms, books which were orthodox Marxian. His lack of liberty was certainly less rigid than that of the Russian communists who, as Professor Laski chose to say, "no doubt" have "a full sense of liberty."

Professor Laski took pleasure in repeating the truism that liberty in practice always means liberty within law. He went on saying that the law always aims at "the conference of security upon a way of life

3 Cf. ibid., pp. 445–46.

which is deemed satisfactory by those who dominate the machinery of state."[4] This is a correct description of the laws of a free country if it means that the law aims at protecting society against conspiracies intent upon kindling civil war and upon overthrowing the government by violence. But it is a serious misstatement when Professor Laski adds that in a capitalistic society "an effort on the part of the poor to alter in a radical way the property rights of the rich at once throws the whole scheme of liberties into jeopardy."[5]

Take the case of the great idol of Professor Laski and all his friends, Karl Marx. When in 1848 and 1849 he took an active part in the organization and the conduct of the revolution, first in Prussia and later also in other German states, he was—being legally an alien—expelled and moved, with his wife, his children, and his maid, first to Paris and then to London.[6] Later, when peace returned and the abettors of the abortive revolution were amnestied, he was free to return to all parts of Germany and often made use of this opportunity. He was no longer an exile, and he chose of his own account to make his home in London.[7] Nobody molested him when he founded, in 1864, the International Working Men's Association, a body whose avowed sole purpose it was to prepare the great world revolution. He was not stopped when on behalf of this association he visited various Continental countries. He was free to write and to publish books and articles which, to use the words of Professor Laski, were certainly an effort "to alter in a radical way the property rights of the rich." And he died quietly in his home, 41, Maitland Park Road, on March 14, 1883.

Or take the case of the British Labor Party. Their effort "to alter in a radical way the property rights of the rich" was, as Professor Laski knew very well, not hindered by any action incompatible with the principle of liberty.

Marx, the dissenter, could at ease live, write, and advocate revolution in Victorian England just as the Labor Party could at ease engage in all

4 Cf. ibid., p. 446.
5 Cf. ibid., p. 446.
6 About Marx's activities in the years 1848 and 1849, see Karl Marx, "Chronik seines Lebens in Einzeldaten" (Moscow: Marx-Engels-Lenin-Institute, 1934), pp. 48–81.
7 In 1845 Marx *voluntarily* renounced his Prussian citizenship. When later, in the early 1860s, he considered a political career in Prussia, the ministry denied his application for restoring his citizenship. Thus a political career was closed to him. Perhaps this fact decided him to remain in London.

political activities in post–Victorian England. In Soviet Russia not the slightest opposition is tolerated. This is what the difference between liberty and slavery means.

IV

The critics of the legal and constitutional concept of liberty and the institutions devised for its practical realization are right in their assertion that freedom from arbitrary action on the part of the officeholders is in itself not yet sufficient to make an individual free. But in emphasizing this indisputable truth, they are running against open doors. For no advocate of liberty ever contended that to restrain the arbitrariness of officialdom is all that is needed to make the citizens free. What gives to the individuals as much freedom as is compatible with life in society is the operation of the market system. The constitutions and bills of rights do not create freedom. They merely protect the freedom that the competitive economic system grants to the individuals against encroachments on the part of the police power.

In the market economy people have the opportunity to strive after the station they want to attain in the structure of the social division of labor. They are free to choose the vocation in which they plan to serve their fellow men. In a planned economy they lack this right. Here the authorities determine each man's occupation. The discretion of the superiors promotes a man to a better position or denies him such promotion. The individual entirely depends on the good graces of those in power. But under capitalism everybody is free to challenge the vested interests of everybody else. If he thinks that he has the ability to supply the public better or more cheaply than other people do, he may try to demonstrate his efficiency. Lack of funds cannot frustrate his projects. For the capitalists are always in search of men who can utilize their funds in the most profitable way. The outcome of his business activities depends alone on the conduct of the consumers who buy what fits them best.

Neither does the wage earner depend on the employer's arbitrariness. An entrepreneur who fails to hire those workers who are best fitted for the job concerned and to pay them enough to prevent them from taking another job is penalized by a reduction of net revenue. The employer does not grant to his employees a favor. He hires them as an indispensable means for the success of his business in the same way in which he buys raw materials and factory equipment. The worker is free to find the employment which suits him best.

The process of social selection that determines each individual's position and income is continuously going on in the capitalist society. Great fortunes are shrinking and finally melting away completely while other people, born in poverty, ascend to eminent positions and considerable incomes. Where there are no privileges, and governments do not grant protection to vested interests threatened by the superior efficiency of newcomers, those who have acquired wealth in the past are forced to acquire it every day anew in competition with all other people.

Within the framework of social cooperation under the division of labor, everybody depends on the recognition of his services on the part of the buying public of which he himself is a member. Everybody in buying or abstaining from buying is a member of the supreme court which assigns to all people—and thereby also to himself—a definite place in society. Everybody is instrumental in the process that assigns to some people a higher and to others a smaller income. Everybody is free to make a contribution which his fellow men are prepared to reward by the allocation of a higher income. Freedom under capitalism means: not to depend more on other people's discretion than these others depend on one's own. No other freedom is conceivable where production is performed under the division of labor and there is no perfect economic autarky of everybody.

There is need to stress the point that the essential argument advanced in favor of capitalism and against socialism is not the fact that socialism must necessarily abolish all vestiges of freedom and convert all people into slaves of those in power. Socialism is unrealizable as an economic system because a socialist society would not have any possibility of resorting to economic calculation. This is why it cannot be considered as a system of society's economic organization. It is a means to disintegrate social cooperation and to bring about poverty and chaos.

V

In dealing with the liberty issue one does not refer to the essential economic problem of the antagonism between capitalism and socialism. One rather points out that Western man, as different from the Asiatics, is entirely a being adjusted to life in freedom and formed by life in free-dom. The civilizations of China, Japan, India, and the Mohammedan countries of the Near East as they existed before these nations became acquainted with Western ways of life certainly cannot be dismissed as barbarism. These peoples already many hundreds, even thousands of years ago brought about marvelous achievements in the industrial arts, in architecture, in literature and philosophy, and in the development of educational institutions. They founded and organized powerful em-pires. But then their effort was arrested, their cultures became numb and torpid, and they lost the ability to cope successfully with economic problems. Their intellectual and artistic genius withered away. Their artists and authors bluntly copied traditional patterns. Their theolo-gians, philosophers, and lawyers indulged in unvarying exegesis of old works. The monuments erected by their ancestors crumbled. Their empires disintegrated. Their citizens lost vigor and energy and became apathetic in the face of progressing decay and impoverishment.

The ancient works of Oriental philosophy and poetry can compare with the most valuable works of the West. But for many centuries the East has not generated any book of importance. The intellectual and literary history of modern ages hardly records any name of an Oriental author. The East has no longer contributed anything to the intellectual effort of mankind. The problems and controversies that agitated the West remained unknown to the East. In Europe there was commotion; in the East there was stagnation, indolence, and indifference.

The reason is obvious. The East lacked the primordial thing, the idea of freedom from the state. The East never raised the banner of freedom; it never tried to stress the rights of the individual against the power of the rulers. It never called into question the arbitrariness of the despots. And, first of all, it never established the legal framework that would protect the private citizens' wealth against confiscation on the part of the tyrants. On the contrary, deluded by the idea that the wealth of the rich is the cause of the poverty of the poor, all people approved of the practice of the governors of expropriating successful businessmen. Thus big-scale capital accumulation was prevented, and the nations had to miss all those improvements that require considerable invest-ment of capital. No "bourgeoisie" could develop, and consequently there was no public to encourage and to patronize authors, artists, and inventors.

To the sons of the people, all roads toward personal distinction were closed but one. They could try to make their way in serving the princes. Western society was a community of individuals who could compete for the highest prizes. Eastern society was an agglomeration of subjects entirely depending on the good graces of the sovereigns. The alert youth of the West looks upon the world as a field of action in which he can win fame, eminence, honors, and wealth; nothing appears too difficult for his ambition. The meek progeny of Eastern parents know of nothing else than to follow the routine of their environment. The noble self-reliance of Western man found triumphant expression in such dithyrambs as Sophocles' choric *Antigone* hymn upon man and his enterprising effort and Beethoven's *Ninth Symphony*. Nothing of the kind has ever been heard in the Orient.

Is it possible that the scions of the builders of the white man's civilization should renounce their freedom and voluntarily surrender to the suzerainty of omnipotent government? That they should seek contentment in a system in which their only task will be to serve as cogs in a vast machine designed and operated by an almighty plan-maker? Should the mentality of the arrested civilizations sweep the ideals for the ascendancy of which thousands and thousands have sacrificed their lives?

Ruere in servitium, they plunged into slavery, Tacitus sadly observed in speaking of the Romans of the age of Tiberius.

INDEX

The typeface used in setting this book is Electra, designed in 1935 by the great American typographer William Addison Dwiggins. Dwiggins was a student and associate of Frederic Goudy and served for a time as acting director of Harvard University Press. In his illustrious career as typographer and book designer (he coined the term "graphic designer"), Dwiggins created a number of typefaces, including Metro and Caledonia, and designed many of the typographic ornaments, or "dingbats," familiar to readers.

Electra is a crisp, elegant, and readable typeface, strongly suggestive of calligraphy. The contrast between its strokes is relatively muted, and it produces an even but still "active" impression in text. Interestingly, the design of the *italic* form — called "cursive" in this typeface — is less calligraphic than the italic form of many faces and more closely resembles the roman.

This book is printed on paper that is acid-free and meets the requirements of the American National Standard for Permanence of Paper for Printed Library Materials, Z39.48-1992. ∞

Book design by Erin Kirk New, Watkinsville, Georgia, after a design by Martin Lubin Graphic Design, Jackson Heights, New York

Typography by Graphic Composition, Inc., Bogart, Georgia

Printed and bound by Worzalla Publishing Company, Stevens Point, Wisconsin